PROVOCATEUR

CLIVE HAMILTON

A Life
of Ideas
in Action

Hardie Grant

BOOKS

Published in 2022 by Hardie Grant Books,
an imprint of Hardie Grant Publishing

Hardie Grant Books (Melbourne)
Wurundjeri Country
Building 1, 658 Church Street
Richmond, Victoria 3121

Hardie Grant Books (London)
5th & 6th Floors
52–54 Southwark Street
London SE1 1UN

hardiegrantbooks.com

Hardie Grant acknowledges the Traditional Owners of the country
on which we work, the Wurundjeri people of the Kulin nation and
the Gadigal people of the Eora nation, and recognises their continuing
connection to the land, waters and culture. We pay our respects to
their Elders past and present.

A catalogue record for this
book is available from the
National Library of Australia

Provocateur
ISBN 978 1 74379 857 7

10 9 8 7 6 5 4 3 2 1

Cover design by Kristin Thomas
Cover image: Lightbulb Studio
Typeset in Adobe Garamond Pro 12/15pt by Cannon Typesetting
Printed and bound in Australia by Griffin Press, an Accredited ISO AS/NZS
14001 Environmental Management System printer

The paper this book is printed on is certified against the
Forest Stewardship Council® Standards. Griffin Press holds
chain of custody certification SGSHK-COC-005088. FSC®
promotes environmentally responsible, socially beneficial and
economically viable management of the world's forests.

Contents

CONTENTS

1

Restless

A T THE END of 1983, I returned from England after completing a doctorate at the University of Sussex. Now thirty, I could no longer avoid getting a proper job. I had a family to support – my wife, Janenne, and a two-year-old daughter. Yet after two undergraduate degrees and a PhD I was none the wiser about what I wanted to do, except that I wanted to make a difference in the world.

I had spent years at university deepening my beliefs about the need for radical social change. But now what do I do? The very notion of 'a career' repelled me. As a newly minted left-wing economist, my prospects for employment were dim in a nation where universities and the public sector had been conquered by free-market 'economic rationalism'.

In the newspaper one day, I stumbled on an advertisement for a lecturing position at the Australian National University's Development Studies Centre. It made sense to apply since my thesis had been on the economics of developing countries, specifically South Korea. The director of the centre was Helen Hughes, an Australian economist recently arrived back after fifteen years at the World Bank in New York and with a reputation as a free-market fundamentalist and a bully. Helen called me in to offer me the position.

'Clive,' Helen said, 'I'm not afraid of Marxism because I know my arguments will always win.' Only an ex-communist who's shifted way over to the right would say something like that. Before taking up her job at the World Bank, she was required to formally recant her previous beliefs as a member of the Communist Party of Australia.

I had never been convinced by Marxism as a political program. At university I found the hardliners' dogmatism intimidating and thought their beliefs quixotic, running against the tide of history. Decades later I was sent a transcript of a phone conversation tapped by ASIO in 1972, when I still lived with my parents, in which a recruiter for a socialist group invited me to a training camp for young activists. The typescript records me declining awkwardly. Nevertheless, my understanding of history and social change was heavily influenced by Marxism, and the mathematical model at the centre of my thesis was married with a historical 'class analysis'. It was the maths that got me the job.

In the 1980s the ANU was the national epicentre of dogmatic neoclassical economics, supplying a steady stream of right-wing economists into the public service. A few months after my appointment, Helen remarked that she had been getting a hard time for hiring me from the economics professors on campus. 'I just tell them,' she said, 'that you were the best of the applicants.' She didn't need to add, 'It was a weak field.'

My immediate colleagues were congenial and I settled in quickly. I was required to teach statistics and econometrics, staying two weeks ahead of the students in the textbooks. It was an education that would serve me well. I learned how to perform in front of an audience week in, week out. Not a natural public speaker, I remember the terror when I forced myself to speak up at rowdy organising meetings of student protesters at the University of Sydney, where I studied political economy. It was only by overriding my fear that I began to find my voice. At root, I have a radical's disposition. I have had it since my teenage years. At high school in Canberra in the early 1970s, I'd chafed against authority. I was elected a prefect by fellow students but was disqualified as unsuitable by the principal. I used to say, 'It's not school I hate but the principal of the thing,' but most of the time I hated school. I grew long hair and became politicised. I was arrested at a protest against the Vietnam War and camped outside the South African High Commission on freezing nights in a protest against apartheid.

After two years, Helen appointed me to the position of director of the graduate program, ceding me considerable responsibility and independence. I was competent and it was in our interests to work cooperatively. Helen didn't even interfere after I began teaching the advanced macroeconomics course in the master's program using a neo-Marxist textbook. The content was hard, and I struggled to keep up with it myself, but I thought the students should study alternatives to mainstream economics. The students came to me with their heads full of World Bank recipes, dispensed in the introductory macro course by Graeme Dorrance. Graeme, Helen's husband, was a nice old bloke with a nicotine-stained moustache. At one of Helen's dinner parties, Janenne was seated next to Graeme. While chatting to her he dropped something on the floor, and she reflexively bent down to pick it up. It was his false teeth. Here you go.

While running the graduate program, I twice travelled to China to recruit students. It was a bleak place, with bad food and painful meetings with deans, meetings whose purpose I did not understand. It was a rare privilege then for Chinese students to be allowed to study abroad and it was a pleasure to observe them relax into the Australian learning environment over the first months and begin smiling.

After four years, the academic culture of ANU economics was crushing me. I could make a case that my left-wing politics made acceptance impossible in such a world, but the truth is I just could not compete in the intellectual world shaped by neoclassical economics. When I asked Helen for a reference for a position as a senior economist at the federal government's Bureau of Industry Economics, she said impatiently, 'You write it, Clive.' Hmm, I thought, so that's how the world works. Several weeks later I left academic life behind with relief, even though I felt no real enthusiasm for my new occupation. Although I wouldn't find my niche in the world until I'd turned forty, in retrospect I see my years in universities and the public service as invaluable preparation.

§

Although my father had been a lifelong public servant, the working environment at the Bureau of Industry Economics was foreign to me. Each day the tea lady would come by with her trolley. We mock this symbol of the somnolent public service now, but the opportunity for everyone in your area to stop twice a day for five or ten minutes, drink tea and eat Iced VoVos together cultivated collegiality and strengthened morale. The razor gang from the Department of Finance would soon kill off the tea ladies. Along with divisive performance bonuses, know-nothing consultants and inflated salaries for department secretaries, consigning the tea trollies to the scrap heap was an early step towards the imposition of corporate discipline on the public service, eroding its hard-won reputation for professionalism and 'frank and fearless' advice. We are all the poorer for it.

Although I warmed to the ritual of the tea trolley, office banter has never been something I enjoyed. I can do it when the need arises, but I'm happiest alone in my office. For me, the jolliness of Melbourne Cup gatherings and office birthday celebrations was discomforting. The Germans have a word for it, *plauschplage*, the felt obligation to engage in tea-room banter with colleagues.

Some clever, and quirky, economists worked at the Bureau of Industry Economics, then overseen by a man named Brian Johns (not the SBS one), another introvert. I took a liking to Ralph Lattimore, a lovely man with a warm smile. Ralph was known to be fiercely clever, and productive. He would run from his desk out to the filing cabinet to grab something he needed and run back to his office. One day, changing into his jogging gear at lunchtime, he shut his office door and took off his trousers, at which point an important thought occurred to him. He sat down at his computer and was typing away when Brian Johns knocked and entered. They conversed for five or ten minutes before Brian left; at no time did the boss comment on the fact that Ralph was working in his underpants.

I also came across someone who would become an adversary in later years. Alan Moran ran the energy deregulation unit and was regarded by most of the bureau's economists as a free-market fanatic. He would soon join the Institute of Public Affairs, the right-wing Melbourne think tank that I would often come up against later. Moran would become a central player in spreading climate science denial and organising opposition to renewable energy.

The middle-of-the-road bureau was seen as an outlier in a Canberra gripped by economic rationalism, where the centres of ideological purity were Treasury and the Industries Assistance Commission (IAC), now the Productivity Commission. Rather than advocate old-style industry support, the bureau understood that industry policy was now acceptable only through beefing up skills and investing in infrastructure.

So for me, the IAC was the adversary. To get under its skin, and to go against received wisdom in Canberra, I wrote a discussion paper advocating 'strategic trade policy', a suite of interventionist policies to help firms capture so-called first-mover advantages and compete against foreign corporations. Strategic trade policy was developed by hot-shot US economist Paul Krugman, nowadays a mainstay of *The New York Times* and a Nobel Prize winner. The editor of *The Bulletin*, owned by Kerry Packer, got wind of the heretic in Canberra and sent a reporter. It led to a flattering story with a photo of me on the front cover posed outside the bureau's office 'looking like I owned the place', as one colleague put it. I was amused to hear that Helen Hughes described me as 'Kerry Packer's stooge'.

When an invitation arrived to speak at the IAC over in Belconnen, I thought: Screw it, no one else is willing to challenge the high priests, so I will. I had heard the stories. The commission had a section, known as 'the thought police', whose job was to check all of its reports for conformity with pure neoliberal theory. On one occasion, a recent recruit suggested at a meeting that more account be taken of the social impacts of a recommendation, at which point a senior staff member pulled an atomiser from under the table and sprayed him. The message: his suggestion was too wet.

To a full auditorium, I put my case for strategic trade policy. To prepare for combat, I'd decided I would stick closely to the arguments Krugman had made, because his arguments had passed through the refereeing sieves of top journals. Still, I expected to be monstered. Instead, I received a series of challenging but polite questions, none of which threw me. Jon Stanhope, the deputy director of the bureau, had come to watch. Back at the bureau, I heard he had reported with some amazement that 'they didn't lay a glove on him'. I guessed they'd been instructed to pull their punches, with the higher-ups alert to mounting criticism of economic rationalism in Canberra.

§

In 1989 I was applying for promotion to the senior executive service when the public servants' union called a strike to improve pay rates for junior staff. The demands did not affect me but I felt I ought to strike in solidarity. My father, a highly principled man who'd spent his working life in the public service, warned me that if I did so I would damage my promotion prospects. I was in a bind, but if I stayed in my office while others went out, I would be putting my own interests above my conscience. I decided to join the strike.

I tell this story because most people have found themselves facing a crisis of conscience of this kind. When young people come to me with an ethical dilemma, I suggest they follow their conscience because they will always feel good about their decision. Besides, 'the universe' often has a way of rewarding those who stick to their principles. As it turned out, joining the strike did me no harm.

Late in 1989, as I sat in my office at the bureau, I received a phone call to tell me I had won the job as head of research at the Resource

Assessment Commission. It was the promotion I'd sought, and I was so elated I had to take a walk around the block. The RAC was a new body created by the Hawke government. Organisationally, it was modelled on the Industries Assistance Commission and tasked with carrying out inquiries to help resolve major resource-use and environmental conflicts. Heading the research branch was a plum job and my appointment caused gnashing of teeth among those who saw me as a left-wing interloper. So it was with satisfaction that early in 1990 I moved into the new commission's offices in East Block, a beautiful, refurbished heritage-listed building that once served as Canberra's main post office. The building was soon humming with bright, hard-working and enthusiastic people, drawn mostly from other government departments. It helped that it was located bureaucratically in the prime minister's portfolio, the most prestigious in the service.

In the Canberra bureaucratic hierarchy, there is a rough rule that the more important the organisation, the closer its offices are to Parliament House. No building is closer to Parliament House than East Block.

2

Kakadu lessons

AFTER A QUIET two years at the bureau, I was about to be pitched in to the middle of the hottest political dispute in Canberra. I would come out the other end singed but more worldly wise.

The first brief of the Resource Assessment Commission was to inquire into the pros and cons of a proposed mine at Coronation Hill, an area located in the headwaters of the South Alligator River that had been excised from Kakadu National Park in the Northern Territory. Environmental groups and the mining industry were at loggerheads, and the issue had become a headache for the government.

A year of intense engagement with the Coronation Hill inquiry taught me how the world of political decision-making works – the convergence of media and politics at the highest level, the influence of ideology, big-money lobbying, clashing personalities and the sheer grubbiness of the tactics. And it taught me something else: just how influential evidence-based arguments, if they are the right arguments at the right time, can be in shifting public debate and political outcomes.

I watched with dismay the dishonest and brutal campaign mounted by the mining industry in support of the gold mine. It was their attack on the traditional owners' spiritual beliefs that disgusted me most. Coronation Hill is known as Guratba to the traditional owners, the

Jawoyn clan (pronounced *jar-won*), numbering around three hundred people. Guratba, a registered sacred site, lies in 'Sickness Country'. The hill is said to be the resting place of a powerful ancestral being named Bula, and disturbing it would bring calamity.

The proposed mine caused an acrimonious split in the Hawke cabinet, with a majority in favour of mining, so the commission's report was meant to clarify and help resolve the conflict. But the company, Newcrest Mining, backed by BHP, and the mining industry were not going to wait for the umpire to adjudicate and mounted a relentless media and lobbying campaign to pressure the government, the commission and the public. It turned to two right-wing think tanks, the Institute of Public Affairs and the now-defunct Tasman Institute, to do 'research' backing mining. Then it relied on its friends in the media to promote its reports.

The pressure was unremitting and almost no one was pushing back, so the miners' views dominated the headlines. At one point, a senior person from Hawke's office phoned the commission saying they were being killed in the media and pleading for the commission to put something out that would help the prime minister. The answer, properly, was, 'No, you'll have to wait for the report.'

The conservatives were determined the mine should proceed, but when elected in 1983, Hawke had talked up his environmental commitment, promising to stop the damming of the Franklin River, which he'd done. Environmentalism as a political force was new and instrumental in Labor's re-election in March 1990. The mining industry loathed the greenies. The companies had always had their way and now, in Kakadu, relentless pressure was being put on a handful of traditional owners to agree to the mine. The company was practising divide and rule, trying to turn one traditional owner against another.

One of the most vociferous supporters of the mine was Hugh Morgan, at the time CEO of Western Mining Corporation and a previous president of the main mining lobby. A few years earlier, he had given a speech to the IPA in which he declared that Aboriginal people had forfeited any rights to their land because they had practised 'infanticide, cannibalism and cruel initiation'. They had particularly liked the taste of the Chinese, he said. That kind of gutter racism was not uncommon among mining executives and their political supporters. Morgan would become John Howard's closest business confidant and be appointed president of the Business Council of Australia, where he would be one of Australia's most influential climate science deniers. In 2002 he received an AC, Australia's highest award, for, among other things, his contribution to sustainable development and cultural research. If ever an award brought the honours system into disrepute it was Morgan's.

The mining industry had supported the Hawke government's proposal to establish the Resource Assessment Commission as a 'neutral umpire'. It was confident the facts would expose the environmentalists' claims as emotional nonsense and confirm the obvious benefits mining brings to Australians. In particular, it was convinced that hard-headed economic arguments based on the evidence would blow away the handwringing of the greenies.

Yet the evidence had its own momentum. Some of it was gathered by my research branch in the form of a 'contingent valuation survey', a new economic technique of 'non-market valuation' that had sex appeal at the time. The survey would 'put a price' on the environment by asking people how much they would be willing to pay to protect it. The gains from mining could then be compared with the lost environmental value.

I wasn't sympathetic to this kind of environmental economics. Posing such a question converts ecological values into market values, which cannot legitimately be measured on the same scale. And if comparing the money value of the gold to the ecological value of endangered species seemed awkward enough, putting the spiritual value of Guratba on the scales seemed inhuman. But that was the brief.

The commission had plenty of money to spend and everyone was interested. Given the potential traps, I wanted the study to be bulletproof, so we hired the most reputable expert from the United States to advise us, Richard Carson from the University of California,

San Diego. Carson did most of his work for industry so could not be dismissed as a 'greenie'.

Carson arrived at our offices bleary-eyed from jetlag. After we had outlined the dispute and our brief to put a dollar value on the environmental costs of the mine, he said, 'I think the mining industry is not going to like this.' To protect Kakadu from the mine's chemical spills, heavy vehicle disturbance, wastewater flows, waste rock piles, and wildlife deaths (some bored miners like to shoot animals), Carson guessed that Australians would be willing to pay a lot more than the $500 million the gold mine would be worth to the economy. His guess proved accurate.

We spent a small fortune hiring a survey company to administer thousands of face-to-face questionnaires across the nation. Sure enough, when the results came in it was obvious that Australians valued protection of the Coronation Hill environment much more highly than the worth of the mine. Our study's novelty and the striking results guaranteed heavy media coverage. Industry reps denounced the survey and Peter Walsh, Hawke's acerbic finance minister and future climate science denier, labelled it a 'shoddy piece of work'. The mining industry liked the idea of using hard-headed economics but hated the results, while the environmental groups were deeply suspicious of this kind of economic valuation technique but liked the results.

While all this was galling, it was the trashing of the Jawoyn people that sickened me. From first European contact the Jawoyn had been dispossessed, dispersed and decimated by white man's diseases. Now they were a deprived and scattered clan just hanging on to their connection to their land. They faced the might of the Australian mining industry, backed by the Northern Territory government and powerful ministers in Canberra. Through reports, media releases and backgrounding to journalists, the miners and the IPA denigrated and insulted the Jawoyn people. They claimed that they were incapable of making a decision, that they had no claim to the land in question, that they had invented religious beliefs to pursue territorial ambitions, that they were pressured by outsiders into an anti-mining position, that they contradicted themselves, that they were internally split, and that they were motivated by primitive superstition.

The IPA hired an anthropologist named Ron Brunton who wrote a report claiming that the Jawoyn, inspired by a land grab, had invented the sacred significance of Guratba. Brunton's submission to the Coronation Hill inquiry argued that, if mining were permitted, then the apocalyptic consequences anticipated by some Jawoyn would prove to be false, and the Jawoyn would learn the error of their belief in the spirit-being Bula. The Australian Mining Industry Council criticised the commission for failing in its draft report to recommend to the government mechanisms for 'educating the Jawoyn on the fallacy of some of their mythological beliefs'. Today, it's hard to believe they could get away with this.

Various commentators expressed the view that it would be absurd to allow religious beliefs to stand in the way of progress. Hawke's environment minister, the political headkicker Graham Richardson, referred to the Jawoyn's creation story as 'Bula-shit'. In an opinion article, Canberra historian Bill Mandle described the spiritual beliefs of the Jawoyn people as 'fantasy', 'mumbo-jumbo', 'nonsense', 'garbage' and 'primitive superstition'. This was in 1991. The contempt was breathtaking. They were brazenly advocating cultural genocide.

During the dispute and its aftermath, I felt ashamed as a white person in the presence of dignified Indigenous activists like Jacqui Katona, with so much pain in her eyes caused by people like those I have mentioned. It was heartbreaking to be in the presence of the old custodians, this voiceless mob of impoverished people, almost destroyed by white colonisation while hanging on to their land by a thread, yet enduring vilification and bullying.

I sat in my office seething over what the mining industry was doing to the Jawoyn people. I asked myself, 'Where are the progressive think tanks pushing back against these lies and distortions?' There were none. It was then that the seed of what would become the Australia Institute was planted in my mind, although it would be another three years before it germinated.

§

When in March 1991 the Resource Assessment Commission decided to celebrate its first anniversary, it chose Vivaldi's, an upmarket restaurant on the ANU campus, as a venue. As a sign of his support for the commission, the prime minister agreed to give the after-dinner speech. His office asked the commission to draft his speech and the task fell to me. As I worked on it, one of my staff, David Imber, entered my office with a suggestion. David had come over from Treasury. He was hardworking, smart and entertaining to have around. In his best deadpan voice, he proposed we have Bob Hawke saying: 'I'm not pro-mining. And I'm not pro-environment. I'm pro-Austraaaalia.' He was taking the piss out of politicians, but I thought it was such a funny line that I included it, without the extra a's.

A day or two later, the draft was sent to Hawke's office. I soon received a call from Hawke's speechwriter. Uh-oh, I thought. He told me that speeches drafted by public servants are almost always awful and have to be rewritten from scratch. But mine, he said, was the best speech he'd seen from the public service. 'Congratulations.' I was chuffed, of course.

When Hawke gave the speech at the dinner it had been rewritten somewhat, which was to be expected. David's line was gone, but something very similar came out of Hawke's mouth. He returned to the top table. 'Excellent speech, prime minister,' said one of the commissioners. Hawke gestured towards me and said, 'Well, he wrote it.' I basked in the glory, but it was overshadowed by the excruciating atmosphere at the table where the commissioners and senior execs made awkward small talk with the prime minister. Hawke soon took charge, regaling us with a series of colourful stories. He laughed heartily at them. Awed by his presence and terrified of saying something out of place, we all laughed along. Yes, prime minister, excellent story.

Conservative commentators were doing their best to blacken my name. My advocacy of environmental protection using economic arguments irritated them. In a splenetic opinion piece in 1991,

John Stone, former Treasury secretary and right-wing columnist, branded me 'the new arch-priest of the environment movement', which didn't do my reputation any harm.

That same year, I was in Adelaide to speak the next day at a business conference on the economics of the environment. I was in my pyjamas, about to get into bed, when an envelope was slipped under the hotel room door. It contained the speech of the other speaker in my session, an economist from the IPA. A note said: 'You should see this.' The text was filled with invective, painting me as a dangerous greenie-communist fanatic. It took me a while to get to sleep, but before I drifted off, I decided on a strategy.

Next morning, there was an air of anticipation as I stood to speak, dressed in my most respectable suit and tie. Over half an hour I presented the most even-handed talk in my most reasonable tone, then sat down. The IPA guy, who had prepared for a fight, knew that giving the hostile talk he had prepared would make him look like a lunatic, and so, with a copy of his speech in front of me, I watched him stumble through his talk, trying to cut out or moderate the nastier bits. He flopped, and the audience looked on, wondering what had just happened. It was a lesson in how to prevail in a debate: know your opponent, know your audience, prepare thoroughly and be ready for surprises.

§

Our contingent valuation study of the Coronation Hill mine was the Rolls Royce of such studies – it should have been for the money we spent and the expertise we hired. Although no one other than a few economic wonks took the numerical results too seriously, the survey results demonstrated beyond any doubt that a large majority of Australians opposed the Coronation Hill mine, many of them strongly. The final report of the inquiry, published in May 1991, assessed the pros and cons of various options without making a recommendation. The impression, though, was unambiguous: approving the mine would be bad policy.

Prime Minister Hawke decided to ban the mine in the face of fierce opposition from various ministers, including Paul Keating. But as cabinet brawled in public, another influence had been working on Hawke. His son Stephen, who was working with Indigenous communities in the Kimberley, was persuading his father that the mine should not proceed. In June, during a visit to a Catholic girls' school in Sydney, where he was mobbed, Hawke announced his unilateral decision to ban the mine.

Many years later, in 2009, I was on a stage at the Woodford Folk Festival with Bob Hawke and Greens deputy leader Christine Milne. I briefly recounted the Coronation Hill story and the credit due to Bob Hawke. I finished by saying that his decision was the beginning of the end of his prime ministership. Hawke commented, 'That's about right.'

Although the proposed mine was small, the Coronation Hill ban was an enormous setback for the mining industry. For decades it believed it had a *right* to mine anywhere it chose. Any obstacle was bulldozed, metaphorically or in practice. Politicians cowered before it; Indigenous people had no chance.

Now, the miners were livid. Hugh Morgan, ever prone to feverish outbursts, gave a speech to the libertarians of the Adam Smith Club in which he said that Bob Hawke 'seeks to impose his own religious, neo-pagan obsessions on the whole nation', and argued that the decision would 'undermine the moral basis of our legitimacy as a nation, and lead to such divisiveness as to bring about political paralysis ... Like the fall of Singapore in 1942, Coronation Hill was a shocking defeat.' Completely bonkers, but it illustrates the symbolic impact of the government's decision on the mining industry.

§

One lesson I took away from the RAC was confirmation that a fish rots from the head. The commission was held together by the superb managerial skills of the head of the secretariat, Richard Mills, but it soon became clear that the appointment of Justice Donald Stewart as chief commissioner was a blunder. Stewart, a former policeman, barrister, Supreme Court judge and royal commissioner, was a fearless crusader against hardened criminals, but his management style was at the psychopathic end of the scale. Hard as nails, entirely ignorant of the subject area and dismissive of expertise, within months the staff had come to fear or loathe him. From its brilliant start, after a year, staff morale was plunging.

Bruised from the Coronation Hill imbroglio and dismayed as the Resource Assessment Commission fell apart and lost political support, my stress levels were elevated. One day we had a guest from the United States named Lyuba Zarsky visiting the research branch. One of my staff was hostile to her, referring to her as 'Lubra'. I was so angry with the bad behaviour that, while alone in the kitchen afterwards washing the crockery, I pushed a tea towel so hard into a glass that it shattered, slashing my knuckle. Blood spurted. White-faced, I wrapped a handkerchief around my hand and took myself to the GP, who sewed it up.

After nearly two years at the commission it was clear to me I could not survive much longer. Around this time, Richard Mills called me into his office to say, 'Clive, you are not a public servant.' His verdict was delivered, I think, after I had been invited onto ABC Radio to debate macroeconomic policy with Des Moore, a right-wing ideologue who had joined the IPA after resigning as deputy secretary of the Treasury. The debate had become animated and I referred to Moore as a 'sado-monetarist'.

In agreeing to go on radio I was within the public service rules because my duties had nothing to do with macroeconomic policy. Even so, for senior executive service officers that kind of activity was frowned on. I got that. Yet with Australia changing in ways that alarmed me, I felt a strong urge to speak out.

3

A Jakarta sojourn

WORKING ON THE Coronation Hill inquiry had changed me. About halfway through it, in late 1990, a few commission staff members had accompanied the three commissioners on a field trip to the Sickness Country in the hinterlands of Kakadu. The sun was harsh and the country dry. We stood on Coronation Hill, Guratba, with senior custodian Nipper Brown standing shyly to the side. I gazed across the country and could almost feel the spirit of the land rising like heat from bitumen on a hot day. It felt to me that mining this place would be sacrilegious. I think it was at that point that I became, in my heart, an environmentalist.

I now knew people in the environment movement and began to wonder whether a role at an organisation like the Australian Conservation Foundation (ACF) might be my destiny. In fact, a few months later I applied for the position of executive director. The selection committee whittled the contenders down to two, including me. A drawn-out deadlock ensued, but in the end they chose the other candidate.

In the meantime, an offer came from a most unexpected quarter. Towards the end of 1991, I received a phone call out of the blue from Vermont. A US consulting company had been commissioned by USAID, America's aid agency, to put together a team to advise the Indonesian government on resource and environmental management. Someone had recommended me. I did have a doctorate in the economics of development and had taught development economics at the ANU, so I suppose I had some claim. It sounded exciting.

Janenne and I discussed it. We now had a second child, and both children were at a good age to experience immersion in another culture. And we were ready for a change. I wrestled with the question of whether accepting a job like this would be any kind of endorsement of the repressive Suharto government but figured the project would be supporting those interested in taking the environment seriously. Within a couple of months we were living in the bustling Jakarta neighbourhood of Kemang.

After the first months in a hot, packed, polluted city, with my senses overloaded every day, I was exhausted. It seemed important not to look away from the destitution that afflicted so many, but it took a toll. My workplace was in a large, shabby house in the administrative district of Menteng. I had a separate office in the jungly backyard. *Cicaks* (house geckos) clung to the walls and the pungent odour of hot fish oil wafted in when the local staff cooked their lunch nearby.

The team leader was an Englishman, one of those expatriates found all over Asia so habituated to the climate and lifestyle that visits home become intolerable. He was a control freak who opened and read my personal mail and insisted on signing off on trivial matters. For my part, I was stressed and demanding, so we clashed. The office manager was a thirtyish man named Budi who'd lived in the United States for a time. He was worth his weight in gold. Budi came to my rescue one day after a speeding motorcyclist clipped my car door in a carpark and crashed. A menacing crowd formed. It took the view that the *bule*, a derogatory name for whiteys, should pay up. Budi arrived and extracted me.

I expected to leave the RAC behind, but it followed me. Several months in, I was at an expat gathering in Jakarta. When I mentioned to the Australian mining executive I was chatting to that I previously worked for the Resource Assessment Commission, he flew into a rage. I had been burned by the experience at the RAC and thought, God, I can't get away from it even in another country. I despised those mining bastards, with their bullying sense of entitlement. I would learn a few years later just how thuggish they could be.

§

The advisory project was attached to the national planning agency, BAPPENAS. Its formation expressed the dawning recognition on the part of a handful in government that resource depletion and environmental decline deserved some attention, if only to gain the right to participate in international processes. 'Daunting' is an inadequate word to describe the educational task for those who could see Indonesia's dire predicament. And 'rapacious' is an inadequate word to describe the attitude of the political-business-military elite reaping fortunes from trashing the environment.

The mantra was: Indonesia is too poor to be concerned about the environment. As I made my way through the city, I wondered what the kids playing next to sewage-choked ponds and the adults washing in the stinking Ciliwung River would think of that, not to mention the tuktuk drivers who spent every day breathing in the most toxic air in the world.

My task was numerical and covered the whole economy. I teamed up with two people at New York University, Faye Duchin and Glenn-Marie Lange, to construct the first input–output model of the Indonesian economy, augmented by indicators of resource depletion and environmental damage. The big boss at BAPPENAS liked the idea of owning a complex bit of economic hardware. It gave him more bureaucratic heft. He had heard somewhere that a dynamic model has even more cachet than the static one we planned. We didn't think the extra effort was worth it, but Faye had made her name by solving the conundrum of how to make this kind of model dynamic, so we knew how to do it in principle. With the help of an experienced

Australian consultant, Sean Foley, I employed and supervised half a dozen young graduates to collect what data we could, making educated guesses for the rest. When the report was finished, the big boss at BAPPENAS had a prestigious-looking report to wave around at global conferences.

Our project had a forestry research station in the remotest part of Borneo and a small office in the Department of Forestry on the other side of Jakarta. Forestry was probably the most corrupt bureaucracy in one of the most corrupt nations on earth. I visited Kalimantan in Borneo where vast tracts of rainforest were being cleared and converted into oil palm. Much of the logging was illegal but the whole operation was run by the military. The generals used their income from bribery to build hotels in Bali and Sumatra.

Kalimantan was the wild west. The Javanese immigrants exchanged lurid stories about the headhunting proclivities of the Dayaks, the indigenous people of Borneo. As we headed out of the city, my driver showed me the handgun he kept in the glovebox. Some Dayaks still practised shifting cultivation in the deep forests. I met an American anthropologist, Fran, who'd been working with them for many years. She had been commissioned to prepare a comic book for children explaining the importance of conserving wildlife. Orangutans and toucans were among the charismatic creatures threatened by human intrusion. At a meeting of village leaders, she asked them to nominate a forest animal of special significance to represent the conservation effort. 'Special animal?' they said. 'We shoot whatever we see.' In the absence of a well-informed understanding of how an indigenous community relates to their natural environment, the lure of romanticising them is ever-present. Fran's story was another blow to my white romanticising.

§

While our time in Indonesia slaked my thirst for the exotic, it also cemented my determination to no longer be a technocrat. And certainly not in a foreign country where, of course, my ability to influence public debate was zero. (Although when I later returned to Australia I carried in my suitcase a confidential report by an American consulting firm detailing the Indonesian energy minister's plan to build seven nuclear power plants around an 'extinct' volcano. I passed it to *The Age*, which ran a prominent story that set alarm bells ringing.) I began to think again about setting up a progressive think tank, so in February 1993 I wrote to several prominent people on the left describing my idea and asking them what they thought. They included Hugh Stretton, the eminent historian, Julian Disney, a past president of the Australian Council of Social Service (ACOSS), Phillip Toyne, who'd not long stepped down as president of the Australian Conservation Foundation, and John Langmore, a left-wing Labor MP, Keating critic and my local member.

I also sent the letter to my lecturer in political economy and sometime mentor at the University of Sydney, Frank Stilwell. A couple of years ago, Frank stumbled across the letter, dated 9 February 1993, in his archives and sent me a copy. It's a reminder of the political currents of the time. After describing my work in Jakarta, I wrote:

> I am writing to test your reaction to an idea I have been developing.
>
> When I was at the RAC I was struck by the influence of right-wing think tanks on public debate ... their publications are often quoted by politicians and journalists, both those with a pre-existing sympathy for libertarian positions and those who are less committed but swayed by apparently coherent arguments ... Of course, the power of economic rationalists in the Canberra bureaucracy is absolute; those in the bureaucracy with an alternative view simply do not get heard.

I then commented on the particularly pernicious effects of applying free-market economics to environmental and cultural issues.

> Before I left Australia a year ago I began talking to some progressive friends and colleagues about the establishment in

21

Canberra of, for want of a better description, a progressive think tank … The purpose of such an institute would be to help counter the influence of economic rationalism on the policy debate and develop alternatives … [It would tackle] any issue in which a strong progressive influence is important and in which we could attract a well-written forceful contribution.

All those I wrote to replied expressing firm to strong support, with Hugh Stretton complaining that setting up such a think tank would not be necessary if universities were doing their job, a sentiment I shared. From that point, my mind was made up to return to Australia and carry out my plan.

4

A think tank

WHEN WE RETURNED to Canberra from Jakarta in August
1993, I set about making contact with potential supporters
for my progressive think tank. For the first few months, I worked
some of the time from John Langmore's office in Parliament House.
John was a thorn in Prime Minister Keating's side. A self-described
Christian socialist, he criticised Keating's economic agenda as unjust
and flawed. But the tide of neoliberalism, combined with the force of
Keating's personality, saw him marginalised. He would, however, help
shape the early work of the Australia Institute.

As we gathered support for the idea, John and I tossed around
names for the new institute. The Australian Institute for Public Policy,
the Canberra Public Policy Institute and the Canberra Institute were
possibilities, but they seemed forgettable. Memories differ as to who
first suggested the Australia Institute, but it is likely that Meredith
Edwards, a friend of John's and at the time a senior public servant,
came up with the name. I have a strong memory of the day late in
1993, as John and I were crossing Northbourne Avenue, when I said,
'Could we really call it the Australia Institute? It's so audacious.' John
replied, 'Why not?' I chuckled at the thought of the right-wing think

tankers' irritation that a left-wing competitor had taken the high ground and registered the name without delay.

While sharing John Langmore's office I picked up some useful modes of operating. I mentioned to John that I did not use the 'Dr' title that my doctorate permitted me to use because it made me wince. 'In this game,' he said, 'you need to take advantage of whatever you can.' So I became Dr Clive Hamilton, which after a time became a signifier in my media presence.

I also noticed John's propensity to pick up the phone to congratulate effusively someone for an article they'd had in the newspaper or an interview they had done. It did not strike me as insincere but generous and collegial, particularly as we Australians are miserly with praise. So I have tried to make a point of expressing my admiration to people who have done something that impressed me, even to some I don't know. Although I could be an irritable boss, I always tried to give plenty of praise. After love, recognition is what we humans crave more than anything.

John and I shared a dislike for Keating's politics; he'd been captured by Treasury. Some Labor supporters still pine for those days because Keating was colourful, which was true enough. One day a journalist from *The Guardian* in London called in to see me at Parliament House. A friend of a friend, Martin Kettle was in town trying to obtain an interview with Keating. A year earlier, the London tabloids had dubbed Keating the 'Lizard of Oz' after he put a gentle guiding hand on the Queen's back. One outraged red top led with the headline 'Hands off our Queen, cobber'. (English people really do believe we call each other 'cobber'.) The prime minister's press secretary had said he could wait in the outer office and try to catch him for a quick interview. Martin returned to John's office an hour later looking a bit shell-shocked. He told me that Keating had walked through the outer office and, on being told a London reporter wanted to interview him, said, 'An English journalist, eh? The only time you people want to talk to me is when I twang the Queen's bra strap.'

'Did I hear him right?' Martin asked me.

'It sounds like something Keating would say,' I replied.

Sure enough, a day or two later *The Guardian* carried Keating's comment prominently, although, curiously, it changed 'twang' to 'tweak'. There was an uproar, with Keating denying he had said any such thing.

§

I knew that the Australia Institute would only be financially viable if donations to it were tax deductible for the donor. Virtually no philanthropist will donate to a think tank unless it has approved gift recipient status. So, with some pro bono legal advice, I carefully drew up the articles of association with that goal in mind, modelling them on those of the Institute of Public Affairs.

Most of those we approached to join the institute's board agreed. The first directors were drawn from universities and the NGO world and had extensive contacts and deep expertise. Hugh Saddler, an energy expert with ALP links, agreed. He would be a stalwart of the institute, soon offering some space in his offices in Deakin West. Hugh became my guru on all things concerning greenhouse gas emissions. Max Neutze, the esteemed ANU professor of urban studies, came on board as the chair. Max chaired the board for the institute's first five years before succumbing to cancer. For me, he was a font of wisdom, tolerance and compassion, and I came to rely on him for advice. His values were rooted in a quiet Christianity. Looking back at the early board membership, I notice that a number of members were Christians, the kind who only mention their faith when asked.

I was moving quickly; after all, it was my full-time job. In November 1993, only three months after returning from Jakarta, we held the first board meeting. I was formally appointed executive direc-tor for four years, to be paid when funds became available. Along with the flurry of decisions to be made – approving the memorandum and articles of association, agreeing on a statement of philosophy, setting up bank accounts, registering for tax purposes, finding an auditor, setting membership fees, planning a newsletter – an institutional culture was emerging, one that gave me a great deal of autonomy, reciprocated by regular reporting.

The public launch of the Australia Institute was held on 4 May 1994 at Brassey House, a heritage building opened in 1927 as a hostel for public servants. It brings back sepia-toned memories for me because as a boy I had sold newspapers from the steps on freezing Canberra mornings; the kitchen ladies would take pity on me and call me in to eat a hot breakfast. Michael Kirby, then president of the New South Wales Court of Appeal, agreed to be the main speaker. Kerry O'Brien, fronting *Lateline* at the time, was the MC. We were strapped for cash but I wanted the event to be lively, so I hired a quirky barbershop quartet to serenade the tables.

We had a full house and I couldn't have been happier with the mix of people. The idea of a new progressive think tank had caught on. Kerry was smooth, witty and professional. I spoke about the genesis and purpose of the institute, and Max Neutze spoke on what would be an early theme in our work, a return of ethics in the age of economics. In a superb speech, Michael Kirby talked of the neglect and marginalisation of the unemployed and Indigenous people but also of 'druggies, sex workers, lesbians, poofs and other "trash"'. He set the institute a goal. 'May it never forget the neglected, the despised, the underprivileged, the disadvantaged ... let it speak up for the "trash".' We were all moved and inspired.

With speeches over, and the well-juiced crowd in a lively mood, it was time for the entertainment, a little-known comedian by the name of Judith Lucy. But where was she? I found Judith out the back, her face pale, her voice shaky. She was immobilised by stage fright. 'I can't do it,' she told me. She looked like she was going to be sick. I encouraged and coaxed her and soon led her into the room, then sat back down at the head table.

In her trademark drawl, Judith began by commenting on how intimidating it was to be in front of such an intellectual audience. 'It's great to be at an event where no one calls out "Show us your tits".'

Of course, someone called out, 'Show us your tits.'

Without missing a beat, Judith looked over to me. 'Was that you, Clive?'

My God! I shrank at the thought that anyone might believe I could say such a thing. As it happened, the person who called out, a local trade union leader, was at my table and was also named Clive.

Having regained her balance, Judith was soon flying. She was out there, the proto-feminist comedian with her bright red lipstick, hairy armpits and savage wit. Her spiel was excruciating but hilarious, with several edgy jokes about menstruation that made some of the older men blanch. I loved it. Her sharp commentary presaged my intention that the institute should challenge sensibilities; it reflected the early influence on me of the counterculture.

This account of the launch may sound as if the institute were preordained to succeed, but that's the trick of hindsight. At the time, I had no idea where we were going beyond the next couple of months. After two decades of striving to succeed, I had now given myself over to fate. I was following the maxim of an Indian sage, words I had heard second-hand: To get what you want, you first have to give up wanting.

§

Over the next two or three years, the Australia Institute's research focused largely on the perils of neoliberalism, with papers and conferences on privatisation, employment policy and the proper role of government. We argued that neoliberal policies were cultivating selfish individualism at the expense of community, teaching us to think of ourselves as consumers rather than as citizens. As I wrote in our first newsletter, we at the institute were motivated by a deepening sense that neoliberal economics had given us 'a society in which there is too much grasping and not enough giving, too much individual and not enough community, too much exploitation and not enough nurturing'.

With no money for staff, I approached sympathetic academics to write papers for us, offering the opportunity to get their ideas out of the scholarly journals, where they had little effect, and into the public debate. One of our best allies was John Quiggin, then at the ANU, who wrote a number of papers for the institute's new discussion paper series. John is a frighteningly intelligent economist, one of only three or four people I have known who qualify as genuinely brilliant, operating on a level way above the merely bright. I found it intimidating but soon learned to be grateful that someone so clever was on our side.

From its earliest days, the institute stayed out of direct politics. The heads of right-wing think tanks had deep connections with conservative politicians, including Labor ones, and spent much of their time working at shifting the Liberal Party further to the right. The Australia Institute was initially set up to oppose the economic rationalist agenda being implemented by the Keating government. The Hawke and Keating governments had adopted much of the conservatives' agenda, so identifying with Labor would not have made much sense.

The wave of economic rationalism had washed over Canberra, soaking the bureaucracy, but there were still a few issues where resistance based on solid argument might make a difference. Finance minister Kim Beazley seemed determined to sell everything not nailed down. John Quiggin and I wrote a paper showing that privatising the Commonwealth Serum Laboratories was gifting $600 million in value to the new owners. Our work made no difference. The new owners duly realised the windfall and used it to expand CSL into one of the nation's biggest businesses.

As a rule, when the more progressive party adopts the conservatives' policy, or vice versa, the game is over. There was no point trying to undo history, even if there was a constituency out there cheering us on. So we broadened our interests, publishing papers on native title, taxation, gambling and greenhouse policy. As the chair of a House of Representatives committee in 1995, John Langmore wangled a few thousand dollars for a paper on a carbon tax. I wrote it with an ANU economist named Mick Common. The analysis showed that if the revenue from a carbon tax were used to abolish payroll tax then employment overall would be boosted while emissions fell. Mick, a pugnacious northern Englishman, was unpleasant to work with. He saw himself as among the elite who didn't need to prove how smart they were by obtaining a doctorate. He was prone to scrawling 'WRONG' across my drafts as if correcting a slow-witted undergraduate, until one day I gave him a blunt character assessment.

That 1996 carbon tax paper was the beginning of my preoccupation with global warming, one that would dominate my work for more than two decades and upend the way I saw the world.

5

Opening climate skirmishes

T HE FIRST DEMOCRATIC elections in South Africa were held in April 1994. A month earlier, I travelled to South Africa at the invitation of officials from the Trade Union Congress and African National Congress to provide advice on the creation of an economic policy centre to help guide the new South Africa after apartheid. Within hours of a dawn landing in Johannesburg, I was in discussions with my counterparts. They were full of ideas and enthusiasm but had a kind of revolutionary consciousness not very conducive to establishing a think tank.

Later in the day I went to my hotel, a good one favoured by business visitors. To stave off the jet lag I went for a walk. As I returned along a quiet sidestreet by the hotel, I was confronted by two black youths, one approaching from the left and one from the front. The latter pulled a knife on me. I glimpsed it, long and serrated, and a couple of feet from my stomach. In the microsecond I had to react, it occurred to me that these guys were going to stab me no matter what. In a flash, I turned and bolted. I heard my glasses clatter on the bitumen. I sensed the guy with the knife lunge at my back and then come after me. After a few paces he decided against pursuing me – chasing a white guy down a street while brandishing a knife has its risks.

I mentioned the incident to my hosts, who were embarrassed. They recommended I move to the Rosebank Hotel, which they said was 'cheaper, safer and better'. I followed their advice. The Rosebank was laid-back, unpretentious and pleasant. Back in Australia, I heard that on the night after I departed, five men brandishing AK-47s burst into the hotel's dining room and stripped everyone of their valuables.

My preference for keeping the Australia Institute aloof from day-to-day politics was reinforced as our focus shifted to larger social issues, but there was a deeper reason for that position. I am an introvert, with an aversion to schmoozing, glad-handing, lobbying and, oftentimes, being in the same room as other human beings. These are not ideal character traits for the head of a think tank. My dealings with various think tanks in Britain, the United States and Australia taught me that CEOs seem to spend the lion's share of their time on precisely the activities I loathe. Moreover, rich people, as a rule, tend to be right wing, so right-wing think tanks have a natural advantage over left-wing ones. It didn't help that I had an aversion to ingratiating myself with rich people. Looking back, I guess I just hoped something would come along.

It's surprising what you can do while living off the smell of an oily rag, as the institute did for its first five years. Apart from a few thousand here and there from an NGO or a government agency for a piece of research, our only source of funds was an untied grant of $10,000 a year from the Oikoumene Foundation, a small Canberra philanthropic trust. The institute was unable to pay me so I accepted some part-time teaching at the ANU offered by Glenn Withers, head of the Graduate Program in Public Policy. Luckily, we had a small mortgage. Janenne's aunt and uncle had offered us their nice little house in Ainslie to rent when they moved to Sydney. After a year, they asked if we'd like to buy it and suggested a price of $50,000. That was way below the market price and we entered an awkward process of pushing the price up to something we would not feel guilty about. It seems hard to believe nowadays. I sometimes think I have been very lucky in life.

The vision of a left-wing think tank inspired some wonderful volunteers on whom I relied. Soon after moving into the office in Deakin West, an older gentleman in a tweed jacket and tie arrived offering to help. Noel Semple was a quiet and methodical man with bookkeeping skills. Over the next three years or so he created a beautiful set of handwritten accounts that always drew praise from our accountants. Technology, in the form of MYOB, made Noel redundant, but he called in periodically to talk about politics.

Another person who turned up to volunteer was Shane Rattenbury, a young man who radiated fitness. A dedicated triathlete aiming for the top, Shane would go on to spend several years working for Greenpeace before entering ACT politics, eventually leading the Greens in their coalition government with Labor. There were other volunteers in the early years (Marilyn Chalkley, John Dargavel and Rod Pickette come to mind). Many people contributed to the success of the institute during my tenure – board members, staff, volunteers, supporters – and I regret that I can't name them all here.

§

Apart from money, a think tank needs credibility above all, and the best way to get it is to borrow some from those who already have it. One of the institute's early successes in this respect was to host in 1996 a public lecture by José Ramos-Horta. It was his first event in Australia since receiving the Nobel peace prize for his tireless diplomacy leading to East Timor's independence. Arranging the event was hard going because Ramos-Horta was disorganised and unreliable. Still, he was a man of great charisma, and when you met him, anything could be forgiven. We hired the Senate chamber in Old Parliament House and in the end could have sold two or three times more tickets than we had. On the night, Ramos-Horta gave a speech of tremendous grace and power. He had an astonishing capacity to speak to the hearts of his listeners. The standing ovation at the end was like none I have ever heard. As Ramos-Horta, hand on heart, bowed again and again, I thought the applause would lift the roof. Of course, some of the love stuck to the institute.

The political environment of the institute changed radically in March 1996 when the Keating government was ousted by a landslide victory to John Howard's Coalition. In a way, life became simpler for us. Those who had made compromises with Labor, like the trade union movement, could be more progressive again. We saw our role as leading the formation of new thinking, the more so as Labor licked its wounds and thought about how to rebuild.

The new government announced that Treasury had found a 'Beazley black hole' in the budget. It was a manufactured fiscal crisis used by Treasurer Peter Costello as an excuse for fierce social welfare cuts. Howard also appointed a National Commission of Audit, staffed by right-wing ideologues linked to the Institute of Public Affairs, whose quick-time report set out a program for slashing government. It was all ideology, much of it too extreme even for the Howard government to get away with, and it sent a chilling message about the influence of the IPA, the epicentre of the hard right in Australia.

The Australia Institute did its own 'audit' of the Audit Commission report, convening a symposium with progressive experts and publishing papers that took apart its shonky reasoning. I didn't expect this work to change anything; as I saw it, the economic battle had been lost. The symposium was more a way of taking stock and building our network.

By mid-1996 the institute had a few thousand in the bank, and so I hired a part-time deputy director, Elizabeth Morgan. Elizabeth, who had a strong background in welfare policy, had been a mature student whom I had taught in the public policy program at ANU. Soon after, the institute went online, announcing its first 'home page' with the URL http://www.ozemail.com.au/~austinst/austinst.html. It wasn't until 1998 that advances in the internet allowed us to simplify it to www.tai.org.au.

Around the middle of 1997, Hugh Saddler's business was expanding and we needed to find new accommodation. We rented a small office in a cheap building at Lyneham shops in north Canberra, enough for three people plus a volunteer or two. Soon after moving, I noticed an uneasy feeling about the place, a 'bad vibe'. I felt it each morning as I arrived, as if someone had been murdered there or the previous tenants had a toxic workplace that had seeped into the walls. After a time, I mentioned it to Elizabeth. She had been feeling it too. I thought it would pass, but it did not seem to fade. We talked it over and I suggested that I ask an Anglican bishop I knew, an institute supporter named Richard Randerson, to carry out some kind of cleansing ritual. Neither of us were at all religious but it was that or break the lease and move out.

Richard arrived a day or two later. He walked around the room softly saying a prayer and waving something. Elizabeth and I quietly followed him. It was all very low-key. Whatever he did, it worked. Arriving the next morning, it was immediately apparent that the unpleasant feeling was gone. Many will scoff, as I once would have. Since my teens I had been a hard-nosed rationalist, but from my late thirties I began to appreciate that there is more to the world than the eye can see.

§

Some of our research papers began to attract attention. A 1997 analysis of 'ecological tax reform' – written by John Quiggin, environmental economist Tor Hundloe and myself – proposed a suite of measures centred on a $6.3 billion carbon tax with the revenue used to abolish payroll taxes. We estimated that implementation of the various measures would cut Australia's carbon emissions by 40 per cent in 2020 and increase employment by around 250,000. Published with the Australian Conservation Foundation, it was widely read. Robert Hill, Howard's new environment minister, asked his department to evaluate our proposals. His openness to ideas was short-lived.

In the same year, 1997, I was approached by Ed Wensing, national policy director at the Royal Australian Planning Institute. With a colleague, land valuer John Sheehan, he had written a paper on the land management implications of the High Court's Wik decision on native title land. At the time, the mining industry had mounted a despicable campaign to undermine Indigenous rights, convincing pastoralists that their properties were threatened. It even funded an advertising campaign in Western Australia suggesting First Nations people were coming to take away suburban backyards. It was the worst kind of dog whistling.

I agreed to publish the paper and had it refereed and edited. So popular did it prove that we had to do three reprints, selling around a thousand copies. Elizabeth and I spent days answering the phone and going to the post office, so I had to employ a part-time secretary for three months. It was all we could afford.

We gained some notice within the Indigenous policy community for this paper and a follow-up one. Our March 1997 newsletter led with a powerful article by Mick Dodson, then the Aboriginal and Torres Strait Islander Social Justice commissioner, in which he argued that the Howard government was emphasising the 'practical' problems of Indigenous disadvantage as a way of undermining their political claims for rights. In September 1999, we published the results of a study, led by Max Neutze, in response to Pauline Hanson's widely believed claim that Indigenous people were receiving excessive hand-outs, disadvantaging white people. It was a complex piece of work covering spending on education, employment, health and housing services, but the conclusion was pretty clear: spending on programs for Indigenous people was not excessive, especially compared with the disadvantages they suffer.

Not long after, I was invited to be a speaker at a large conference of Indigenous leaders, to be held at Canberra's convention centre. I felt honoured but, on reflection, decided to decline. I didn't think I would have anything interesting to say and thought I would feel uncomfortable as a white person dispensing advice to Indigenous leaders. I still wonder whether declining was the right thing to do and whether I had insulted the hosts.

§

In a March 1996 note to the board, I proposed the institute do more work on climate change. It was clear to me that it was an important public policy issue that was not going to go away, and no other players were talking about its implications. Hugh Saddler was years ahead of almost everyone in understanding the implications of the enhanced greenhouse effect, and our early conversations had a deep influence on me. My fascination with and concern about the issue went up several notches when in August 1997 I travelled to Bonn to attend a meeting of the parties to the United Nations Framework Convention on Climate Change. It was a preparatory event for the vital conference in Kyoto to be held three months later, and it opened my eyes to the vast international significance of global warming that we in Australia, asleep in the sun, failed to notice.

It was there I first met Bill Hare, who led Greenpeace International's climate campaign from Amsterdam. At that point, environment NGOs did not give much priority to climate change and Bill, an Australian with a physics PhD, had battled to persuade Greenpeace to commit to it properly. Within the international negotiating community his views carried authority. I soon formed the view that Bill Hare was the most influential Australian in the global climate debate, and one of three NGO leaders internationally whose opinions helped shape the climate change agenda for a decade or more.

In Bonn, I also realised how deeply the influence of the fossil fuel lobby penetrated into the Canberra bureaucracy. I attended a 'side event' put on by the US fossil fuel lobby to reinforce its claim that reducing coal and oil consumption would cause massive economic dislocation. Lined up on stage with the apologists for coal and oil was the head of the Australian Bureau of Agricultural and Resource

Economics (ABARE), Brian Fisher. The message was unmistakable: this public servant was one of them. The Howard government was shameless; even Australia's official delegations to climate change negotiations included lobbyists from the fossil fuel industries.

ABARE had built an economic model to prove how damaging it would be for Australia to cut its carbon emissions. It was a dodgy model, biased from one end to the other, with its skewed results presented in ways designed to mislead and frighten the public. John Quiggin and I would soon take it apart, piece by piece.

The energy minister, Senator Warwick Parer, was later forced to admit under questioning from the Australian Democrats that the ABARE modelling was funded by contributions from the big fossil fuel companies and their lobby groups. In return, the lobbyists earned a seat on the 'steering committee' overseeing the work. It was scandalous. I had grown up in Canberra believing in the professionalism and strict neutrality of public servants in the advice they give government. My father, like his peers, saw himself ultimately serving the public rather than the government.

My criticism of ABARE's collaboration with the fossil fuel lobby was unrelenting. I made enemies and the hostility was directed not only at me. At high school my daughter was berated by a fellow student, whose father was an executive at ABARE. 'Your father's a communist,' he jeered. The incident was part of her political education.

An inquiry by the ombudsman later lambasted ABARE, not least for misleading readers of its reports by hiding its funding sources. Fisher rejected the findings, although he conceded that perhaps he should have anticipated the 'misunderstandings'. The government's chief adviser on climate economics continued to share platforms with fossil fuel lobbyists around the world. Brian Fisher told a conference in London that it would be cheaper to evacuate small island states subject to inundation by rising seas rather than to require rich countries like Australia to reduce their emissions. I suggested he go tell that to the Tuvaluans forced to abandon their homes. That kind of moral failure was common among the conservatives and free-market economists opposed to cutting emissions. The Howard government would award Fisher the Public Service Medal.

All of this was sickening to watch. But it set the pattern for the desperate tactics used by conservative governments in Australia for the next two decades.

§

International anger at Australia's climate stance had been made very real to me in September 1997 when I travelled to the Cook Islands to watch the Pacific Island Forum. The invitation came from the Te Ipukarea Society, a local environmental organisation. As an Australian, I felt ashamed observing John Howard bully tiny island states threatened by rising seas into muting their calls for stronger climate action. And I worried about the likely legacy of resentment it would leave.

The Howard government told lie after lie about climate change. In the lead-up to the December 1997 Kyoto conference, ministers returned from abroad announcing that Australia's position, which amounted to asking for special concessions to keep polluting, was receiving a sympathetic hearing. Energy minister Warwick Parer, previously a Queensland coalmining executive, told a business conference that he didn't believe in the science. Parer, who for years had shared a Canberra flat with his friend John Howard, secretly owned shares in coal companies while he was the minister. Eventually he was forced out and went to work for the coal industry.

When I arrived in Kyoto in November 1997 for the vital third Conference of the Parties (COP 3), the expectation that something globally significant would emerge was palpable. By now I was convinced that global warming was the dominant environmental problem before which all others paled. It was awkward to be an Australian among those who took it seriously. For three or four decades, Australia had built a strong international reputation as one of the environmental good guys, but that reputation was now in freefall over climate change.

The Kyoto conference was sensational. With some five thousand people packed into the vast conference hall, it was nerve-racking as the days passed and negotiations were bogged down in minutiae. Over two gruelling weeks, rumours circulated hourly, drafts were leaked and coffee was drunk in prodigious quantities. Australia joined with obstructionist Saudi Arabia and Russia, relentlessly advocating for narrow fossil fuel interests, squandering decades of international goodwill. We became a pariah nation.

Towards the end, I bumped into the renowned environmental author David Suzuki on a lonely train platform outside the conference centre. He was grumbling about the waste of energy and attention given to these big international conferences; the only solutions were local. For me, coordinated global commitments were essential, but I wasn't up for an argument and said nothing.

As midnight on the last day ticked over, marking the official end of the conference, the clock was 'stopped' so negotiations could continue. Finally, in the early hours an agreement was struck, an extraordinary balancing act between the United States, Europe and the Group of 77 developing countries. At 2 am the conference chair was gavelling through the protocol's various clauses and subclauses that had been agreed to by all 181 parties. It included permission for Australia to *increase* its emissions by 8 per cent by 2010, the only nation so favoured other than Russia. And then, at the last moment, Robert Hill stood and said that Australia would torpedo the entire agreement unless the exhausted delegates agreed to insert what was known as the 'Australia clause' on land clearing.

Forced to accept, the world community was appalled at Australia's tactics and demands. An EU spokesman called it 'wrong and immoral'. Back in Canberra, at the first post-Kyoto meeting of the Howard cabinet, Robert Hill received a standing ovation. In the face of dire scientific warnings, smug Australian conservatives shafted international negotiations to protect coal interests. They would still be doing it at COP 26 in Glasgow in 2021.

The Australia clause enabled emissions from land clearing to be included in a nation's greenhouse gas accounts. In practice, it applied to Australia alone. The clause continues to be fundamental to Australia's emission targets. Infuriated at the statistical sleight of hand enabled by the clause, I went on something of a crusade to explain to the public the Howard government's swindle. The essence of Article 3.7 is this. In the Kyoto Protocol, each nation's agreed reductions in emissions (or in Australia's case, a lower increase) would be counted from the base year of 1990. Australia, alone among developed countries, had very large emissions from land clearing in 1990, much of it for cattle grazing in Queensland. Emissions from land clearing happened to have peaked in 1990 and had fallen steeply by 1997, giving Australia scope to sharply increase our fossil fuel emissions while offsetting them against large reductions in emissions that had *already taken place* and had nothing to do with greenhouse policy measures. As Labor's Duncan Kerr said, reaching our target would be 'a three-inch putt'.

The day after the Kyoto conference ended, I issued a media release saying the Queensland government, which decided on most land clearing, held the key to Australia's Kyoto commitment. Everyone involved knew Australia's Kyoto deal was a scam. Yet it remained the numerical basis for the mantra repeated thousands of times by the Abbott, Turnbull and Morrison governments – that Australia would 'meet and beat' our Kyoto target. It's dishonest. The slogan has been used to create the entirely erroneous impression that the government was doing something effective to reduce emissions. The Australia clause meant we had to do virtually nothing to meet our target.

If that were not enough, two years after Kyoto, Howard reneged on the Kyoto deal, saying Australia would not ratify the treaty it had signed. The deniers were on the ascendant, led in parliament by Senator Nick Minchin, and attitudes in the Howard government were hardening even more. Howard had Hugh Morgan in his ear. The CEO of Western Mining (now part of BHP Billiton), who would soon be president of the Business Council of Australia, was a denialist

fanatic. In 2000, when Robert Hill's environment department published four reports exploring the pros and cons of emissions trading,
Hugh Morgan denounced them as 'Mein Kampf declarations'. This
extremist remained John Howard's closest business adviser.

In 2001 I wrote a book exposing it all, *Running from the Storm*.
No one took much notice.

6

The power of words

F OR A THINK TANK like the Australia Institute, which didn't engage in lobbying, our effectiveness depended largely on our ability to get our messages out through the media. As my staff quickly learned, I could be pedantic; my kids once gave me a t-shirt that read 'I am silently correcting your grammar'. I grew up in a wordy household – correct spellings, pronunciations, meanings and usages were part of the daily back and forth, along with puns and double entendres. The Oxford English Dictionary (the 'OED') was frequently consulted. Fowler's *Dictionary of Modern English Usage* was simply 'Fowler'. Grammar was always gently corrected.

As a teenager, I'd read a lot of George Orwell, the master of plain English, and I honed my writing skills at university, forming the view that if I could not express an idea in clear prose then I did not understand it and should do some more thinking. At the Australia Institute, I edited everything for good English and blanched when mistakes crept into our publications. Without shunning colourful or memorable imagery, every sentence should be distinguished by clarity. Although the staff sometimes rolled their eyes at my editing, I hope they took something away from it, because the ability to write well is a boon to any career.

We couldn't afford a media officer in the early years, so I also taught myself how to write a press release. When each one was finalised, I would make two hundred copies. As the only one at the institute with a Parliament House staff pass (courtesy of John Langmore), I would head over to the press gallery and manually put the releases in the press boxes. I remembered performing the same task when, for a year or so in 1979–80, I worked in the original Parliament House as a researcher for a Labor Party senator. It was slightly embarrassing to be doing this task and I worked quickly, hoping I would not be caught in the act by any journalists. Back at the office I would fax the release to selected journalists outside Canberra then sit back and hope the phone would ring. It was late in 1998 before I acquired my first mobile phone so I included my home landline for after-hours calls.

A deep understanding of the complex, subtle world of the media is imperative for a successful think tank. You first need to know your way around the main newspapers and news and current affairs programs on radio and TV, and nowadays the online world too. Relationships, however transactional, need to be built with the journalists in your areas of interest. It's a relationship of mutual benefit – unless they are nice on the phone and nasty in print, in which case you scratch them off your list. You need to learn to do a meta-reading of news stories. Before reading one, you take note of the outlet, the placement of the story, the headline and, of course, the by-line. In doing a meta-reading of news stories, you are asking yourself: What's the orientation of this news outlet? What's the orientation of the journalist – straight reporting, agenda-driven, tabloid-style? What's the message being communicated on the surface and between the lines? Who did they go to for quotes to reinforce the story and what does that say? How are the editors presenting it – headline, placement, photo – and what does that tell me?

When a new research report was ready for release, as a producer of potential news I had to ask myself: Should we do a scattergun news release or target an outlet for an exclusive? Which outlet is most likely to be interested? How can I craft a story and pitch it in a way more likely to appeal to one news outlet rather than another? Which journalists cover this topic? Is the timing right?

My understanding of the media improved dramatically from 2001 after I employed press gallery veteran Jacqui Rees to provide advice. She was only part-time and I paid her much less than she was worth, but she was committed to the institute. Jacqui was invaluable, on hand to shape a media release, advise me on whether to offer an exclusive, provide background on a journalist and respond to any problems. One of her earliest pieces of advice was to urge me to be the institute's front man for the media rather than have report authors do the media. The institute needs to have a figurehead, the person the media thinks of. It was difficult to get the balance, as I know how much people need recognition for their work, so I juggled it as best I could over the years. Jacqui gave me another piece of advice that stuck with me: if you are going to criticise someone, do it more in sorrow than in anger. I resolved to put it into practice, although my resolve often failed me.

Occasionally, I got it wrong. In late 1997, the tumultuous waterfront dispute broke out between Patrick Stevedores and the Maritime Union of Australia. The company wanted to break the union's influence and push up productivity on the wharves, measured by crane rates. Patrick and Peter Reith, John Howard's industrial relations minister and hardman, insisted crane rates could be raised to twenty-five lifts an hour. Examining international data, I did a piece of analysis arguing that the prevailing rate of around eighteen was already close to the international benchmark expected under Australian waterfront conditions, and twenty-five lifts an hour was out of reach. (You might be wondering how I could present myself as an expert on crane rates, of all things? It's a fair question. The answer is chutzpah, but it only works if you already have credibility as an analyst.) When I put out the report in April 1998 it was the first time the institute was the subject of a media frenzy. I went on *Today Tonight* and, carried away by the tabloid TV environment, ended up saying that Peter Reith had gone into the dispute with testosterone pumping, but had come out with 'pizzle rot'. It was a silly line, embarrassing in retrospect. Although my research was based on highly credible international data and the report had been reviewed by a couple of experts, three years later it became clear that crane rates of twenty-five an hour were indeed possible. I was ready to admit the mistake and waited for someone to call me out. But no one did.

7
Dirty politics

As A RULE, when you enter the public domain, the more influence you have, the more enemies you attract. As the institute kicked into a higher gear and my profile rose, some of the attention we received was less quizzical and more hostile. Before we reached that stage, however, we still lacked the most important element for success – money.

By the end of 1997, the institute's financial position was perilous. We had $20,000 in the bank and could no longer pay Elizabeth Morgan. When I left my previous job to establish the institute my income fell by around two thirds, and I was supplementing the meagre payments from the institute with part-time teaching at the ANU. Janenne had been solidly supportive from the outset, but I began to feel I had tested the family's patience too much. The institute had tried everything and I was at the point of concluding that the venture was not going to work. So in March 1998 I wrote a memo to the board saying we had reached a crunch point and had to consider shutting down. I then listed a few unsuccessful appeals we had made for funding and mentioned in passing that I had made a submission to an obscure philanthropic trust called the Poola Foundation.

I didn't know Karen Alexander very well, but the environmental activist and adviser to the Poola Foundation was responsible for suggesting to Mark Wootton, who managed the foundation, that he meet me. The foundation was a new, progressive philanthropic trust founded by Eve Kantor and Mark Wootton, with a shedload of money to give away. When Mark came to our office at Lyneham shops, he must have been impressed, because a few weeks later the foundation agreed to give the institute $100,000. It was the start of a beautiful friendship. For Mark, it's all about trust. The credibility of the institute's board members provided enough reassurance for him to 'take a punt', as he phrased it. A year later, Poola committed to substantial funding over three years, aided by linked foundations from the same family. The funding kept coming and was the bedrock of the institute's operations for as long as I was executive director.

I enjoyed the irony that Australia's foremost left-wing think tank was funded by Rupert Murdoch's money. As I soon learned, Rupert's sister Anne Kantor had very progressive views, as did her children, including Eve, to whom Mark was married. Members of the Murdoch family had inherited shares in News Corp, but in the early 1990s Rupert decided to buy them out. They were each left with millions to give away. It may sound strange to say but it is not easy to give away millions of dollars in a responsible way. Mark and Eve were down-to-earth and modest and as far from the Dirty Digger's global power politics as you could get. Without the vision of Mark Wootton, Eve Kantor and Anne Kantor, the Australia Institute would not exist today.

With secure funding, I could for the first time appoint someone full-time to run the office and recruit a few researchers. As I did so, we moved to new offices in University House on the ANU campus.

§

In public life, any perceived weakness is liable to be noted and used against you at any time. I had unwittingly opened myself up to some very grubby attacks when in 1994 I agreed, after some hesitation, to speak on Caroline Jones's long-running ABC Radio program *The Search for Meaning*. The program was a platform for people, under Caroline's gentle guidance, to speak of their own spiritual or religious experiences. As it happened, at the end of the 1980s I had had, unbidden and out of the blue, a numinous experience, for want of a better term. The event shook me up and over the next few years, as I explored the meaning of it, I had other experiences. One, which I related to Caroline, was a kind of waking dream or visualisation that centred on an unpleasant character who announced himself as 'Jacob'.

When the program went to air, my doubts were assuaged by the warm response from the public. Many people contacted me to say what a relief it was to hear someone talking about these things in public as they themselves had struggled alone. (I know I'm being vague, but once bitten …)

Fast-forward three years to September 1997 when I received a couple of phone calls from people in Parliament House urging me to turn on the radio and listen to question time in the Senate. I was disturbed to hear Senator Warwick Parer, the energy minister, delivering a sneering personal attack in which he ridiculed my on-air revelations. He had great sport with my mention of the figure of Jacob, making me out as someone who hears voices. It was a premeditated character assassination in response to a Dorothy Dixer asked by Senator Eric Abetz. The government was upset at my criticisms of its abysmal failure to take global warming seriously, not least my role in organising a statement signed by 131 professional economists critical of the government's arguments and calling for a firm policy to cut emissions. Parer set out to trash my credibility under cover of parliamentary privilege.

A few days later, Democrats Senator Meg Lees rose in the Senate to excoriate Parer for his 'manic diatribe'. She denounced Parer's 'unjustified and undignified attack' on me and defended my reputation. Then she tabled the statement by the economists. At the urging of other members of parliament, I wrote a response to the Privileges

Committee, which has members from all sides. Recognising the smears for what they were, the committee agreed to incorporate my reply into Hansard, where it can now be read.

It made little difference. Several years later, in 2006, the dirt file was dusted off. I had been arguing in public that continuing drought assistance to some farmers is counterproductive and it would be better to help them off the land. MPs from both sides were enraged. Prime Minister Howard said my proposal was 'quite absurd and ridiculous', although a year later his government began offering 'exit grants' for exactly the purpose I had described. This time, instead of asking the Dorothy Dixer, Eric Abetz made the same sneering attack on me after a question from Senator Bill Heffernan, Junee farmer and political bruiser. Once again, I wrote to the Privileges Committee, which agreed to incorporate my reply into Hansard.

Although people told me the attacks were a badge of honour, when you have men like Parer, Abetz and Heffernan coming after you in parliament, undoubtedly with the approval of the prime minister, it hurts, even when you have a thickish skin. At times over the years I wanted to retreat from the fray, but then something would come along that annoyed me and I would go on the front foot once more. That was the case with the GST, which had its own lessons for how the institute operated.

§

John Howard had gone into the October 1998 election promising to introduce a goods and services tax (GST) to replace a swag of sales taxes levied by the Commonwealth and the states. He almost lost the election, with Labor winning 51 per cent of the vote on a two-party preferred basis. While retaining a majority in the House of Representatives, Howard was relying on the votes of the seven Democrats in the Senate to pass his tax reform legislation. Over the next months a fierce political battle developed, mostly focused on the welfare implications of the GST package of tax changes.

The government was desperate to have the legislation passed and began courting Democrats leader Meg Lees.

In September 1998, the institute published an analysis of the environmental consequences of the GST package. We had noticed that it included changes that would cut diesel prices, benefiting road over rail transport, reduce petrol prices for businesses, and make cars cheaper. It would also penalise renewable energy. Yet the Coalition's weighty GST policy document made no mention at all of the environmental implications of the reforms. Personally, I was not opposed to the GST as a replacement for the dog's breakfast of sales taxes, but I was implacably opposed to the elements of the package that would increase urban air pollution and worsen our carbon emissions.

With financial support from the New South Wales Sustainable Energy Development Authority, Hal Turton and I did the numbers. Hal was a brilliant researcher who had dropped out of his doctoral studies in biochemistry to work at the institute. We showed that overall the tax changes would see carbon emissions and particulate pollution rise significantly. We published a discussion paper that attracted almost no media attention, although people were buying copies. When the Coalition won the election the following month, I wrote to Senator Meg Lees setting out the issues. She took a keen interest and the Democrats initiated a Senate inquiry into the environmental effects of the GST package with terms of reference modelled on our concerns. Lyn Allison, the Democrats' environment spokesperson, had taken an early interest in our analysis and invited me to her office to discuss it.

When the media asked him about our report, Treasurer Peter Costello was contemptuous. He seemed unable to grasp our simple point: if you cut the price of fossil fuels then people will use more of them and that will mean more pollution. The amount depends on the size of the price cut and the sensitivity of demand for fossil fuels to price changes, for which we had used conservative estimates. Economics does not get any more basic than that, but Costello just didn't get it.

In December 1998, we made a submission to the Senate inquiry reproducing our results on the environmental implications of the tax changes. I was discovering that submissions to parliamentary inquiries can be a very effective way of putting analysis and ideas into the policy assessment process. And, if it's a well-argued submission, the media sometimes regard it as more newsworthy. As long as the arguments are solid and well made, they provide ammunition to committee members who share your perspective, and they force your opponents to respond. You can also say things in parliamentary submissions that cannot otherwise be said without the risk of being sued for defamation. If the committee publishes the submission then you are protected by parliamentary privilege.

Many scientific studies around the world had shown that fine particles in diesel fumes cause respiratory diseases and premature deaths. At the time, the best estimate was that over a thousand Australians died each year as a result of inhaling particulates, mostly from diesel. So I decided to up the stakes. We calculated that, using conservative figures, at least sixty-five more Australians would die each year as a result of the increased particulates due to the GST package's cuts in fuel prices, along with additional road deaths from more trucks on the roads. We made another submission to the Senate inquiry. Costello, Robert Hill and other government members mocked our claim.

The number was robust, but I realised that a robust number is sometimes not enough. So I contacted the Australian Medical Association and, together with the Australian Conservation Foundation, we made a joint submission to the Senate committee restating our analysis, including the sixty-five deaths claim. When the committee brought down its report in March 1999 it said that it found our arguments 'compelling' and that the health implications of the GST package were 'profoundly disturbing'. The report in effect endorsed our sixty-five number, thereby legitimising it. The government knew it had a problem, driven home over the next couple of months as business groups associated with railways and the gas industry (big hitters like BP Amoco, AGL and Boral) belatedly began lining up to criticise the proposed fuel price changes.

As the negotiations between Costello and Meg Lees approached a peak in May 1999, Lyn Allison asked me to be on hand to respond to the government's arguments. She told me that a red line for the Democrats was that any deal must result in 'no net damage to the environment', which reassured me that I would not be embarrassed by association with it. After consulting with the chair of my board, I agreed, and spent the last several days of the high-drama negotiation period in and out of Lyn's office.

A few days later, it became clear that the government was lying through its teeth. It had secretly asked the Bureau of Transport Economics to model the effects of the GST package on air pollution and carbon emissions. When the Democrats managed to extract the results tables from the government and brought them to me to inter-pret, I was shocked by Robert Hill's cynicism. While he continued to claim there would be no environmental damage, his own numbers showed that the damage would be *double* our estimates.

Surely the government would now have to make major modifica-tions to the package's polluting elements to get it through the Senate? But by that point, Meg Lees – having extracted concessions on fresh food – was already locked into a deal. She had accepted government assurances that it would allocate some funds to offset the environ-mental damage and bring forward tighter emission standards, but for me the promises were all on the never-never and would not offset the damage even if enacted. She had forsaken the commitment to no net environmental damage, shafting Lyn Allison in the process.

When I heard Meg Lees was about to do a deal, and still stunned by Robert Hill's duplicity, it all felt too dirty. I didn't want to be asso-ciated with it and walked out of Parliament House. Tom Allard of *The Sydney Morning Herald* got wind of my walkout and phoned. Wanting to distance myself from the imminent deal, I confirmed the basic facts of my decision and expressed the view that the GST package cannot be rescued by any conceivable government offer.

The next morning, the story appeared below the headline 'Democrat adviser quits over push for diesel deal'. My withdrawal made the Democrats look worse. I felt bad for Lyn. She'd brought me into the tent, and when I walked out, she must have thought I had betrayed her. I had, and Meg Lees who had supported me in the past. But I felt I had been misled as I had agreed to help out on the understanding that the Democrats would not agree to a package that harmed the environment. The whole thing was a mess.

As it happened, the Democrats split, with five senators voting for the GST legislation and two, Natasha Stott Despoja and Andrew Bartlett, voting against. A couple of days later I received a call from Natasha. She was shell-shocked. Lees had broken the party's promise at the last election to oppose the GST. Voter support for the Democrats began to collapse, and the rest is history.

That was the closest I ever got to political events while at the institute. I was burnt by it and felt guilty at walking out on Lyn Allison. But the alternative was to be seen as endorsing a deal that was environmentally reckless. While I received plaudits for sticking to principle, I felt grubby. I guess politicians are caught in these traps often, compromising one principle in pursuit of another. Or just sacrificing principle for re-election. The experience confirmed that my predisposition to keep the institute out of politics was the prudent one.

A couple of weeks after the deal was done, I was interviewed for a *Four Corners* program devoted to the Democrats' role in the GST. I was relating the heated moment when one of Meg Lees' advisers had told me Treasury 'would not wear' the changes I was advocating. I retorted, 'Fuck Treasury. No one elected them.' (It was, I believe, the first time the ABC had broadcast the f-word, prompting indignant letters to the editor criticising Dr Hamilton's limited vocabulary.) When I sheepishly expressed regrets at the next board meeting, the chair at the time, Mary Crooks, dismissed my remorse. 'Oh, don't worry, Clive, it's nothing', she said, and we moved on. How I appreciated my board.

8

Advocacy scholarship

FOR ME, THE pinnacle of success for our research was to see stories based on our work splashed across the posters in the wire racks outside newsagencies. Although today devalued by the rise of online, the posters were the most definitive proof of our public impact. I collected them, visiting a local newsagency in the afternoon to ask if I could have the poster. They always obliged. I had them laminated and stuck them on the office wall. The first one I collected, in 1999, was also a sign that our research was making an impression internationally. After the GST debacle, the Australia Institute carried out a piece of research that had an enduring influence and proved that a simple number, in this case 26.7, can change the global conversation.

The United States was typically named as the nation with the world's highest greenhouse gas emissions per person. I knew that was probably incorrect; Australians were almost certainly the world's worst greenhouse gas polluters. The problem was that everyone accounted only for fossil fuel emissions, neglecting emissions from land use change, forestry and agriculture. For most countries the difference was negligible, but Australia had very large emissions from vegetation clearance. I also knew that all of the numbers were buried in the official inventories lodged with the United Nations. No one had put them together because there seemed no need to. The idea of calculating emissions comprehensively would occur only to someone who believed the full picture should be known *and* who had the technical knowledge. That was us.

I was familiar with the annual greenhouse gas inventories compiled by each nation as part of their obligations under the 1992 UN Framework Convention on Climate Change. My guide was Hugh Saddler, who was responsible for compiling much of Australia's inventory and knew the technical nooks and crannies of greenhouse accounting better than anyone else in the country.

I asked Hal Turton to do the numbers. We had some excellent researchers at the institute but Hal stood out in any kind of analysis involving numbers. He amazed me with the speed of his work, and it was no surprise that when he later took a job at a prestigious European energy research agency he moved quickly up the ranks. With Hal's calculations, aided by Hugh's technical advice and with me shaping the interpretation and presentation, we soon produced a paper showing that Australians indisputably have the highest greenhouse gas emission per person in the industrialised world.

At the time, a Senate committee was taking submissions for an inquiry into Australia's response to global warming, so in November 1999 I lodged an eight-page submission including the killer table of numbers. We issued a media release headed 'Australia has world's highest greenhouse emissions per capita: New study'. When all sources of greenhouse gases are factored in, I wrote, 'Australians emit 26.7 tonnes of greenhouse gases per capita per year, double that of other wealthy countries and 25 per cent more than emissions per person in the United States.'

On 5 November 1999, *The Age* and *The Sydney Morning Herald* carried the story on page one. *The Age*'s headline, 'Australia world's worst on greenhouse', shouted from the newsagencies' posters on the footpaths outside newsagents.

Within weeks, all over the world news stories were noting that Australians had the world's highest emissions per capita. The ethical and political significance of this charismatic fact was immense, because international 'burden-sharing' negotiations placed great weight on the polluter pays principle – the more you pollute, the more you are expected to cut your emissions.

The government twisted itself into knots trying to explain away this devastating statistic, based on its own figures, offering all kinds of excuses and special pleading, all of which we shot down in a subsequent submission to the Senate inquiry. It is not true, we argued, that our high fossil fuel dependence makes it harder for Australia to cut emissions because, unlike other rich countries, we had not yet picked the low-hanging fruit. Yes, our cities are far apart, but the vast majority of transport emissions occur within cities. And our reliance on coal exports is irrelevant because the carbon emissions from exported coal are counted against the nation that burns the coal. Over the next months, the institute made six submissions to the Senate inquiry covering various aspects of greenhouse policy and politics.

Throughout it all, environment minister Robert Hill spun the government's climate messaging in devious and absurd ways. Each evening, as we listened to *PM* or watched the seven o'clock ABC news, Janenne had to put up with me hissing, 'You rotten lying bastard.' Curiously, I react more strongly against politicians who know they are bullshitting than against the 'maddies' like Tony Abbott who are convinced that climate change is a hoax. On matters like this, it seems to me to be more wrong to tell lies cynically than to tell lies when you are deluded.

§

From 1998, with our funding secured for three or four years, the institute was shifting into top gear. We became the foremost critics of the Howard government's stance on greenhouse gas emissions simply because we did the research and put the arguments out there. We became a thorn in the government's side, not least because our research was influencing the way other nations viewed Australia.

When Tim Currie representing the European Union arrived in Australia in 1998 for talks, the government declared that the EU now understood, meaning accepted, the Australian position on climate change. I knew they were verballing Currie; the EU was furious with Australia. So I wrote to the environment commissioner of the EU, Ritt Bjerregaard, seeking clarification of the EU position. She wrote back to me in very blunt terms: 'I would like to emphasize that, while they may wish to portray it in that way, Mr Currie did not endorse or support the Australian Government's position.' The EU, she said, continues to be concerned about the level of the Australian target. And in a nice endorsement of our work: 'We will continue to need the support of the Institute in assessing the realism of Australia's target, which will be important as we move towards reviewing current levels.' Of course, I made the letter public, as Ritt Bjerregaard would have anticipated. I imagined John Howard and Robert Hill fuming in their offices.

In 1999 alone there were some forty mentions of our work in federal parliament. By 2001 newspapers were referring simply to 'the Australia Institute', without the need for a descriptor. One prominent academic said the institute had been the best thing to happen in progressive politics in Australia over the previous decade.

Our productivity was high because the staff were excellent and the projects were chosen for brevity and impact. Although we did a few projects with other organisations, I preferred to rely on projects that could be completed quickly by institute staff. We moved faster than other organisations. In choosing a research project, it was essential that it could be done by one or two researchers in three or four months, six at the very most. When people came to visit, they were always surprised at how few of us there were. With no more than half a dozen staff, supplemented by research from outside academics, many progressives told me that the Australia Institute was a beacon of light through the dark decade of the Howard government.

Of all the think tanks, the Australia Institute was the most transparent about its finances and operations. At times I asked myself if there was anything that would embarrass us if it appeared in newsprint. There was nothing, but that did not prevent the *Financial Review* columnist P. P. McGuinness describing us as 'a shadowy leftist think tank'. Piers Akerman, at the time the nastiest right-wing commentator, devoted a full column in *The Daily Telegraph* to trashing me and the institute, calling it a 'secretive left-wing think tank that doesn't publish a list of its supporters or sponsors, and doesn't intend to'. His piece was so chock-full of false claims that I contacted the editor and demanded a right of reply. Sometimes editors wave articles through then, when challenged by the target, look again and think, 'Shit, that is over the top, and defamatory.' The editor agreed to publish a letter from me and reluctantly accepted two hundred words, long for the *Telegraph*. I called out Akerman's fabrications about our opaque funding sources and said if he had bothered to phone me, I could have disabused him. Obviously stung, Akerman then claimed he had phoned the institute but been brushed off. I checked with the staff. The man had just lied outright.

§

When beginning a research project built around data collection, the outcome is often predictable. Sometimes, though, the numbers go against expectations, or complicate the picture in unexpected ways. I always welcomed that: if *we* were surprised then the final product would be surprising to others and therefore more newsworthy. Of course, the institute had an ideological orientation, but I always followed the protocols of academic research. I described what we did as 'advocacy scholarship'. In this we were much more intellectually honest than the right-wing think tanks. Some of the reports put out by the Centre for Independent Studies and the Institute for Public Affairs were no more than polemics, did not stand up to any kind of scrutiny and were often paid for by interested parties.

As this suggests, I take research integrity and academic freedom very seriously. When in the later 1990s I began to hear grumbling among academics about subtle curbs on their academic freedom, my ears pricked up, and in 2000 I initiated a research project to look into it. It was led by Pam Kinnear, a sociologist by trade whose talents, unappreciated by her previous employer, were obvious to me from her academic work. While at the institute, Pam was responsible for some highly influential reports, including a critique of mutual obligation – the Howard government's toxic policy of stigmatising the disadvantaged – and one on 'new families' to counter the prime minister's 1950s romantic vision of what families should look like. But none caused an uproar like the one on academic freedom, which brought the wrath of the varsity gods down upon us.

On 8 January 2001, *The Sydney Morning Herald* poster outside newsagencies blared 'How unis lower standards: New study'. The story was based on preliminary results from a survey we had conducted of academics. Although our survey was designed to test views on academic freedom, many had complained about pressure to lower standards for international fee-paying students. From the moment the *Herald* story appeared, and for some weeks afterwards, we were under siege. I learned that those who live atop ivory towers are just as capable of pulling on hobnail boots as any coal industry lobbyist.

Caught off guard, the university mandarins were incensed, reflexively denying there was any problem with the quality of their degrees. It seemed to me that their primary anxiety was the threat to the $3 billion education export industry. Each time they mentioned it, they reinforced our point about the commercialisation of universities. Their tempers worsened when the story about soft marking ran prominently in the *South China Morning Post* and *The Hindu*. The government panicked, instructing its embassies throughout Asia to issue a media release denying the allegations. The Australian Vice-Chancellors' Committee (AVCC) began accusing us of shoddy work. It even wrote a letter to my board complaining bitterly about our report. The board told them to bugger off.

I knew we were right – and so did the AVCC, including the more prestigious universities in the Group of Eight. It was a bruising encounter, and at times I was nervous. Within weeks, though, we were vindicated by the flood of stories and scandals that emerged after the dam wall broke. That was our job, in a way – dam-busting. In the most celebrated case, biologist Ted Steele at the University of Wollongong was dismissed for revealing that he had been instructed to upgrade two honours students. There was a backlash against the university. Steele was gutsy and the union backed him. The federal court would later order the university to reinstate him.

A Senate inquiry into soft marking was established. It was another avenue for academics to make their complaints public, although most feared reprisals if they spoke out against their employers. Nevertheless, the universities saw the writing on the wall. No longer did they deny they had a problem with soft marking, grade infla-tion and plagiarism; they announced they would investigate and do everything to root it out. Despite the brutal campaign against us by the universities, our reputation seemed to emerge unscathed. By the end of 2001, our role in the debate was deemed important enough for me to be invited by the Group of Eight to Christmas drinks. I didn't go; I suppose I should have, but drinks with important people is not my cup of tea.

While the furore was happening, our lease at the ANU was coming up for renewal. Vice-Chancellor Ian Chubb was the president of the AVCC and I spent a few anxious weeks wondering whether he would kick us off the campus. I would not have gone quietly, already imagining the headline – 'Researchers expelled from ANU after exposing malpractice'. But Ian Chubb is more sensible than that.

9

Walking a tightrope

IF YOU ARE going to make an impact and be noticed, you have to operate at the edge. For me, an Australia Institute that was worthy and safe was anathema; I liked to stir the pot. On the other hand, the coin in which think tanks trade is credibility, a currency hard to accumulate and easy to squander. Striking the right balance requires the daily exercise of judgement.

Apart from the quality of the work, the main means of building credibility is to surround yourself with credible people. Respected experts like the 'the architect of HECS' Bruce Chapman, 'the architect of Landcare' Phillip Toyne, and Victoria's former auditor-general Ches Baragwanath agreed to write papers for us.

People didn't necessarily agree with us, but they knew that our position would be well argued and backed by evidence. In 2002, the secretary of the environment department, Roger Beale, addressed a group of businesspeople about matters environmental. According to a journalist present, when he mentioned the Australia Institute, the audience expressed 'a mix of outrage and dismissive indifference'. Beale responded, 'You may not like what they say, but you've got to take them seriously.'

The best defences against attack are to make the research as watertight as possible and to explain it in clear, unambiguous terms. Usually when doing a research project, it's prudent to consider the likely reactions from various parties and shape your message accordingly. In truth, I was pretty cavalier. As long as I thought the analysis was robust and on the right side of defamation law, my attitude was, 'Screw it, let's see what happens.' As a general rule, provoking ire is better than being ignored.

Sometimes those we expected to react angrily did not take the bait. Hal Turton and I wrote a thorough report detailing the massive subsidies being swallowed up by the aluminium industry, mainly in the form of artificially cheap electricity, which it used in prodigious quantities. We estimated the subsidies at $157,000 per employee each year. The smelters had been getting away with it for years and liked to keep it hushed up. It offended me. I wanted to force the industry on the defensive and, in language a bit over the top, described it in a media release as 'the spoiled brat of Australian industry'. But the lobby group was clever and did not respond. Sometime later, the chief of the aluminium lobby group told me they had bought a copy of our paper and, in a breach of copyright law, photocopied it for wide distribution to their members. It was, he said, the most thorough analysis of the industry available.

Often, I decided to intervene in a matter of public importance because the received wisdom was harmful and contradicted by the evidence. In 2004 I asked Judith Healy, an ANU health policy academic, to write a paper debunking the ageing population panic that seemed to infect everyone. The ageing scare animated Treasurer Costello in particular. He built a looming crisis on the basis of a Treasury 'Intergenerational Report' as a justification for all kinds of regressive measures. An ageing population was a threat, a burden, a crisis, we were told. No one was challenging the rhetoric, which stigmatised older people as a social liability. Using hard data and strong arguments, Judith showed the 'crisis' was overblown and there were many benefits of an ageing population. Rather than being a burden on society, most health costs occur in the last year of life, whenever that year occurs, and older people make a huge contribution to society in the forms of unpaid childcare, voluntary work and lower crime rates. (Personally, I look forward to fewer hoons on the road.)

The 'ageing crisis' was the justification for budget cuts, postponement of retirement and higher immigration. The latter added to aggregate GDP growth but had virtually no effect on growth per person, in other words, on Australians' wellbeing. The environmental implications of endless growth were massive, but people like Costello, a narrow-minded thinker, could not grasp this simple fact. The cargo cult of growthism seemed unassailable to 'serious people', that is, economists and financial commentators and all who took their lead from them. I pointed out often that basic demography shows that the population profile *must* age sooner or later, unless the population is to keep growing forever. So why not bite the bullet?

Our work on the benefits of ageing was so contrary to ingrained myths that it had little effect. Too many were invested in blaming older people for all kinds of problems and stoking false notions of intergenerational warfare, which continues today in the 'blame the boomers' trope, even though gen Xers now run most organisations, including government. These were not only socially divisive but also, on any familiarity with the relevant data, fallacious. Sometimes social beliefs are so deeply held that no amount of contrary evidence can change them.

§

One of the secrets of the Australia Institute's success was its ability to be a year or two ahead of the zeitgeist – the spirit of the age or, less grandly, the prevailing mood of society. Some of our best work articulated the subterranean concerns of the community, or at least large segments of it, anxieties yet to emerge into the public domain. Picking the zeitgeist is more important for think tanks on the left than on the right. If we consider the far-reaching neoliberal revolution that conservative think tanks helped bring about, their success was not due to anticipating the public mood. The public never supported the program of privatisation, corporatisation and small government. Instead, they won over the intellectual, political and corporate elites.

Perhaps the zeitgeist we explored to greatest effect was the heightened materialism of the late 1990s and 2000s, until the financial crisis of 2008 brought the era to an end. By 2002, Australia was in the middle of a long economic boom. Our first, early intervention was in 1997, when we published an alternative to GDP as a measure of national wellbeing. Rather than accounting only for the market value of final goods and services, the genuine progress indicator took account of worsening inequality as well as measures of the costs of pollution, unemployment, traffic congestion, crime and so on, none of which are measured by GDP yet all of which reduce our wellbeing. It was extremely exacting work, but the analysis showed that while GDP had been growing strongly over the decades, national wellbeing was lagging well behind when measured by the new index. In 2000, Richard Denniss and I produced an update of the genuine progress indicator. With a pretty good economic pedigree, the new index attracted strong interest from unexpected quarters. I was even invited to give a lecture at Treasury.

Consumerism was rife. Brands, lifestyles, luxury spending, McMansions, retail therapy and the making of the self through consumption were the preoccupations of Australians. After the neoliberal revolution of the 1980s and 1990s, the market and marketing were shaping society in ways they never had before. Overwork and its effects on children were explored for us by Barbara Pocock from the University of Adelaide. (She was also a board member.) While caught up in the new world, it seemed to me that Australians also felt uncomfortable about the changes these trends were bringing to their families, their communities and the nation.

Over the next several years, the institute produced a stream of research designed to speak to Australians about these concerns. The centrepiece of the research was a survey I commissioned from

Newspoll in 2002, a time of unprecedented affluence. Among other things, it revealed that 62 per cent of Australians believed they 'cannot afford to buy everything they really need'. It was a powerful number. Nearly half of those in the *highest* income group expressed the same sentiment. I coined the phrase 'middle-class battlers' to highlight the contrast between the national myth of who we are and how we actually behave. The survey also revealed that when asked to stand back and reflect on their lives and on society, more than eight in ten believed their society was 'too materialistic, with too much emphasis on money and not enough on the things that really matter'. What really mattered, they said, were more time with family and friends, less stress and pressure and more fulfilling lives. Here was the contradiction of the age.

To illustrate the striking fact that that nearly two thirds of citizens in one of the world's richest countries believed they couldn't afford to buy everything they really needed, I wanted to show that, although family sizes had been shrinking over the decades, the sizes of houses had grown rapidly. I soon discovered that there were no consistent national statistics on the floor spaces of new houses. However, I managed to cobble together some pretty good data from various sources. They showed that while the average household size had declined from 3.6 people in 1955 to 2.6 in 2000, the floor space of new houses had risen from 115 square metres to 221 square metres. In response to our work, a couple of years later the ABS began collecting data on the floor space of new housing.

These bigger houses had to be filled with more stuff, so I listed some of the luxury products people were buying. One Saturday morning, I happened to be at Barbeques Galore and came across the Turbo Cosmopolitan, 'Australia's most prestigious gourmet out-door entertainment system', priced at $4990. Bingo! How does the gourmet outdoor entertainment system square with the mythos of the backyard barbie, put together by Dad from bricks and a hotplate and used for burning a few snags? In truth, a backyard arms race was underway. It was a headline made in heaven.

And so it proved. I gave our report as an exclusive to Adele Horin, and *The Sydney Morning Herald* splashed her story across the top of the front page of the Saturday edition with the headline 'Rich cry poor, then put another prawn on the outdoor kitchen'. In addition to the main story, the edition included a human-interest story, a comment piece by Adele, an op-ed by me and an editorial about our report. Media impact never gets any better than that. The Turbo Cosmopolitan became a national talking point in interview after interview, from highbrow outlets to lowbrow ones. I was amused several months later when out of the blue the postie delivered a parcel containing an aluminium box with a set of top-range barbeque utensils and a letter from the national marketing manager of Barbeques Galore. The utensils were 'a small gesture of appreciation' for the publicity. The bastards.

Developing these themes, I wrote a book exploring how modern politics is built on the unchallengeable assumption that a better future hinges on higher economic growth. *Growth Fetish*, published in 2003, analysed the 'sicknesses of affluence' and described a politics beyond growthism. It was a bestseller here and abroad and was the beginning of a strong relation with the publisher, Allen & Unwin, and Elizabeth Weiss in particular. What I always appreciated about Allen & Unwin was that the company, rather than simply chasing profits, was committed to the promotion of progressive ideas and improving society.

How many Australians, I now wondered, had made an attempt to escape the pressures to work more, earn more and spend more? The institute's study of downshifting, the antidote to the consumerist life (written by me and Elizabeth Mail), was once again built around a Newspoll survey. The results showed that, excluding retirees, a quarter of adult Australians had voluntarily decided to accept lower incomes in order to improve their quality of life. The report garnered many headlines and turned the 'seachange' debate from a TV fantasy into a real-life phenomenon. There was so much interest that we followed up with a second report, using focus groups to delve more deeply.

What led them to make the change? How hard was it? How had their friends and colleagues reacted? Had the change made them happier? The results were fascinating. Good qualitative research is hard and requires expertise. Luckily, Christie Breakspeare, who'd recently moved from Sydney to Canberra, had walked through the institute's door volunteering to help. She was experienced in 'qual' and, over the next months, I watched admiringly as Christie turned a random collection of nervous strangers into a group willing to talk about intimate aspects of their lives and aspirations.

§

Having developed its modus operandi and recruited excellent research staff, the Australia Institute became highly productive, with a disproportionate impact in the media. Successful research begins with topic selection. The topic had to be one with currency or likely to resonate, which means having one's finger on the social and political pulse. It had to have a high chance of being noticed. I had a crude test. If a staff member came to me with an idea for a project, I would listen to the proposal, explore the research strategy with them, and then ask, 'So what would be the headline?' In other words, if the results of the research turned out as expected, what would be the first line in a media release or the headline in a newspaper? A dull or predictable headline ruled it out.

Richard Denniss, who arrived at the institute from the University of Newcastle in 2000, understood this. Richard, a heterodox economist, was a prolific researcher and entertaining public speaker. We shared a critique of neoliberalism when it is used to gloss over market failures or spread market values into areas of life where they do not belong. We knew its faults and how to make them glare.

We were also both natural stirrers. There was nothing we enjoyed more than putting forward perfectly reasonable economic arguments that we knew would get up the noses of privileged groups. Richard left the institute for a while to work as chief of staff to

Natasha Stott Despoja, then leader of the Australian Democrats, before returning. We continued to explore the themes of advertising, overwork, indebtedness and materialism. In 2004, Richard came to my office and said we needed to write a book putting together all of our research on these, and we should call it 'Affluenza'. I agreed immediately and in 2005 *Affluenza* was published by Allen & Unwin. It would sell some 40,000 copies and change the national conversation. It was also the cause of a falling out between us. Although he seemed relaxed about it as publication approached, Richard felt he was not given enough recognition as the co-author of the book and in the launch publicity. It was a legitimate grievance, and I should have pressed the publisher to ensure he received more acknowledgement. Richard resigned soon after. Over the years I made a few efforts to break the ice, but the ice was not for breaking.

§

Around this time we had had a run of prominent stories in the Fairfax papers. The late and admired Adele Horin, the *Herald*'s social affairs reporter, was an excellent journalist who showed a keen interest in our work. Adele told me that when she took one of our reports to the editors' meeting – one showing that a third of Sydney fathers spend more time commuting to work than playing with their children – one of the editors asked, 'Does Clive Hamilton sit around all day working out how to get on the front page of *The Sydney Morning Herald*?'

Bold research ideas ought to challenge one's friends sometimes as well as one's political opponents and, perhaps more than any other, our work on the harm to children of internet pornography had that effect.

In 2002, I read a story in *The Guardian Weekly* about a French-government study concluding that almost all boys and girls aged sixteen and seventeen had viewed one or more pornographic films and that hardcore porn had become the principal vehicle for even quite young children's understanding of love and sexuality. It reported an investigation into eight teenaged boys accused of the gang rape of a fifteen-year-old classmate.

I tore out the story. At the time, porn was taking over the internet. In contrast to tame men's magazines, the internet had emerged as the wild west of sexual deviancy. Scattered comments by Australian doctors and child psychologists indicated they were becoming worried about the effects on children of early exposure. I guessed that parents across the country felt under siege, with no one articulating their concerns other than people dismissed as religious moralisers.

For me, working on this problem went beyond child protection. I also wanted to challenge, from the left, the spread of uncritical, anything-goes libertarianism fuelled by a de facto alliance of marketers, postmodern intellectuals and cultural elites. My own roots from teenage years were in that kind of libertarianism but, observing some of the social consequences, it seemed to me to have been taken too far, as if any constraints on personal behaviour were oppressive by definition.

There were few better qualified to write a report on children's access to pornography than Michael Flood, who had a doctorate in gender and sexuality studies, and experience working with violent men. He was teaching at the ANU when I asked him to lead a research project on the subject and would later come to work full-time at the institute. My worries about what some of our supporters might think were allayed not only by Michael's progressive credentials but also by the way he spoke, with the calm logic of the well-informed expert.

Our target was not erotica as such but what Michael termed 'extreme and violent' sexual practices, the kind of thing too extreme even for an X classification – bestiality, incest, rape. In our early discussions, I asked Michael, 'What about S&M, where both parties freely consent?' He replied, 'Mixing sex and violence is never okay,' which made sense to me. Consent had always seemed a simple matter; I was now realising it is an ethical minefield.

As the junior author on the study – and the senior author on a follow-up paper on regulatory responses to the problem – I felt I ought to know more about what I was researching, so I drove to a sex shop in Fyshwick to inspect the X-rated videos. I bought two using the institute's Mastercard. Returning to the office, I made a note to file and mentioned to one or two staff what I had done. I took the videos home. When I told Janenne I'd be watching some porn that night, I couldn't resist the punchline: 'It's purely for research purposes.' I didn't get far into them; the badly acted bump and grind was tacky. Maybe I should have switched off the analytical brain. A few years later, our office manager, Kelly Bruce, who had been with us only a few months, was cleaning out our storage shelves before a move. She came to my office holding two dust-covered videos. 'What do I do with these?' she asked, raising an eyebrow. I can't imagine what must have been going through her mind.

To gauge the extent of youth access to porn, we commissioned Newspoll to survey sixteen- and seventeen-year-olds. Younger people were our main interest, but they could not be surveyed for ethical reasons. As expected, nearly all admitted to looking at internet sex sites. But the real heart of the research was a content analysis of internet porn carried out by Michael. Too many people still visualised *Playboy* when porn was mentioned, so I wanted him to describe in blunt terms what was easily available. The result was truly shocking, so confronting in its dispassionate descriptions of the genres, extreme fetishes and misogynistic violence that I felt the discussion paper ought to include a warning at the front. After the content analysis, the report summarised the evidence of harms to children from accessing porn. We called for better education of kids in sex and sexuality, including incorporation of pornography education into school curricula to help inoculate children against the disturbing effects of seeing it.

When published in March 2003, the immediate strong reactions to our work were multiplied by the release of a second report soon after in which we called on the government to require internet service providers to apply filters to all pornographic content, while allowing adult end users to opt out of the filter. After all, we noted, the government already censors TV, books, magazines, films and videos, all with strong public support, so why should the internet be exempt? There was a lot about X-rated porn we didn't like, particularly the routine dehumanising and degrading of women, but our target was extreme and violent imagery on the internet that was banned on videos sold in Australia.

We discovered that parents of teenagers strongly supported our concerns through another Newspoll survey we commissioned. It showed 85 per cent of parents said they were worried about their children's access to internet porn and a whopping 93 per cent were in favour of our proposal for mandatory filtering, with an opt-out for adults.

First out of the blocks to come after us were the 'sex-positive' pro-porn libertarians, who from start to finish misrepresented our argument. Kath Albury from the University of Sydney, for example, claimed we wanted to limit adult access to porn, that we were hostile to non-hetero sexualities and that we wanted to deny minors access to materials about sexuality. Any reading of our reports shows we said none of these. We argued explicitly in favour of 'pornography education' in schools to teach teens how to critically evaluate porn to counter its worst effects. 'Sex-positive' libertarians like Catharine Lumby and Kath Albury defended porn, unwilling to recognise the distinction we drew between mainstream and extreme and violent porn. Another expert, Helen Pringle, later noted that these pro-porn academics ignore the harms and 'treat pornography as an *avant garde* political gesture'. They adopt a superior stance: I'm so sophisticated, nothing shocks me, so if it shocks you then you are uptight, or worse. Against this kind of free-for-all that glosses over the difficult questions, Michael had been working towards a progressive sexual ethics for years.

Anticipating misrepresentation, Michael and I had been careful to express our views clearly, but some people have their buttons pressed by a headline and off they go. For the 'sex-positive' clique, *every* expression of sexuality is valid, ergo, we were just like the conservatives who want to 'control the sexual activities of others'. They argued that all 'texts' have meanings only in the minds of the readers, and since all readers, including children, have agency, they cannot be manipulated or exploited. Seriously.

Then there were the internet libertarians. I had not appreciated until then how fanatical these people are. I soon understood that their whole identity is bound up with the 'freedom' they enjoy on the internet. In reaction to our reports, they exploded in a rage, led by Electronic Frontiers Australia. Regulating porn would lead to censoring political speech and thus authoritarianism, they insisted. The internet is the people's mode of communication that has evaded control by big corporations, they claimed. For them, the internet was sacrosanct.

It irritated me that these people presented themselves as progressive. There is nothing left-wing about this stance. At bottom, it's the same self-obsessed individualism and anti-government messianism that drives tech billionaire Peter Thiel and Julian Assange, both of whom backed Donald Trump.

We received a flood of emails, some very creepy, along the lines of 'How dare you take away my porn'. The internet service provider industry mounted a strong attack, making all kinds of hyperbolic claims. Internet speeds would be slowed by 90 per cent and half the industry would go bust, they said, the usual bluster industries spew out when faced with regulation. Before publication I had, of course, explored the feasibility of our proposal with internet industry experts. They said it was quite doable. The Internet Industry Association was out arguing that if there is a problem then it should all be left to parents to fix. Labor's IT spokesperson, Senator Kate Lundy, echoed the industry: 'It's up to parents to be more vigilant. Filtering pornography simply would not work.' (Three months previously she had called for laws to ban spam.) I had little time for this 'blame-the-parents' attitude, which presents social problems as matters of individual responsibility (as some do for climate change). Parents were doing what they could but were overwhelmed. They didn't want to be looking over their children's shoulders twenty-four hours a day and were appealing for government help.

The communications minister Richard Alston's first reaction was to criticise our report, picking out the 'small sample size' of the Newspoll survey. That criticism used to frustrate me. The sample size was quite big enough; it's the *representativeness* of the sample rather than the size that matters more. Alston said the government's existing policy was highly effective at keeping the internet safe and protecting children. This was manifestly absurd.

He quickly changed his tune. Prime Minister Howard raised the issue at a party room meeting, telling Coalition MPs of the need to do more to protect children. The government was expressing concern but seemed locked into a regulatory system that was not working. Here was an opportunity for Labor to wedge the government, but a staffer for Opposition leader Mark Latham told me that Latham was not going to go there. He had once been accused of hosting porn nights in his garage.

Beyond the industry, libertarians and the cultural studies academics, we also came under fire from prominent gay activists, including David Marr on *Media Watch* and Brian Greig, the Democrats' spokesman on family services and IT. We knew that homosexual erotica often played a particularly significant role in the lives of gay men and had acknowledged the positive role that some pornography could play for same-sex-attracted young people. Yet everyone had an entrenched view.

The main parties were conflicted, so when a Senate inquiry was held into children and internet porn, its report was a whitewash. At the time of our reports, the research linking viewing hardcore porn with subsequent sexual violence was suggestive only. Since then, the evidence has become firmer and the potentially damaging effects on children are now accepted. They say that revenge is best served cold, but, as I have learned many times, vindication served cold means everyone has forgotten you said it first.

10

Unaccustomed as I am

Requests for me to speak multiplied in the early 2000s. It was the long Howard era, when the ALP appeared lost and there was a demand in sections of the public for new voices. By 2006 I was giving thirty or forty public talks and lectures each year, at universities, bookshops, writers' festivals and NGOs. Speaking to large audiences is not inconsistent with introversion. And, of course, it's part of the job. From a wide range of conversations at these events, I soaked up impressions about what was happening out in the world.

I rarely spoke with politicians, although there was an exception in May 2002 when, at the invitation of Senator Kim Carr, I addressed the national conference of the ALP and trade union left, held annually in Canberra. The venue was Old Canberra House, the former ANU Staff Centre, where I happened to have been married a long time ago. In thinking about what I would say, I had a sense of the growing irrelevance of the traditional left, arising from its inability to develop a politics that resonated with the times. I tossed up whether to play it safe and state the usual about social injustice and the Howard government's penchant for penalising the most vulnerable, or to take a risk. I decided on the latter a week or so before the event when, looking down from a plane coming into Sydney, I saw stretched below an expanse of ordinary suburbs where half had backyard swimming pools glinting in the sun. This is the new reality of consumer lifestyles that the left had to grapple with.

It was a Sunday and, when my time came, I began speaking about how the left had failed to keep up with the times. In an era of unparalleled affluence, the 'deprivation model' – politics based on the assumption of widespread material want – is not a useful way to characterise society. Poverty is unforgiveable, even more so amid affluence, but it doesn't help to claim it's the lot of the majority. We had no coherent alternative to neoliberalism, no social democracy for an era of global consumer capitalism. We needed to admit that neoliberalism had been very successful on its own terms but had failed to make for a more contented society. Ask the person next to you, I suggested to the audience. Do they believe that on the whole Australians are happier today than they were forty or fifty years ago?

I made some scathing observations about the so-called Third Way, then big in Blair's Britain, suggesting it was little more than Thatcherism with a human face, a label in search of a meaning. And I mocked its chief Australian proponent, Mark Latham, as the 'Sage of Werriwa'. Latham, of the Labor right, was not present, but his prominent advocacy of a new politics based on 'aspirational voters' whom Labor should help to climb the 'ladder of opportunity' struck me as vacuous lifestyle politics. He irritated me, although it could not be denied that Latham was out there with policy ideas, some of them worthwhile, in a way other Labor leaders were afraid to do. He was always on the front foot.

My speech flopped. I had gone after the most sacred verity of left politics – the deprivation model. While rooted in historical fact, the idea of the struggling masses flew in the face of the reality that Australia was an enormously wealthy country. Materially, a large majority of people led a comfortable life. Doug Cameron, the left-wing union leader, was the first to go after me from the floor: I was betraying the left by ignoring the poor and disadvantaged. At the tea-break, as I stood wondering how quickly I could get out of there, one or two delegates quietly said my talk was a breath of fresh air. Later, Kim Carr told me he didn't think he would be entrusted again with the job of inviting the guest speaker. However, the speech was widely reported and debated. Geraldine Doogue referred to it on ABC Radio National as a 'watershed in the history of the left in Australia'. It wasn't anything like that, sadly, but it did me no harm for it to be seen that way by some.

Mark Latham's reply was not long in coming and took the form of an op-ed in *The Australian*. He began by suggesting my ideas belong to the Institute of Public Affairs rather than a left-wing think tank. They revealed the poverty of green-left thinking. A left-of-centre politics must focus on poverty and economic insecurity, he wrote, while Hamilton 'wants working-class people to hold middle-class, environmental values' without the higher incomes. It was, he thundered, 'the ultimate betrayal of the green Left: post-materialist basket weaving for gentrified inner-city types … Hamilton can keep his wickerwork and rabbit food.'

It was tremendous fun. Latham and I continued to trade barbs until he was elected Labor leader in December 2003, which began a wild ten-month ride for the Labor Party. In 2006 I read *The Latham Diaries* – one of the most readable political memoirs – and realised that, although our politics seemed far apart, we had something elemental in common: we were both driven by the belief that bold ideas change the world. Latham had now withdrawn but I found an email address and wrote to him praising the book, saying that I had not realised how powerful was the opposition in the Labor Party to a person expressing fresh ideas. I apologised to him for being so harsh in my public comments.

Some weeks later I received a reply that truly surprised me. He said that he too regretted going after me in the way he had. You were right, he wrote, Australians are materialistic and obsessed with consumption. It was a gracious reply. In recent years, I have looked on with sadness as Mark became entangled in Hansonite politics.

Latham's criticism of my position, and Doug Cameron's, had some truth to it; I had been implicitly downplaying poverty and inequality. But I have always taken the view that sharp differences generate debate. My true position is sometimes more moderate or less certain than the one I express, but a rusted-on conventional belief is best blown up by a direct assault rather than a wishy-washy 'maybe we should take this into consideration'.

§

By 2004, with no more than five or six paid staff at any time, the Australia Institute was on a roll, turning out paper after paper on health insurance, work and family, carbon emissions, climate refugees, Indigenous rights, drug prices, funding of private schools and much more. I look back now and am astonished that our productivity was so high. The institute had some brilliant young researchers over the years, and I sometimes thought that my biggest legacy would be training a cadre of them.

In August that year, the institute held a tenth anniversary dinner at Old Parliament House. Geraldine Doogue agreed to be the MC and did so with the trademark sparkle in her eyes. Tim Flannery happily agreed to give the keynote speech, although he was upstaged by Sharan Burrow, Australian Council of Trade Unions (ACTU) president and a member of our board. Sharan began: 'This is a fantastically precocious ten-year-old and I think she is fantastic. She is gregarious, she's loud, she's opinionated, she's determined, she's provocative and aren't we glad she is.' It was a sign of how far we had come as a force in public debate.

After the lies of the Iraq war and the despicable children overboard ruse, not to mention repudiation of the Kyoto Protocol and shameless middle-class handouts while squeezing the poor, Howard's election victory over Mark Latham in October 2004 sent progressives around the country into deep despondency. Two days after the election, *The Sydney Morning Herald* published an opinion piece in which I attributed Howard's win to a decade of Australians turning inward, absorbed by their own material circumstances with little room left for building a better society. Occasionally, an opinion piece perfectly captures a mood and it went viral, as we would later say. Rather than being composed, articles like this pour out onto the page as controlled rage. The reaction from readers was enormous and for me bittersweet. It was redoubled when the ABC republished the article a few days later.

It is usually impossible to know how much impact, if any, one's work has. Among the exceptions was our intervention in the debate over the privatisation of Canberra's electricity, water and sewerage utility, ACTEW. Chief Minister Kate Carnell, who led a rare Liberal Party government in the ACT, was red-hot on selling the territory's most valuable asset, one that as a long-term Canberran I felt I part owned. As always, privatising politicians talk up the immediate pile of cash from the sale while ignoring the long-term decline in public revenue. That's exactly what John Quiggin's analysis showed in a paper for the institute. Canberrans' net worth would fall by $700 million if ACTEW were sold at the mooted price. He also showed that the high-powered Sydney consultants (one a former New South Wales Treasury secretary) that Carnell had hired had made some basic accounting errors.

Kate Carnell was attacking our credibility in the media. She was worried because she needed the support of three independents in the Legislative Assembly and they were undecided. In January 1999, the local chamber of commerce and the trade union council co-sponsored a debate at the National Press Club where the suits from Sydney would face off against John and myself. It was billed as a showdown and everyone turned up, including Carnell, the independents and several potential buyers.

We were winning the debate and Kate Carnell began heckling us from the front table, sparking an exchange from which she came off second best, according to the *Canberra Times* story the next day. When the vote on privatisation came in the Legislative Assembly, the Carnell government lost. The independents quoted our work to explain their shift from initially favouring to opposing the sell-off. For me, it was a sweet victory.

§

Public debates where the outcome is cut and dried, as in the ACTEW case, are rare. But speaking in public repeatedly can help shift the national conversation, even when speaking to sympathetic audiences. It is often said of people like me that we are preaching to the converted. That's true, but I took the view that my role was to provide the converted with new insights, arguments and ways of thinking so that they could use them in their interactions with the unconverted. Over time, the process can shift the public conversation.

That's the theory. But there was one domain where nothing I did seemed to make any difference, even though I devoted more of my life to it than anything else – climate change.

11

The greenhouse mafia

I N EARLY DECEMBER 2005, while sitting in my ANU office, a call
came through from Janine Cohen, an investigative journalist from
Four Corners. She was just phoning to see whether I had any story ideas
for 2006. It was almost as if I had been waiting for such a call because
in my back pocket I had been carrying around a stick of dynamite.

About five years earlier, the head of the ANU's Graduate Program
in Public Policy, Glenn Withers, had asked if I would serve as a
co-supervisor for one of his PhD students. The research topic was
industry engagement in greenhouse policy. It was right up my alley,
but the candidate was a Liberal Party staffer, which made me a bit
suspicious. How could someone who worked inside the Coalition
government analyse the issues objectively? It turned out that
Guy Pearse, who wrote speeches for Robert Hill and shared a house
in Canberra with George Brandis, was a young man of independent
mind who understood the seriousness of climate change. He had a
unique insight into the workings of the Liberal Party and corporate
lobbying and, perhaps above all, his conservative credentials meant
he was trusted by the power players, the ones telling lies to the public
and playing the dirty tricks. So I was keen to see where his research
would lead.

Guy was wary of me, given my reputation as a harsh critic of the government, but over time we began to get on well. Doctorates can be a crushing undertaking. As a part-time student, it was a struggle for Guy, the more so as he had moved on to work as an independent consultant, mostly for industry and federal agencies. By early 2005, he was wrestling with the thesis write-up. He emailed Glenn and me and said that due to pressure of time to complete, he wanted to cut out a planned chapter, the one featuring his research into the role in policy formation of a group of powerful fossil fuel lobbyists who called themselves 'the greenhouse mafia'. Guy had coaxed leading members of the group into making admissions about how they operated. Oh no, I thought, that's the most important chapter. So I urged him to do the work and keep the chapter. Glenn agreed and he pushed on with the thesis.

Guy submitted the thesis a few months later and it was passed by the examiners. In its pages were quotes from the greenhouse mafia boasting about how they drafted and vetted confidential cabinet sub-missions, about their mateship with the public servants formulating policy and about their direct line to Howard and his chief of staff, Arthur Sinodinos. Drawn largely from senior levels of the bureau-cracy, the greenhouse mafiosi claimed they knew 'more about energy policy than the government does'. One said that the reason he gets out of bed each morning was to defeat the environmentalists. The thesis exposed corruption of democratic governance at the highest level, all done in collaboration with senior ministers, from Howard down.

The final thesis was lodged in the Menzies Library at the ANU, with restricted access. There it was, sitting there, a bomb that only needed detonation. So in December 2005 I mentioned it to Janine Cohen, outlining its contents and its provenance, a Liberal Party insider. She saw it straightaway: it had 'scoop' written all over it. I said I couldn't promise anything; it would be up to Guy. I phoned Guy, told him why I thought it important for his thesis to see the light of day and described what he could expect to happen if he appeared on *Four Corners*. I then left it to him to contact Janine.

There was a second big greenhouse politics story I knew about that also needed to see the light of day. Graeme Pearman, an internationally respected climate scientist and someone I knew pretty well, had been the head of the climate science division at CSIRO. He often spoke frankly about what the research was telling us about the risks of global warming, the need to cut carbon emissions and the importance of targets. The Howard government was suppressing climate science and behaving like a child with its fingers in its ears. Public servants had been instructed to avoid using the terms 'climate change' and 'global warming' in their ministerial briefings. By speaking the truth, Graeme was making life awkward for his politicised bosses at CSIRO. He told me he had been gagged by top CSIRO management on several occasions and that he had in effect been fired from his job as chief of the division. In 2004 he had been made redundant – for speaking the truth. I knew a lot of scientists through my climate change work and had heard several stories about CSIRO researchers being muzzled and their reports censored. I told Janine what I knew. I then phoned Graeme, told him to expect a call, and suggested he think about what he wanted to do.

On Monday, 13 February 2006, the first *Four Corners* program of the year went to air. Titled 'The Greenhouse Mafia', it was a blockbuster. It opened with: 'A whistleblower steps forward with claims that industry representatives have burrowed deep inside the federal bureaucracy in a successful bid to hijack greenhouse policy.' Guy was at the centre of the program, revealing what the fossil fuel lobbyists had told him. A squirming environment minister, Ian Campbell, denied everything. The second half of the program was devoted to Graeme Pearman and the gagging of climate scientists, with a senior CSIRO executive trapped like a roo in the head-lights by Janine's questioning. To say it created a sensation would be an understatement.

We lionise whistleblowers, but the fallout for them is often disastrous. And so it was for Guy Pearse. He lost all of his consulting income and his reputation was trashed in the Liberal Party, where a bright future had beckoned. The big bullies of the greenhouse mafia were after his blood, claiming he had lied about what they'd said. Guy had them all on tape, so none of them were going to sue. He was instantly in high demand as a speaker, but that doesn't pay the rent. Penguin offered a lucrative book deal, leading to the 2007 publication of his book *High and Dry*. Another round of interviews and speaking engagements followed. Everything he said was factual and he did the Australian public a great service, yet the pressure on him was immense and took a severe toll. At times I felt guilty for being the catalyst of the situation he found himself in, but we both understood the stakes. His decisions were his own.

Guy was unusual as a whistleblower. In my experience, those plucky enough or ornery enough to blow the whistle on malfeasance tend to be quirky and difficult characters who rub their workmates the wrong way. When they go public, they often don't get support from their colleagues, even when the colleagues know they are right. Their quirks make it easier for their bosses to make them out as unstable or with an axe to grind. Against this, Guy was thoughtful, likeable and responsible, with a promising career ahead of him. But he had a conscience, and courage, and that was the cross he had to bear. The service he performed was heroic.

Another sign of just how closely the Howard government was collaborating with the fossil fuel companies in setting greenhouse policy was revealed in 2005 when confidential notes of a meeting were leaked. Howard had called a secret get-together with big polluting companies (Rio Tinto, BHP, Alcoa, Origin Energy, etc.) because, as he told them, the government was losing control of the debate and being outmanoeuvred. *The Sydney Morning Herald* was 'a problem for the government'. Industry minister Ian Macfarlane then told the group that the renewable energy investment scheme, itself pathetic, 'worked too well', with investment in renewables growing too quickly. He called for ideas to kill it off. Strict confidentiality was emphasised to those present because if the renewable industry heard about it 'there would be a huge outcry'. It confirmed for me just how corrupt was the relationship between the Howard government and the fossil fuel lobby: they worked tightly together to prevent any effective action to limit Australia's carbon emissions. It was criminal.

§

In the mid-2000s, I was becoming increasingly alarmed by what the scientists were telling us about global warming and the blighted future for the world if we failed to rein in emissions. And I was dismayed at the growing intensity of the opposition to taking the scientists' warnings seriously. I tracked the way right-wing operators, notably the Institute of Public Affairs in Melbourne, were importing the ideas and tactics of industry-backed science deniers in the United States. It frustrated and offended me that they were gaining so much influence and that few people seemed to understand what it meant. Apart from the disastrous climatic consequences of failing to heed the scientists' warnings, it struck me as a challenge to the European Enlightenment itself: they were repudiating the use of reason and evidence to understand and respond to the world around us.

The Murdoch newspaper *The Australian* was the foremost purveyor of climate science disinformation. For years, story after story cast doubt on the science, vilified scientists, undermined respected scientific bodies and disparaged renewable energy. Everyone could see it, yet *The Australian* denied its denialism. It claimed to accept the need to reduce emissions then trashed every carbon-cutting policy put forward, other than worthless ones used by the Coalition as a fig leaf.

The opinion pages were edited by Tom Switzer, who was succeeded in 2008 by Rebecca Weisser, then by her husband Nick Cater. They turned over the pages to blowhards with no scientific expertise who had nevertheless managed to discover fundamental errors in basic climate science. Conspiracy theorists were preferred over eminent climate scientists with decades of published research. Soon, *The Australian* would be publishing the ravings of charlatans like Lord Christopher Monckton and the crazed conspiracy theories of Maurice Newman.

Newman, chair of the ABC board and Tony Abbott's chief business adviser, informed his readers that the world is actually cooling and unless we stop the 'climate change madness', most of us will 'descend to serfdom' because climate science is being used by the UN to impose authoritarian rule over the world. This kind of proto-Trumpian rant was published regularly in *The Australian* by Tom Switzer and his successors. Switzer now has a current affairs program on ABC Radio.

When *The Skeptical Environmentalist* by Swedish statistician Bjorn Lomborg was published in 2001, the newspaper went into overdrive. At last, someone from 'the other side' had broken ranks to expose environmentalism. Lomborg was perfect – a gay, vegan, Nordic left-winger who claimed to be a Greenpeace member. He was all over the paper for days, promoted with an air of triumphalism that was indecent. On visits to Australia, Lomborg was hosted by the IPA. Andrew Bolt sang his praises. Lomborg's political strategy was to formally accept the science but claim global warming was greatly exaggerated. He emphasised 'the positives' of a warming globe and argued that all kinds of other problems deserve more attention.

The Skeptical Environmentalist was a woeful book by any scholarly standard, full of factual errors, exaggerations and non sequiturs. In places, it was gobbledegook. Cambridge University Press was castigated by serious scientists for publishing a work chock-full of scientific mistakes. A year or so later, Cambridge approached me to write a book responding to Lomborg. It was tempting, but, on reflection, spending a year or two doing the exacting work of unpicking Lomborg's text, followed by months of going head-to-head with Lomborg around the world, thereby giving him even more oxygen, did not seem like a productive use of my time.

To keep track of *The Australian*'s lies and distortions, a blogger named Tim Lambert kept a log from 2006 to 2013 titled '*The Australian*'s war on science'. In one of many notorious episodes, in 2014 *The Australian* ran a series of stories by Graham Lloyd claiming that the Bureau of Meteorology had been manipulating raw temperature data to create the false impression of a warming trend. The whole story was based on the absurd claims of a denialist blogger, claims easily disproved by the bureau. Without a shred of credible evidence, Lloyd's articles suggested the climatologists at the bureau – a great Australian scientific organisation admired around the world – were engaged in scientific fraud by doctoring data and then covering up their cheating. In January 2022, I was astounded to see *The Australian* still running stories by Lloyd suggesting the bureau was fiddling the figures. Predictably, the story attracted hundreds of triumphal comments from the newspaper's posse of denialist readers.

Chris Mitchell, the pugnacious editor-in-chief of *The Australian*, appeared impervious to criticisms of his paper's climate change reporting. Although Robert Manne, Tim Flannery and one or two others copped it worse than I did, a campaign of ridicule and vilification was conducted against me. One of the most effective distortions was the paper's claim that I had called for a suspension of democracy to deal with climate change.

At public talks over the years, I had often responded to audience members expressing exasperation at the unwillingness of elected governments to take action. They asked me whether democracy was the problem. So in a speech I gave in Brisbane in 2007 I attempted to pre-empt the question by saying that 'the implications of 3°C, let alone 4°C or 5°C, are so horrible that we look to any possible scenario to head it off, including the canvassing of "emergency" responses such as the suspension of democratic processes'. An extract from the speech was published in the *Sunday Mail* newspaper. A few days later, *The Australian*, in its 'Cut & Paste' section, carried the quote with a heading indicating I wanted to suspend democracy.

I wrote a letter to the editor pointing out that I have never advocated the suspension of democracy; on the contrary, I have often called for its reinvigoration. But by then the slander had had the desired effect, passing into the folklore of denialist bloggers and commentators like Andrew Bolt, who reproduced the furphy a number of times. Each time Bolt went after me in his column I received a slew of abuse and threats from his followers.

§

Malicious distortion is one of the many traps in public debate. Wilfully misinterpreting data was another favourite tactic of *The Australian* and its editors. In 2007, the institute commissioned an opinion survey that showed three quarters of Australians (including 60 per cent of Coalition voters) wanted their electricity supplied by renewables and energy efficiency. Only 8 per cent preferred nuclear energy, which was in sharp contrast to claims made by *The Australian* to the effect that people were becoming more supportive. *The Australian* had misinterpreted Newspoll data to support its campaign for nuclear power plants. I had no in principle opposition to nuclear power, but it made no sense as a response to Australia's urgent need to cut emissions. It would take at least twenty years to get the first one started and the cost would be much greater than that of renewables.

The conservatives were using calls to debate nuclear as another stalling or diversionary tactic. When in 2006 Prime Minister Howard called for a 'full-blooded debate', we decided to take him at his word. We asked ourselves: if Australia were to build nuclear power plants, where exactly would they be located?

I began looking into it with Andrew Macintosh, who had arrived at the institute in June 2005. A lawyer by training, Andrew had worked at Parliament House for the Democrats, helping craft legislation to protect the environment. Andrew was furious at the political cover being given to the Howard government by environment group WWF, so we wrote a detailed exposé of the money flowing to WWF and its frequent praise of the government. Now we turned our attention to the nuclear 'debate'.

We first spoke to a number of experts about the criteria for siting nuclear power plants. It turns out that nuclear power plants need a lot of water for cooling, which in Australia means on the coast. They need to be near major transmissions lines and adjacent to big electricity load centres. And they need to have rail and port access for transporting the fuel rods. It wasn't hard to work out the suitable areas.

So on 23 May 2006, we issued a media release nominating the likely sites for nuclear power plants: Westernport Bay, Portland and Port Phillip Bay in Victoria; Port Stephens, the Central Coast and Wollongong in New South Wales; and the Sunshine Coast in Queensland.

There was uproar. The media went crazy. For two days, Andrew and I barely came up for air between the scores of interviews, a large proportion with local radio stations in the areas we had mentioned. Coalition MPs in those areas ducked for cover, forced to say they would not support a nuclear plant in their electorate. The government, on the back foot, dismissed our claims as a stunt. Maybe, but a good one. We wanted to keep the government honest. You can't have nuclear power without building the plants somewhere. If the government disagreed with our assessment, let it say where it believed the plants would be sited, which of course it could not do. Once the punters began asking themselves where the plants would be, the conservatives' tactic of debating nuclear in the abstract became impossible. Howard stopped calling for a debate.

When the story blew up, supporters of the institute began phoning the office. Some were confused. Is the Australia Institute now backing nuclear energy? Our office manager, Kelly Bruce, had to explain it to them. Letters and emails arrived from angry anti-nuclear activists accusing us of supporting nuclear energy. Sigh.

§

It was not all seriousness and angst at the Australia Institute. We had our lighter moments, not least a bit of research we decided to do on owners of four-wheel drives. Massive gas-guzzling 4WD vehicles, now called SUVs, had been flooding onto city streets. Personally, I wanted to see these monsters taxed off city roads. As it happened, a Roy Morgan database we could access included information about the types of vehicle people drove. I dug into it to see what distinguished 4WD owners demographically and socially from other drivers.

It didn't take long to find gold. It turned out that drivers of large 4WDs like Toyota Land Cruisers and Nissan Patrols were on average more individualistic, obese, aggressive, homophobic and intolerant. Our report was an instant hit, although it did not slow the deluge. Interviewed by John Laws, as soon as I mentioned Land Cruisers he jumped in to tell me that Toyota 'makes very good cars' and that the company is a sponsor of his program. I agreed Toyota makes very good cars. 'I drive a Prius.'

Satire is a risky tactic in public debate. In 1997, the Australian Koala Foundation approached me and Tor Hundloe, an environmental economist and member of the institute board, to assess the contribution of koalas to the Australian economy. Koalas had become a drawcard for foreign tourists, especially from Japan. So we carried out a survey of Japanese tourists, stationing Japanese-speaking researchers at airports with a questionnaire asking visitors how important koalas were in their decision to come (72 per cent wanted to see them) and what kind of koala-based activity they spent money on – petting zoos, wildlife parks and 'koalabilia'. We came up with an estimate of the contribution of koalas to the economy of $1.1 billion. Deborah Tabart, the CEO of the foundation, was happy.

A few years later, in 2002, I appeared on *Ockham's Razor*, Robyn Williams' forum for provocative ideas on Radio National. The idea for the talk, 'Cashing in on Koalas', was prompted by a conversation I'd had with my friend Dan Lunney, a koala expert. I began by noting the study Tor and I had conducted on their 'economic value' and calls to allow people to keep native animals as pets, creating a market for them. I began to speculate on how this economic approach to valuing wildlife might be extended to solve the problem of severe overpopulation of koalas on Kangaroo Island in South Australia. Could we lucratively exploit overseas demand for 'koala experiences'? Noting the popularity of hunting ranches in the United States, I proposed that numbers on Kangaroo Island could be reduced if we charged American tourists to shoot koalas. I went on to propose that, for inexperienced hunters and children learning to use guns, it may be feasible to capture some koalas and place them in enclosures so that they could be shot at close range. Based on prices for various animals at Texas hunting ranches, I suggested a fee of $1000 per koala with at least $1500 for a mother and baby. Additional fees could be charged to have the koalas stuffed so they could be taken back to the United States to be displayed on loungeroom walls.

One could hardly lay on the satire more thickly. However, letters and emails arrived accusing me of being a monster for proposing that those innocent koalas be shot for money! Deborah Tabart came under pressure from her members, including Girl Guides, to defend koalas against this outrage, so she wrote me a letter expressing her horror at my proposal. How could I! In 2009, Andrew Bolt would suggest that I had no credibility as a commentator on climate change because I had advocated charging tourists to shoot koalas.

§

My conflict with *The Australian* would escalate when threats of defamation began flying around. In 2006 I was approached by Robert Manne, who at the time was a commissioning editor for the progressive publisher Black Inc. in Melbourne, to write a book about the politics of climate change. Rob hoped that the book would do for the politics of climate change what Tim Flannery's *The Weather Makers* had done for the science. (It didn't.) In *Scorcher: The dirty politics of climate change*, I argued, inter alia, that the Howard government had been secretly collaborating with the fossil fuel industries to sabotage effective action on climate change against the wishes of the public and had been working to destroy the Kyoto Protocol. The book also explored and documented the rise and spread of climate science denial in Australia, a topic on which I had written often. It was peppered with references to the way *The Australian* had systematically promoted climate science denial, undermined the reputations of climate scientists, and published news stories that wilfully distorted the truth.

Following standard book publicity practice, around two weeks before the publication date of *Scorcher* the publisher sent the page proofs to Patrick Lawnham, editor of the 'Inquirer' section of *The Weekend Australian*, testing his interest in bidding for extract rights.

A few days later on 4 April, I received a phone call from Chris Mitchell. In a cordial conversation he suggested that my comments in *Scorcher* on the role of *The Australian* in the climate change debate were unduly harsh. The next day a package arrived by courier enclosing materials collated by various staff and designed to persuade me that the paper's news coverage, editorials and opinion pieces provided a balanced perspective on the climate change debate. Mitchell's accompanying letter argued that his paper's coverage had not been 'anti-green' but instead emphasised a 'practical approach' to the issue which 'sits easily with the views of the people who pay for the paper each day'. He invited me to visit the paper's offices at Holt Street and speak with the editors. (I wasn't going to do that. When you get to know people personally it becomes awkward to criticise them in print.)

For reasons I didn't understand, Mitchell made strenuous efforts to ensure I received the package of material overnight so that I could read it over the Easter break. Having spent years reading and assessing *The Australian's* coverage, the material made no difference to my perceptions, although the determination to get me to change my views suggested a sensitivity to criticism at odds with the paper's bullying style. At my request, Australia Institute researcher Christian Downie had spent many days in the National Library examining all opinion pieces and editorials over the first three months of 2006, a fairly typical period. In that period, *The Australian* published nine opinion pieces or editorials in favour of the Howard government's position and one against, ten against the Kyoto Protocol and one for, and ten against the consensus view of the science and six for, including one 'for' by Prime Minister Howard. The latter should be seen in the light of studies showing 97 per cent of all articles in refereed scientific journals backed the main propositions of climate science.

In the meantime, another, less cordial correspondence was taking place between staff at *The Australian* and Black Inc. Patrick Lawnham wrote to Morry Schwartz, founder and chair of Schwartz Publishing, owner of Black Inc., complaining that *Scorcher* 'greatly misrepresents' the newspaper's coverage of climate change. He claimed to have been shocked by the book! The letter went on to say that *The Australian* wanted an 'addendum' to be inserted into the book, including ones already printed, 'stating that *The Australian* rejects the book's representation of its coverage of greenhouse and other environmental issues, and of its staff's motives and intent'. Of course, such a demand is unheard of in the world of publishing and could not be taken seriously.

This was all the more breathtaking for the fact that the demand was made by a powerful national newspaper against a small publisher. It suggested a puzzling desperation to avoid criticism, perhaps explained by the dramatic shift some months beforehand by the newspaper's proprietor, Rupert Murdoch, from climate sceptic to greenhouse believer. (The conversion was a pretence and short-lived.) *The Australian* had locked itself into such a trenchant denialist position that change seemed too threatening, and the only avenue was to deny its denialism and excoriate those who pointed to the truth of its stance.

Of course, Black Inc.'s publishers rejected *The Australian*'s demand out of hand. Robert Manne was also engaged in an email correspondence with Tom Switzer, the paper's opinion editor, who frequently gave space to denialists and anti-science fanatics. Defending his stance, Switzer wrote that 'a strong case could be made that no scientific consensus on climate change exists', which was news to the scientific community around the world. In Australia, the CSIRO, the Bureau of Meteorology and the Academy of Science must have been making it all up.

Switzer ended his 16 April email with an implicit threat. 'Finally, I would not be surprised if certain individuals here do indeed decide to take action over the chapter.' Rob was unmoved; like me, he is the kind of person who digs in his heels when someone tries to intimidate him.

The signalling by senior staff at *The Australian* that defamation action was being considered struck me as bullying typical of the newspaper. With a daily circulation of 130,000 and double that number on Saturdays, *The Australian* was in a strong a position to defend itself against any criticisms, and it was in a class of its own when it came to bagging people it did not like.

The threats were also profoundly hypocritical. I emailed Chris Mitchell to point out that as editor-in-chief he had for years campaigned vigorously against Australia's unfair defamation laws, with many editorials making a strong case against them for restricting free speech. One bewailed the 'ludicrous defamation laws, which act to suppress free speech and enrich lawyers … Book-burning through defamation means control of the historical record goes to the people with the deepest pockets and the smartest lawyers.' In the same year, I reminded him, the newspaper had opined that the 'whole legalistic approach ignores a fundamental truth: freedom of speech and a vigorous and open marketplace of ideas are essential to a democratic society'.

Mitchell's response was swift: 'Neither the paper nor I would ever sue.' I stored that away. But *The Australian*'s denunciations of me and the institute only escalated. In June 2007 it carried a bizarre editorial headed 'Reality bites the psychotic left', arguing, if that's the right word, that the work of the Australia Institute 'fits the dictionary definition of the word "psychosis"'. Robert Manne and David Marr were also named among the psychotic left.

Three years later, Mitchell took legal action against a journalism academic, Julie Posetti, claiming he'd been damaged by a tweet she had sent out reporting words allegedly spoken by Åsa Wahlquist, who had for many years been the rural reporter at *The Australian*. Posetti tweeted that Wahlquist had said Mitchell is inclined towards conspiracy theories and believes those who want strong action on climate change follow an 'eco-fascist line' and are 'aiming to destroy everything he loves and values'.

The Australian always has a few good, straight journalists, and Åsa Wahlquist was one of them. I'd dealt with her on a few occasions. After I once questioned a story under her by-line, which struck me as a distortion of my views, she confided that the published story was not the one she wrote, and that she was sick of her stories being rewritten to give them an ideological slant.

Mitchell eventually backed down on his legal action against Posetti. Justifying his decision, he complained about how hurtful it was to be criticised. He then let it be known that he regretted not suing me over *Scorcher*.

I used to read *The Australian* every day as part of my job and was often dismayed – no, disgusted – at the character assassinations in which it specialised. The way the paper would target and then, day after day, mercilessly pursue an individual they disliked for political reasons was something to behold. Although nowadays she presents as the affable 'PK' on ABC Radio National, I will never forget the vicious and unrelenting campaign that Patricia Karvelas, then a journalist at *The Australian*, mounted against the respected Indigenous academic Larissa Behrendt in 2011.

Behrendt, who did not share *The Australian*'s preferred position on Indigenous policy, had sent a late-night private Twitter message with a nasty comment about another Indigenous woman. It was a mistake and she apologised, but *The Australian* had an excuse for a campaign of character assassination. Week after week it dug up dirt on her, much of it inaccurate, discrediting her, dividing the Indigenous community and trying to have her fired from her job. In his *Quarterly Essay* entitled *Bad News*, which eviscerated *The Australian*, Robert Manne wrote a damning account of what Karvelas had done to Behrendt and its devastating personal effect. After interviewing Behrendt, Manne wrote: 'I asked her to comment on the impact the *Australian*'s campaign had had upon her life. She could not speak.'

One day I received a call from one of *The Australian*'s journalists asking me to comment on a story she was writing that involved me. I did not trust her and said I did not want to comment. She told me that if I wouldn't speak with her, she would send a photographer to wait outside my house and photograph me unawares. This journalist was exposed a couple of years later using the same blackmail technique on someone else.

When Ian Fry, an Australian representing Tuvalu, made a powerful and moving speech to the 2009 Copenhagen climate conference, *The Australian* published a sneering front-page story by Samantha Maiden ridiculing his 'tear-jerking performance' and featuring a photograph of Fry's house, along with shots of his car and air-conditioner. It was at a time when climate campaigners and their families were receiving grisly death threats.

Public life in Australia can be brutal, but News Corp takes it to another level. It thrives on finding and then vilifying ideological 'enemies'. That's the business model, so to speak. It has left a trail of collateral damage, lives blighted by attacks from out of nowhere. For those willing to enter the fray, social media now competes with the Murdoch media to make public participation like a swim in a shark-infested sea. By the time I left the Australia Institute, I was scarred and bruised. There was some time to go before I reached that point; in the meantime, I would discover that there are other sharks in the waters.

12

Climate, climate, climate

CREDIBILITY CAN BE built a number of ways. In Australia we admire international links, and I had been building these in the climate arena, the global issue par excellence. Back in 2003 I had spent three months as a visiting academic at Cambridge University – desirable in itself but also something that stands out on a bio. It was a kind of sabbatical break with no specific task, just an opportunity to read and think. I had organised the invitation to come from an old acquaintance, Geoff Harcourt, a Cambridge economics professor originally from Adelaide. Way back in 1978, when I was a student at the University of Sydney, Geoff had stayed a night or two at our house in Glebe when he spoke at a political economy conference. Geoff was a delightful man who wore his eminence lightly. I was a bit in awe, of course.

I'd turned down the opportunity to do a PhD at Cambridge, preferring the more radical Sussex, a decision I have sometimes regretted. At Cambridge as a visiting academic I was attached to the Department of Land Economy, although I never quite understood what it was. When I turned up on the first day, I was taken to a small, dark and dust-caked room. This was my office and it was an omen: they would ignore me completely. Over at my college, Clare Hall, it was the same. When I gave an evening seminar to college fellows arguing that, beyond a certain level, higher incomes do not make people happier, they were so outraged that I should challenge the unalloyed marvels of growth and progress that a pile on ensued.

Nevertheless, I enjoyed my time at Cambridge, spending day after day alone in the stacks of the university library reading philosophy books. To break up the highbrow, before I left Canberra I had commissioned a British polling company to replicate for Britons the survey that showed two thirds of Australians believe they cannot afford to buy everything they really need. The results were very similar, so I wrote a shortish paper modelled on the Australian one, with British examples of luxury consumption, excessive debt and the stresses of materialism. I asked the media office of the university to issue a release and put the paper on their website; it would then become a 'University of Cambridge study'. I was surprised they agreed so readily.

The story attracted quite a bit of attention, although there was something not quite right about an Australian lecturing British people about their profligacy. Nevertheless, I was approached by the BBC's *Panorama*, the equivalent of *Four Corners*, although it had gone downmarket in style. They soon began filming a program about excessive consumption in Britain. The producers hired a big black Rolls Royce and drove me to Oxford Street, where I was filmed getting out of the Roller and entering upmarket shops. I couldn't see the point, really, and when the program went to air, I felt foolish, the 'don from Cambridge' doing tabloid stunts.

§

It was while I was in Britain that the idea for an International Climate Change Taskforce was cooked up. I took the train to London to give an informal talk at the Institute for Public Policy Research (IPPR), a kindred think tank with offices near Covent Garden. Afterwards I had lunch with Matthew Taylor, IPPR director and later head of Tony Blair's policy unit. He was savvy and matter-of-fact and I liked him. We were eating a sandwich at a table outside a café, talking about the cracks appearing in the Kyoto Protocol. The Bush administration had repudiated it and was pressuring scientists to be silent. The Howard government, now dominated by deniers, had pulled Australia out of the agreement.

Matthew suggested a high-level taskforce aimed at finding a way forward, with members drawn from the United Kingdom, Australia and the United States. The idea of a global collaboration on a high-profile issue appealed to me and we agreed to do it. Neither of us could think of a suitable think tank in the United States to be the third leg. Back at IPPR, someone mentioned a think tank called the Center for American Progress (CAP). Looking into it on my return to Canberra, I saw that it had only recently been set up, after George W. Bush won the presidency. Someone later described it to me as a parking lot for ex-Clinton staffers waiting for the next Democratic presidency.

CAP's president was John Podesta, who had been Bill Clinton's White House chief of staff. He would later come to global attention when, as chair of Hillary Clinton's 2016 presidential campaign, Russian agents hacked his computer and gave a trove of emails to WikiLeaks. I emailed him out of the blue with the outline of the proposal and he expressed interest. A month or two later I was in Washington, DC, and called in to the centre's offices on H Street. Podesta was an athletic, taciturn man. I didn't warm to him. As our conversation progressed, I was unsettled to discover that he knew virtually nothing about climate change, just enough to know that it might become an issue and that CAP could benefit from being the American leg of the three-legged stool. But only if he could find some money, which would prove difficult for him. Leaving Washington, I took doubts about teaming up with the Center for American Progress, but by then it would have been awkward to uninvite them, and there was no obvious alternative.

The Australia Institute did almost all of the intellectual work and supplied the bulk of the funding, thanks to Mark Wootton, who immediately saw the potential of the taskforce. Being able to come up with our share of the funding quickly, while the other two partners struggled for months, improved the institute's standing and influence in the process. I employed former ABC journalist Alan Tate and his consulting partner Justin Sherrard to undertake much of the high-level organisational work.

Podesta brought in a hard-nosed lawyer, Todd Stern, a Podesta protégé who would later become Obama's chief climate envoy and be accused by some of blowing up the 2009 Copenhagen conference. Podesta also drafted in Jonathan Pershing, another of his colleagues in the Clinton administration. Pershing would succeed Stern as Obama's chief climate negotiator.

We began three-way discussions about whom to invite onto the taskforce. On the American side we chose Senator Olympia Snowe, a moderate Republican who agreed to be a co-chair, along with John Holdren, a brilliant Harvard environmental scientist who later worked for President Obama. Timothy Wirth, who ran the Clinton–Gore campaigns and served them as undersecretary for global affairs, was drafted in, although for the most part he was MIA.

The first British member of the panel was co-chair Stephen Byers, a transport secretary under Tony Blair who'd been forced to quit in an expenses scandal, although he remained influential in government. Jonathon Porritt, a well-connected environmentalist and writer whom I had known for a while, and Adair Turner, chairman of the Financial Services Authority, joined too.

The three from Australia were Bob Carr, who as New South Wales premier had adopted a progressive stance on climate change, Tony McMichael, the renowned epidemiologist from the ANU, and Cathy Zoi, who had worked in the Clinton White House before settling in Sydney to work in green finance. To add a diversity of perspectives, we also invited experts or senior politicians from China, Malaysia, Germany, Switzerland and France.

While working with the IPPR was a pleasure, working with CAP was exasperating. On our three-way think tank phone calls, Jonathan Pershing and another DC lawyer were hard-bitten, rude and unpleasant. They treated us, especially the Australians, as sub-ordinates. At one point it got the better of me and I bit back, telling them what shits they were to deal with. They backed down. That collaboration disabused me of the notion that Democrats are more internationalist in sentiment than Republicans. They are all schooled to believe that the United States is the exceptional nation and others need to just play along. It was dispiriting to realise this was where progressive Americans were at.

The first meeting of the taskforce was held at Windsor Castle, a venue suggested by Stephen Byers. When we arrived we were told the Queen was not in residence, but a bit of royal magic dust could only enhance our credibility. The Australia Institute had written the background paper and we made good progress at Windsor. One night, when the Australians gathered at a restaurant, Bob Carr launched into an hour-long disquisition on the history of the American Civil War. At first it sounded impressive, but our eyes soon glazed over. On and on he went. I reflected on the difference between a history buff and a historian.

The second get-together of the taskforce was held in Sydney at Government House, a stately venue for a high-powered group of overseas visitors. Over the following weeks, the Australia Institute wrote the draft of the taskforce's final report. The first reaction of our Washington partners was to express concern about the title. 'Towards a low-carbon future', they wrote, would not fly because Americans would confuse 'low-carbon future' with 'low-carb diets'. I am not making this up.

The report was published in January 2005 and attracted intense media attention internationally, with some two hundred newspaper and online stories in the first two days. The reporting in Australia was modest, although the Howard government felt obliged to 'welcome' it. Taskforce chair Stephen Byers received a complimentary letter from Prime Minister Tony Blair commending the work and pointing to its importance in the coming year. In all honesty, while I learned a lot, I'm not sure that the whole effort made any difference.

§

Life has a habit of presenting unexpected opportunities. In July 2005, Mark Wootton visited me at our ANU offices. After the tragic death of Eve Kantor's brother Tom, Mark and Eve found themselves having to decide how to spend the $10 million in Tom's philanthropic fund. Mark was keen on some kind of circuit-breaker in public understanding of climate change and asked me to come up with a way to 'cut through'.

I was a bit overwhelmed by the responsibility; it was not obvious what could best be done with $10 million to bring about a step change in the political landscape. I thought about it for a few days then proposed that we set up a non-profit organisation modelled on the Australia Institute but devoted mainly to communications rather than research. And so the Climate Institute came into being. I registered a company limited by guarantee and structured to permit tax-deductible donations. We found offices in George Street, Sydney, courtesy of Adam Kilgour, a marketing executive whom Mark and I had come to know at a strategy retreat for environmentalists. We put together a board with me as the chair. Now I was running two organisations. I really should have known better.

We formed a three-person committee to recruit a CEO. We were not flooded with strong applications but two appeared to be well-suited. We did all of the due diligence but could not decide between them. It was left to me to make the decision. Although I had collected three additional informal references from his close colleagues, I chose the wrong one. To cut a painful couple of months short, it was my job to fire him. We searched for a replacement. To add to the pressure, I sent a private email that included an uncharitable remark about one of the board members, an email she subsequently read in an email stream. When I heard what I'd done, I wanted to hide in a cave.

I was so stressed by this stage, I wasn't coping. The Climate Institute was going through a messy birth and I was neglecting the Australia Institute. I'd been meditating every morning for many years, but even during this quiet period my mind was swirling. I was juggling too many balls, and when I began to drop some it belied my belief in my own competence. I felt I had to resign from the Climate Institute board. In bailing out so suddenly I knew I had let down the others. It was a low point as I retreated to my office in Canberra. As always, the best way to drag oneself out of a slump is to get plenty of exercise and be productive at work.

§

In 2006, the ANU informed me that it would not be renewing the lease on our offices in the Innovations Building. It claimed it had run out of space. I managed to secure a meeting with Vice-Chancellor Ian Chubb to put our case, but he was unmoved, and in February 2007 the institute took up residence in a street behind the now trendy Manuka shops. Manuka is a familiar part of town for me; my father took me there as a boy to have my hair cut and my shoes resoled, and at high school I bought milkshakes and played pinball there. Soon, however, an incident occurred that turned the vibe less friendly. It was in the middle of the millennium drought and farmers were suffering badly. It was the op-ed I wrote arguing that, with the climate changing, droughts would become more frequent, so the government should no longer be handing out drought relief for farms that cannot survive in the longer term. Within hours, our office manager, Kelly Bruce, began fielding calls from stressed farmers who wanted to vent. A few days later, an envelope arrived, postmarked Victoria and with no return address. Gingerly opening it, inside was a letter composed of words cut out of magazines and glued to the page. It was angry, and the author said he was coming to get me with a gun.

I'd had a few death threats from climate science deniers, but this was the most unsettling one I had received, and it made me anxious about the staff. The police were called. They took the letter and advised on some security measures. Each morning for the next year or so, as I stepped out of the front door of our house I hesitated, scanning the wooded reserve across the road for any sign of a madman with a rifle.

This was not what I had imagined think tank life to be when I returned from Jakarta in late 1993, full of enthusiasm. It's true, I played the game pretty hard. It got results but naturally invited backlash. The fact was that after twelve years of being out there, it was starting to wear me down. I had stopped enjoying it, and that was before David Jones came after me.

13

SLAPPed

ONE SATURDAY MORNING in early 2006, I was shopping at Harvey Norman. I can't remember what I was looking for but as I passed the rows of whitegoods, I came to a large wall at the back of the store covered by television screens. They were all tuned to a music video showing a rap singer engaged in simulated sex with several barely clad dancers. They bent over while the rap singer rhythmically thrust his genitals against their backsides. I looked around. Am I the only one thinking this is just wrong? There were parents with young children wandering around the store. I was dismayed that soft porn had become so normalised that it could serve as the wallpaper for a furniture and electrical goods retailer.

Around the same time, I began to notice twenty- or thirty-something women dressed and made up in the trashy style of Paris Hilton, celebrated for a leaked sex tape showing her engaged in fellatio. What bothered me was the eight- or ten-year-old girls with them, evidently their daughters, dressed and made up in the same way. Why would a mother allow her little girl to be presented as sexually desirable?

Soon after I mentioned it to Emma Rush. Emma had not long arrived at the institute from the University of Melbourne, having completed her thesis on the ethics of consumerism. She had already written two papers for the institute on corporatisation of child-care. I asked Emma if she had noticed that kids were becoming more sexualised.

'Oh yeah,' she exclaimed, 'you should see the magazines tweens read.' The issue had had some play in the media with Ariel Levy's book on 'raunch culture', but I suggested there might be a research project in it. Emma, along with research assistant Andrea La Nauze, began working on a systematic analysis of the way children were being sexualised through various media. Since so many people, not least department stores, had become habituated to the practice, the underlying purpose of the analysis was to defamiliarise the common practice of presenting children in eroticised ways.

Not long before the report was due to be released, I was looking through the *Good Weekend* magazine from *The Sydney Morning Herald* when I came across several full-page ads for children's clothing brands sold by David Jones. One image in particular, for Alison Ashley apparel, showed two girls who I guessed were around ten or eleven looking into the camera with the kind of smouldering come-on expressions commonly adopted by women models. To me it was blindingly obvious. On Monday, Emma said she'd seen the same ads.

A few of us sat around discussing possible titles for the report. I'd noticed that in 1995, Phillip Adams had used the term 'corporate paedophilia' in a semi-jocular way to describe the way businesses exploit children in their marketing, and it struck me as an appropriate, if provocative, term for the rampant sexualisation of children in Australia. It was too good not to put on the cover. 'Let's use that,' I suggested to nervous chuckles.

On 9 October 2006, we issued Discussion Paper Number 90 along with a media release headed 'Corporate paedophilia: Sexualising children by advertising and marketing'. The release began by saying that children were being sexualised, exposing them to a wide range of risks from a young age. After referring to Emma and Andrea as the authors of the study, it then quoted me:

> Major retail chains such as David Jones and Myer have jumped on the bandwagon. When family department stores show no conscience on these issues, or are inured to the effects of their behaviour, the situation is very unhealthy.

The media response to the report was a little disappointing. Emma did seven radio interviews that day, but only two major ones, on ABC's *PM* and ABC Sydney *Drive*.

The next morning, 10 October, David Jones made a terrible mistake, the opening shot in what would be a drawn-out and difficult episode for the institute. At 10.30 am, Kelly Bruce buzzed through to tell me that David Jones's CEO, Mark McInnes, was on the line and wanted to speak with me. Uh-oh, I thought, I know what this is about.

McInnes, affecting a deliberate and menacing tone, told me that they had seen our media release and that unless we removed all mention of David Jones from our report, he would take immediate and forceful legal action against the institute. He told me I had 'two hours' to do it. I asked him to put it in writing. He said he wasn't going to do that and hung up.

Gulp. I thought about it for a few minutes then phoned my friend Brian Walters SC, a Melbourne barrister. Brian had written a book on SLAPPs, strategic lawsuits against public participation, used by corporations to silence their critics in civil society. He was highly regarded and did quite a bit of pro bono work for environmental groups. I told Brian what had just happened and asked, 'What should I do?'

He turned it over in his mind for a minute or two, aware that recent changes to the defamation law had made it impossible for corporations to be defamed, and said, 'Here's what I think you should do.' It was the kind of advice I love to hear – go on the front foot.

An hour later I issued a media release describing exactly what had happened, that is, DJs' CEO had threatened legal action unless the institute removed all references to the company from its report. I wrote that the institute had been advised that it has not broken any law and that it stands by the quality of its research and the claims made in it.

It took an hour or so then the world went crazy. The David Jones threat was the top story on Channel 9 news that night, with the *Good Weekend* image of the two sultry girls prominently featured. Channel 7, Channel 10 and the ABC all followed suit. Over the next couple of days we were caught in a media frenzy. Emma and I did some forty or fifty radio and television interviews. Dozens of newspaper stories raised the temperature, reporting that retailers had reacted 'furiously'. A national debate began about corporate sexualisation of children, with anger over corporate bullying adding fuel to the fire.

More than any other report the institute had published, our emails and phones were flooded with messages of congratulation and support. Of the hundreds of emails thanking Emma and the institute, many began with 'as the mother/father of young girls' and went on to speak of how they had worried in silence about the phenomenon we were describing and how they were 'despairing' about how they were going to protect their girls from the 'bombardment'. Many complained bitterly about 'bralets' for six-year-olds, lingerie for pre-teens and highly sexualised music videos watched by kids on Saturday mornings. Others had stories of their children being drawn in by media and peer pressure and how parents can only do so much to resist the tide. Many denounced David Jones, with some forwarding the retailer's replies to complaints they'd made to DJs before our report. Some identified as feminists, others as conservatives. Wrote one supporter: 'it's about time someone had the balls to say what most parents are thinking.' TV producers and opinion page editors commented to us on the overwhelming viewer and reader reaction to our story.

A surprising number who made contact were lawyers expressing their support and offering to give advice. Support also came from psychiatrists, child psychologists and people working in children's mental health. A Queensland lawyer wrote to say that, while putting herself through university, she had worked as a security guard at Myer where 'the children's clothing area was the best area to catch a paedophile'. A month later, a dozen well-known experts in child health and wellbeing wrote a public letter backing our claim that sexualisation of children by 'commercial forces' is making them much more vulnerable to sexual danger and harm.

§

In the days after the story broke, I took note of the experts quoted in the media. A large majority, especially those with clinical experience, agreed with our report. Then there were the critics. The immediate ones included Catharine Lumby, the 'sex-positive' cultural studies expert who had authored a report praising porn, Mia Freedman, who had made her reputation by selling women's magazines, and Russel Howcroft, the advertising industry advocate who would later make a name on *The Gruen Transfer*, where the other panellists often mocked him for his refusal to criticise any ad for overstepping ethical boundaries.

Alan McKee, a Queensland academic who co-authored Lumby's pro-porn study, declared that no reasonable adult would see any sexualisation in the images we drew attention to. He later told a Senate inquiry that there was no sexualised representation of children in the mainstream media. Another of these postmodern defenders of sexual liberation for children, Duncan Fine, wrote that Paris Hilton is a good role model for young girls because she is 'an escape from the Western Taliban'. He wrote: 'No 10-year-old looks sexually provocative to me, nor to any adult I know. Want to know why? Because children cannot provoke sexual desire in an adult. They are children.'

When Channel Nine's *Sunday* program showed the Alison Ashley ad to Catherine Lumby, she had no hesitation: 'There is no sexual behaviour going on in this image.' After a *7.30 Report* story on the issue went to air, online commentary was scathing of Lumby, also a member of the Advertising Standards Board, which we would soon criticise as little more than an apologist for the advertising industry.

The backlash was not restricted to 'pro-sex' cultural studies academics. Simone Bartley, the CEO of Saatchi & Saatchi, which handled DJs' advertising account, was indignant; the suggestion that they would sexualise children was 'repugnant'. 'We have never, ever eroticised children in any way for any client in any communication.' As we'll see, a document released later, after a freedom of information tussle, would show this was a lie. DJs' head of marketing, Damian Eales, was 'appalled' by the allegations. Eales, the brother of former Wallabies captain John Eales, had told the media he took 'great offence', insisting on the company's 'family values'. I think Eales was genuinely shocked and offended by our accusation. But that was our point: people like him had become so inured to the creeping sexualisation of children that they were unable to see it under their noses. Emma responded in *The Australian*: 'We expect them to deny they are doing it, but the truth is, they pose children like adults.' *The Australian* itself wrote a typically narky editorial blaming the problem on 'the Left'. It was inundated by cranky letters from its own readers supporting our argument.

All of this might have been expected. But we discovered that mixing children and sexuality brings some creepy people out of the woodwork. 'SHAME ON YOU,' wrote a man who could not see anything 'sexual' in the photos, adding, 'I hope you get taken for everything.' An academic at the University of Adelaide emailed Emma to tell her the paper was just a leftist rant, finishing with: 'I hope they rape you financially. You should have stayed in the kitchen.' I informed the university of what this person had done, indicating that he ought not to be teaching young women (or young men, for that matter). Despite the enormous support she was receiving, the hate directed at

Emma must have been disturbing. This kind of trolling was new. She kept a brave face, but I was worried about her welfare and checked in with her during the worst periods.

The most upsetting reaction to our report came from a direction that I should have anticipated but did not. The day after TV news bulletins led with the DJs' story, Emma received an email from the extremely distressed parents of the ten-year-old girl in the Alison Ashley ad. They felt that we had 'dragged our gorgeous little girl into your dirty allegations' and wrote of the deep distress of the family as it responded to calls from people they knew. Worst of all, the girl had been ridiculed at school. On the same day I took a phone call from the distraught grandmother of the same girl. She asked me to remove the David Jones advertisement from our report's electronic appendix. I agreed to do so.

Later that day I received a faxed letter from a solicitor representing the family. It spoke of the family's distress; they felt they had been violated, even more so when they learned we had used the image in our report, thereby alerting voyeurs or paedophiles to the image. He noted the image had been removed but threatened legal action if we were to use it again.

I recognised that it must have been a shattering experience for the family, and I worry about whether bringing it all back up now is the right thing to do. At the time, I had an urge to apologise to the parents, even though, in my opinion, they like many other parents had been naïve to allow their daughter to be presented in the way she had been. The parents too were victims of the culture of sexualisation. As I saw it, we had merely pointed to the obvious, but there was a taboo on pointing it out in public, a taboo we had seemingly broken.

Of course, we waited eagerly to see the next issue of the *Good Weekend* featuring DJs' kidswear ads. When it came, the contrast was stark. The way the children were now dressed and presented, they could have been Amish. A panicked message must have been sent to Saatchi & Saatchi to strike out anything even vaguely erotic. Although Saatchi had indignantly denied they ever present children in sexualised ways, they knew exactly what to change. We stored the contrasting imagery away for possible use in court.

§

One of my first urges after receiving Mark McInnes's phone call was to pull out our professional indemnity insurance policy. Alert to the possibility of a defamation action, I had taken it out in the early days of the institute. I notified our insurer of the threatened action.

It took a few weeks before the letter from David Jones's lawyers arrived. They were coming after me personally as well as the institute. It was the beginning of my crash course in how the law really works when the big end of town is involved.

Soon afterwards, I travelled to Sydney to meet Adrian Howie of Kennedys, the solicitor appointed by the insurance company to look after this case. I was relieved to find a genial, experienced and very sharp lawyer. He knew my brother Roger, a Sydney barrister. Adrian was not one of those control-freak lawyers who believe the law operates divorced from the rest of the world, insisting you say nothing more in public. Adrian understood that our greatest advantage was in the court of public opinion, a court in which a win for us was virtually certain.

Adrian's associate was a young lawyer named Rebekah Rivkin. I found her pleasant, efficient and on side. Rebekah was still recovering after being badly pummelled in the 2005 tsunami. Nowadays, she is Rebekah Giles, a celebrity defamation lawyer with a list of devoted high-profile clients. At our first meeting, it was explained to me that ultimately the insurance company calls the shots. Kennedys were being paid by the insurer. If it decided we should apologise and settle then that was it, unless I decided to go it alone, risking a very large legal bill and the possibility of losing my house, even if I won. (When courts order the loser to pay the costs of the victor it's never for the full amount, so you may still end up out of pocket by a couple of hundred thousand.) However, I was assured that the insurance company would not seek to settle the matter against my wishes, which was a great relief. On our second or third meeting, Adrian confided to me that the insurance company was strongly backing the institute and me in the legal action because the CEO had two teenage girls and was himself worried about the problem we had publicised. I was grateful to hear it, but also a little disconcerted at this insight into how the system works. What if the CEO were otherwise inclined?

McInnes had hired attack-dog lawyer Mark O'Brien, then at Gilbert + Tobin, who had a reputation for a take-no-prisoners approach. I soon came to loathe the man for his bullying tactics and, now with my back up, looked forward to defeating him.

Mark O'Brien was casting around for a law we may have broken. His initial line of attack was to claim that we had defamed Damian Eales, DJs' head of marketing. Although we had nowhere mentioned Eales, O'Brien argued that many people in retail and marketing knew that he oversaw DJs' advertising, so we had damaged his reputation by implication. Adrian Howie reckoned it was a try-on, and he replied to O'Brien to that effect.

O'Brien dropped the defamation route and began to argue that we had engaged in 'deceptive and misleading conduct', contrary to section 52 of the *Trade Practices Act*. David Jones wanted the court to order us to make a public apology, which they had helpfully drafted, saying that DJs does not sexualise children. They wanted damages awarded under section 52 and costs. Apart from truth, we had a number of defences, the first of which was that, as a non-profit think tank, we didn't engage in trade or commerce and are therefore not covered by the Act.

To me, blind Freddy could see that the institute – a charity with tax deductibility receiving some 80 per cent of its income from donations – was not a commercial enterprise. But the law does not always recognise blind Freddy. Nevertheless, Adrian would later express the view that a judge, in all likelihood male and a social conservative, may desire to avoid expressing an opinion as to the sexiness or otherwise of the children in the ads and find in our favour on a technical issue.

I had been told that legal cases like this were all-consuming. From go to whoa it probably took up an aggregate of seven or eight weeks of my work time and a couple of months of other staff time. However, it hung like a spectre over me, ever-present. I was sure our case was rock-solid, but you can never be certain with the law. Judges can be capricious. So I was incensed to have been put in this situation, anxious that it might not go our way and determined not to let the bastards defeat me.

14

Exit

WHILE THE DAVID JONES issue ground away – through subpoenas, expert testimonies, legal manoeuvrings and preparatory hearings – the Australia Institute was busy pushing out more research and participating in public debates.

After several years in power, the Howard government had become intolerant, although there had been signs from the beginning. To illustrate, in 2001 I was nominated to be one of six finalists for the Prime Minister's Environmentalist of the Year Award. With John Howard in the Lodge, I thought there was no chance I would win. But as the big night approached, I learned some of the backstory to the award. The previous year, an independent judging panel, including the ABC's Robyn Williams and Clean Up Australia's Ian Kiernan, chose as Environmentalist of the Year the environmental scientist Ian Lowe. When the decision was communicated to the environment minister, his office phoned to say that Ian Lowe, a critic of the government, was unacceptable. After some deliberation, the panel asked the awards manager to phone the minister's office and tell the government 'to get fucked' (or so it was put to me at the time). At the gala awards night, John Howard, with gritted teeth, handed the prize to Ian Lowe. Within months, management of the awards was soon handed to a more compliant organisation. I sat through the gala awards night in 2001 to see the award go to water expert Peter Cullen, worthy but safe.

For some years I had been hearing stories about NGOs becoming more reluctant to say anything critical of the government, so in 2004 the institute carried out an online survey of NGOs. They reported tactics including bullying, harassment, intimidation, public denigration and threats to withdraw funding, sometimes directly from ministers or their offices. Ninety per cent said that organisations critical of the government risk having their funding cut. Cutting funding, and even threatening to deny tax deductibility, were not the only tactics. Another was personal vilification carried out by the government's hardmen, notably Senator Eric Abetz. He even threatened the RSPCA for campaigning against live sheep exports. Meanwhile, Treasurer Peter Costello was praising voluntary organisations and saying how the government would protect them from threats.

One of the most troubling moves was the government's effort to take away the charitable status of NGOs, especially environmental ones. This followed an extended campaign by the Institute of Public Affairs targeting environmental organisations for engaging in 'political' activity. The double standard was breathtaking: no tax-deductible organisation in Australia, other than the political parties themselves, was more heavily engaged in politics, and more secretive about its funding, than the IPA. At the urging of the IPA, the government pressured the taxation commission to go after Aid/Watch, a very small outfit that had been lobbying in favour of a larger aid budget. The ATO disqualified it as a charity, a decision that ended up in the High Court. After four years, Aid/Watch won but at crippling expense.

Disturbed at the way the Howard government was suppressing critical voices, I teamed up with Sarah Maddison at the University of New South Wales school of politics to edit a volume, *Silencing Dissent*, analysing the muzzling of NGOs, the politicisation of the public service, the stacking of statutory authorities, restrictions on academic freedom, and more. Published in February 2007, the book sold strongly, clearly speaking to a widespread anxiety. Commentators at *The Australian* mocked us, as if we were complaining about being gagged ourselves. They hadn't read the book but brayed about our 'hypocrisy'.

§

There was no let-up in our work exposing the dangers of climate change and the deceptive claims of the Howard government. In 2007 the institute published papers on the public's preference for renewables, the siting of nuclear power plants, Australia's carbon budget, problems with carbon offsets, the myth of clean coal, emissions from coastal shipping, emissions from land clearing, and a critique of the work of the government's preferred modeller. In December 2006 we had published a paper, prepared by Christian Downie, drawing together the evidence on increased bushfire risk due to a warming climate. The frequency of very high and extreme fire danger days would increase markedly and so would the damage caused by fires. Prime Minister Howard dismissed our report as 'esoteric'. In early 2020, the report was cited on the front page of *Le Monde* to explain the infernos of our 'Black Summer'.

After noticing a similar analysis in Britain, Andrew Macintosh and Christian Downie used best-available data to make projections through to 2050 of greenhouse gas emissions from aviation. International aviation had been exempted from all proposed emissions trading schemes and was subject to no other policy measures. The numbers showed that if nothing is done about aviation emissions while other sectors cut theirs, aviation would account for the nation's *entire* emissions allowance by 2050, with nothing left for other sectors, notably agriculture. To meet targets, Australians would have to take fewer flights.

It was a simple argument based on robust data, but that didn't prevent Deputy Prime Minister Mark Vaile denouncing our report as 'whacky'. The costs of including aviation in an emissions trading scheme would 'wreck the economy', he said. Labor's Martin Ferguson told parliament that the Australia Institute wants to deprive working families of their hard-earned holidays. I despaired. Why is it that so many of our politicians say such dopey things? These ideas are not so hard to understand.

Business leaders were no better. The boss of Virgin Blue declared, 'I just don't fathom what they are on about.' Imagine that: a top executive in one of the main carbon-polluting industries unable to understand the implications of greenhouse policies for his industry. Meanwhile, the UK government had just issued a white paper arguing that aviation emissions are rising rapidly and should be included in any emissions trading scheme. International aviation organisations were moving in the same direction.

It's clear from what I have written that I often took a jaundiced view of the economics profession. Yet the profession as a whole is not as conservative as I may have made out. Many economists in Australia have centrist or centre-left views. Even conservative economists were capable of reading the science of climate change and concluding that Australia should be doing much more than the intransigent Howard government was willing to do, that is, sweet FA. It was with this in mind, and noticing a similar effort in the United States, that in 2007 I got together with John Quiggin and Peter Dixon, the Monash University professor and a highly regarded economic modeller, to ask the nation's academic economists to sign a statement. It declared that Australia will be severely affected by heatwaves, droughts, bushfires and sea-level rise, that we could cut our emissions sharply for minimal economic cost, and that we should ratify Kyoto and demonstrate international leadership.

It was a strong statement, and the response was well beyond our expectations. Among the 271 academic economists who signed it, 75 were professors. That's a lot of economics professors. The statement made it much harder for the Howard government and its tame economic modellers to argue that climate change was not a big problem and cutting emissions would cripple the economy.

I was pleased to be able to escape the fray for a while when in June 2007 I was one of three guests on a panel with the Dalai Lama at an event held in a packed auditorium at Sydney's Darling Harbour. The theme was materialism and happiness, a subject on which I had written extensively. The Dalai Lama greeted each of us on stage by bowing and placing a white satin scarf around our necks, which was oddly moving. Geraldine Doogue was in the chair. On the panel were the director of the Black Dog Institute, Gordon Parker, a man who radiates human kindness, and Magda Szubanski, glowing from the success of *Kath & Kim*. The Dalai Lama was all grace and good humour, if not very profound. My friend and publisher Elizabeth Weiss, a serious devotee of Tibetan Buddhism, later told me that the Dalai Lama saves his more difficult teachings for committed students in small groups.

It was a bright spot in a tough year, one in which the David Jones case loomed over everything.

§

From the outset, our lawyer Adrian Howie and the insurance company shared my determination not to take a backward step. This kind of case rarely ends up in court, but after nine months of mounting pressure, I found myself hoping that the case would go to trial. It would be a world first and I knew we had massive public support. There were parents and women's groups ready to demonstrate against David Jones on the steps of the federal court, a PR debacle for the company.

The discovery process requires each side to hand over to the other all documents of possible relevance to the case. Louise Collett, who worked part-time in our office, was assigned the exacting task of trawling, line by line, through the trove of documents that arrived by courier in fifteen or so boxes. We were entertained by emails between Saatchi staff about how wasted they were at weekend parties. Louise, who was studying law at ANU, came across documents that gave us some valuable insights. Before our report was published, the company had been receiving complaints from the public about the eroticisation of children in its advertising. And the guidelines it was claiming would have ruled out any sexualisation of children had only been written down in a mad scramble after the media blow-up.

We were informed by letter that many relevant documents – like the 'presentation boards' Saatchi created for the ads and DJs' sign-off on artworks – had been destroyed as part of the 'ordinary course of business'. I would never suggest that David Jones or Saatchi & Saatchi destroyed evidence they were legally obliged, under heavy penalty, to produce. While the boxes of subpoenaed documents were not the bonanza I had hoped for, Louise did find one explosive email that may have been missed by the shredder deployed in the ordinary course of business. It was an email from Saatchi & Saatchi to the Office of the Children's Guardian detailing the forthcoming shoot, including the Alison Ashley images. The email included an instruction to the photographer that the two girls in the Alison Ashley ad should be made to look 'slightly more adult and sexy'.

One of those girls was ten years old, the other twelve. So Saatchi instructed its photographer to make these girls look more adult and sexy, and David Jones signed off on it. The Office of the Children's Guardian, whose function is to ensure that children used in advertisements are not exposed to any risks, waved the shoot through.

Although our lawyers, experienced in the vagaries of the law and the quirks of judges, were more cautious, I thought with this piece of evidence we had David Jones on toast. But I could not help thinking of the parents of the girl who, through tears and rage, had told Emma she must be sick to see their little girl as sexualised. How would they react once they knew that David Jones, through its advertising company, had knowingly presented their daughter as 'more adult and sexy'? In March 2007, I phoned the parents' solicitor to tell him what we had found and that, if the case went to trial, the email would be a key piece of evidence. I said that, although the parents may not see it this way, we are on the same side.

We had also been informed by a reliable source that a man claiming to be a paedophile had contacted David Jones to tell them that 'he struggles with images of girls and the images of girls in DJs catalogues were especially disturbing to him'. He supplied his phone number and said he was willing to give evidence to the court. In our office, we also received a couple of phone calls from men claiming to be paedophiles saying they obtained sexual gratification from looking at the kinds of ads our report highlighted. The title of Discussion Paper No. 90 had been only a metaphor for the sexualisation of children, but increasingly the court case seemed to be focusing on the behaviour of real paedophiles.

David Jones had form for sexualising children. In 1999 the retailer had been lambasted by women's groups for putting a heavily made-up nine-year-old girl with a come-hither expression on the front cover of its fashion catalogue. The Women's Electoral Lobby and a group of professional women had written to David Jones with the accusation it 'has calculatedly exploited a child as an object of sexual fantasy'. Just as it did in response to our report, DJs whined that it has a policy to 'maintain the highest standards in relation to the portrayal of children'. What a crock. The Women's Electoral Lobby also criticised the Advertising Standards Council for being 'a toothless tiger run by advertisers'. Naturally, as part of the exchange of letters aimed at convincing the other side that they would lose in court, our lawyers forwarded the 1999 news story to Mark O'Brien.

We had to produce documents for David Jones too. With the help of one or two staff members, it took a couple of days to print or make copies of everything that might be relevant. There was only one document that gave me heartburn, an email exchange with our media adviser, Jacqui Rees, a few days before publication. Jacqui had noted that there had been a lot about the issue in the media so we might not get much traction. I replied that I had pitched the story to someone from ABC Radio's *Life Matters*. When she did not express much interest, 'I said the paper fingers David Jones and Myer, which seemed to stop her in her tracks.'

I confess that I thought for a moment about making the document disappear, destroyed in the ordinary course of business. But the penalty, if caught, was severe. Of course, Mark O'Brien made as much of the email as he could in the back and forth between the solicitors. As I was learning, it's normal for lawyers to exchange letters trying to ramp up the pressure on the other side by displaying their strengths, hoping to psych them out. Our lawyers were not letting up and flagged our intention to issue further subpoenas.

§

I have noted that a number of academics in cultural studies and media departments came out in defence of David Jones. Heavily influenced by postmodern French philosophy, they claimed that children are already sexual beings and can't be 'sexualised'. And they are savvy media consumers who should not be regarded as unwitting victims. Besides, there are as many 'readings' of advertisements as there are pairs of eyes, so there is no objective way to assess the effect of marketing. I am not caricaturing their arguments here; that is precisely what they argued. While ostensibly from the left, these academics were in practice defending a wealthy corporation using the law to attempt to crush a small, progressive think tank. And I enjoyed the irony that the most vocal academic defenders of David Jones, a company that spoke earnestly of its 'family values', were also vigorous defenders of the porn industry.

David Jones's lawyers commissioned an expert report from a professor of media and cultural studies. One of the first claims in his book-length expert opinion was that the Australia Institute was 'anti-capitalist', suggesting that leftist ideology was our true motive for criticising David Jones. In his opinion, our report failed to recognise that childhood is socially constructed, that children are erotic beings anyway, and everything depends on who is doing the looking, so there is no objective truth. In response to the institute authors' claim that the child models had 'sultry' and 'pouting' expressions, he wrote that these are 'subjective terms' and their accuracy 'rests entirely in the eye of the beholder'. 'It is therefore impossible to conclude from the pictures themselves that the models have been "exploited".'

This was standard cultural studies blather – there is no truth, every reading of a text is down to the interpretation of the viewer. It doesn't matter how children are dressed and presented, they can *never* be sexualised or exploited, except in the eyes of the, presumably perverted, beholder, in this case beginning with the two young women who wrote our report.

On our side, a professor of semiotics, dismayed at David Jones's abuse of the law, had volunteered to provide expert advice, writing that he could see exactly what the authors meant about the posing of the girls. Kennedys obtained an expert opinion from a forensic psychiatrist with a string of high-quality publications and long experience working with sex offenders in prisons. He confirmed that paedophiles are likely to use images such as those of David Jones for sexual gratification. In the mind of the paedophile, he wrote, these ads legitimise their proclivities. His expert report was devastating and one of my regrets is that we never had the opportunity to see him in the witness box, up against the cultural studies enthusiasts that David Jones was relying on. Like the documents Saatchi & Saatchi destroys in the ordinary course of business, our barrister would have shredded them.

§

One of the strangest incidents of the DJs saga occurred in January 2007 and involved author Tom Keneally. We had published a follow-up paper to 'Corporate paedophilia', this one on the failure of the regulatory system. In it, Emma and Andrea had carefully analysed the performance of the Advertising Standards Board, concluding that the industry's self-regulatory agency was failing to protect children. (After our first report, the CEO had dismissed claims of the sexualisation of children as a 'non-issue'.) The nation was awash with ads eroticising children, all overseen by the board, which blithely batted away the torrent of public complaints. Our report, 'Letting children be children', argued that governments should act to help parents protect their children from the onslaught of sexual imagery by advertisers, something we knew parents desperately wanted.

Late one night, Tom Keneally, a member of the Advertising Standards Board, sent an impassioned email to Emma and Andrea. They had defamed him, he said, by implicitly accusing him of complicity in the sexualisation of children, something that 'as a father and grandfather' he found offensive. He followed up with an email the next day talking of 'imputations', 'slander' and 'defamation'. He claimed his reputation had been damaged and listed his memberships of prestigious international organisations.

Already under intense pressure, I was seriously displeased at Keneally's threats of legal action and replied uncompromisingly, reproving him for attempting to suppress debate over a matter of great public concern. I wrote that 'I would have thought a writer of your standing would have an unwavering commitment to intellectual freedom'. If you don't like what we have written then, I suggested, pick up your pen, adding that we would defend ourselves to the utmost against 'corporate bullies, anti-democratic governments or famous writers'. I was furious that he had threatened my staff and said he owed them an apology.

Keneally responded a day later with a half-indignant, half-whining email claiming he had not mentioned legal action and that his initial email was 'the plea of a citizen seeking discourse'. I took it as a backdown and the whole thing blew over.

§

Although a trial was still several months away, on 6 February 2007 the first stage of formal legal proceedings began in the Federal Court. The hearing was over technical issues, yet it was the first time, probably globally, that a court had been asked to consider the sexualisation of children in advertising. Mark McInnes was still up in arms, claiming we had accused David Jones of something 'abhorrent'. It would take him and the DJs board another year before they realised that as long as they persisted with their foolish action, 'David Jones' and 'corporate paedophilia' would keep cropping up together in the media. Down in Melbourne, Myer, whom we had mentioned alongside David Jones, said nothing. They must have been laughing behind their hands.

With such a public uproar over sexualisation of children, it was not surprising that politicians took up the issue. In parliament, Labor senator Ursula Stephens asked the communications minister, Helen Coonan, whether she shared the concerns expressed by the Australia Institute. She did. Stephens followed up by asking the minister whether she believed it appropriate for big business to use the *Trade Practices Act* to 'bully non-profit researchers into silence'? Coonan did not accept that David Jones's action was an abuse of the system, adding that the government was reviewing the national system of advertising. In August, Coonan agreed to establish a Senate inquiry into sexual images of children in advertising. The Democrats' Lyn Allison had been pushing hard for it.

The big advertisers were spooked. Early in April 2007, noting reports about the sexualisation of children and complaints by consumer and parent groups, the Australian Association of National Advertisers announced it was reviewing 'with all speed' its children's advertising code to make it consistent with 'community standards'.

Campaigners like Melinda Tankard Reist were reinvigorated, and new community groups sprang up, notably Kids Free 2B Kids, the brainchild of Melbourne comedian, mother and activist Julie Gale. A wonderful presence at any gathering, Julie was indefatigable. She was not averse to taking a spray can to billboards that objectified women. She challenged retailers for displaying highly explicit pornographic magazines. In 2008 she lodged a freedom of information application at the Office of the Children's Guardian for documents relating to DJs' advertising. Over months, Saatchi's lawyers fought tooth and nail to prevent the release of documents, but Julie was persistent. Eventually, the office was forced to hand over 225 documents, although it withheld nine, claiming they were commercial-in-confidence. Julie appealed to the ombudsman and the Office of the Children's Guardian was eventually forced to hand over most of the remaining documents, including a copy of the Saatchi shoot brief instructing the photographer to make the girls appear 'more adult and sexy'.

However, days before Julie received the incriminating evidence, Saatchi & Saatchi played a really dirty trick. They leaked the documents, with their own heavy spin, to a friendly journalist at *The Daily Telegraph*, Janet Fife-Yeomans. The story claimed the email ('obtained by *The Daily Telegraph*') was written by a freelance photographer (who had since been fired) and that David Jones only became aware of it in the course of its legal action against the institute. The fault, the story suggested, all lay with the Office of the Children's Guardian, which should have stopped the shoot.

To anyone who thought about it, it was preposterous to suggest that the photographer pulled the wool over the eyes of everyone, including Saatchi & Saatchi and David Jones, submitting to them sexualised images of the girls that they then innocently approved. Yet *The Daily Telegraph* published Fife-Yeomans' story, buried deep in the newspaper, so it became old news. It was a cynical use of the media: a story planted and buried to kill the real story before it was on the front page of *The Sydney Morning Herald*.

Tragically, Julie Gale died of breast cancer in 2018. She was mourned at a gathering of 350 friends, family and fellow campaigners.

§

As the months passed, I wondered what sort of advice Mark O'Brien continued to give Mark McInnes and whether McInnes was being candid with his board about the weakness of their case and the damage a trial would do. So after consulting Adrian Howie and my board chair, Tony McMichael, in November 2007 I wrote a letter to DJs chair, Robert Savage, pointing out relevant facts and stating our resolve not to give way. I received a reply from the deputy chair, John D. Coates AC, Olympics chief and a doyen of the Sydney establishment. He affirmed DJs' commitment to 'traditional family values', said the board backed the executive team and indicated a willingness to reach a settlement if we admit error.

By now I was even less willing to give ground, so I wrote back to Coates, gloves off, pointing out: that we had obtained a copy of the 'shoot brief' for the Alison Ashley ad in which the photographer had been instructed to make the girls appear 'more adult and sexy'; that the parents of those girls would likely take legal action against DJs; that we were aware that immediately after our report, DJs issued an urgent instruction to remove and destroy a Fred Bare children's catalogue; and that DJs lied about the existence of its child advertising policy. I added that DJs' reputation is being damaged in the public domain, not least for trying to silence a public advocacy group. And I made sure he knew that we were prepared to take the case to the High Court on the grounds that any finding against us would breach the Constitution's implied right of free speech, and that we had notified the Commonwealth attorney-general to that effect.

In his book on SLAPPs, Brian Walters noted that one of the objectives of these lawsuits is to divide opponents. It pains me to write this but the dispute began to create tensions within the Australia Institute. At the beginning, the institute's board fully backed me in standing up for the integrity of our research, but as the law ground its way towards a court showdown, board members began to waver. After a while, some wanted the institute to reach an agreement admitting we had erred and apologise. When it was suggested to me that 'it's not our core business', I replied that if standing up to a big corporation trying to drive its critics from public debate is not our core business then I don't know what is. In the view of some, I was taking an 'absolutist' position, which was not wholly untrue. Apart from the dangerous precedent a David Jones victory would set, throughout the saga my actions were dominated by one sentiment, put bluntly: 'Screw you, you're not going to bully me into submission.'

By the end of 2007, the board wanted out and was willing to compromise by admitting error. I was resentful at what I saw as weakness. Besides, as Kelly Bruce pointed out, so many people were cheering us on in our battle to expose the eroticisation of children that backing down would have meant betraying them. I dug my heels in further.

The truth was, though, that after fourteen years running the Australia Institute, I was worn out. I'd stopped enjoying it before the David Jones blow-up. Now I knew my time was up and I flagged an intention to move on. But I did not want to give an advantage to David Jones so stayed on through the last months of 2007, hoping the case would be resolved. By the end of the year, with the board no longer behind me and no sign of the case concluding, I gave notice that I would be leaving in a few weeks.

Adrian Howie now acted for the institute and, separately, for me. Any proposal by the institute to settle would need my endorsement. By this stage, despite the enormous pressure, I wanted the case to proceed to trial and even welcomed the prospect of ending up in the High Court. I could see myself as Darryl Kerrigan.

On 4 April 2008, David Jones capitulated. They withdrew their action in the Federal Court. We'd won.

The relief I felt was so sweet, yet I was angry too for being put through the wringer over a report that told the truth. Of course, I felt vindicated in adopting a resolute stand and hoped those who had accused me of taking an 'absolutist' and 'unreasonable' position would acknowledge that standing firm was the right thing to do. (None did.) Interviewed on ABC Radio's *PM*, I said DJs' dropping of the case was a victory for free speech and that I had no regrets about naming the company.

David Jones had wanted me to agree to abstain from any further public comment on the company's sexualisation of children, but I had made it clear to Adrian that I would not agree to any gag. I'd agree only to keeping silent on the terms of the settlement. Adrian told me that, if asked by journalists, I can say that I am 'very pleased with the outcome'. They know it's code for 'we won and the other side lost and had to pay costs'. The media reported that DJs' strategy had 'backfired spectacularly'. When I phoned Brian Walters with the good news, he suggested there would be many red faces around DJs' board.

They say schadenfreude in not an admirable sentiment, but I enjoyed it in bucketloads two years later when Mark McInnes's true character was exposed in a sexual harassment suit. The case was brought against him by Kristy Fraser-Kirk, a twenty-five-year-old publicist who described her ordeal in excruciating detail. DJs chairman Bob Savage denied the retailer had a culture of harassment and bullying, despite complaints from several other female employees. The company tried to tarnish Ms Fraser-Kirk's reputation. She said, 'I just wanted to be treated with respect.' DJs avoided a court case by settling with her. McInnes was soon forced to resign.

15

Finding a new role

T HE AUSTRALIA INSTITUTE was established because I believed that powerful ideas can change the world. I'm not sure I believe that anymore, at least not in the same way. The prevailing system is so entrenched that no serious alternative vision of the world can get oxygen. Social democracy has become neoliberalism with a human face, and socialism is either used interchangeably with social democracy or represents a new kind of totalitarianism.

Once, the new social movements envisaged the liberation of minorities and women as contributions to a new kind of society, but the decentralisation of left activism into various forms of identity politics has scuppered that dream. A 'let's build this' politics has become a 'don't do that' politics. And the white noise and white heat of social media is perfectly suited to a politics of issues rather than ideologies.

The think tank world today reflects these changes. The monopoly of right-wing think tanks is long gone; they did their job. A number of centrist and progressive think tanks have sprung up – the Grattan Institute, the Lowy Institute, Per Capita, the Centre for Policy Development, the Green Institute, and a couple of others. Most of the funding and media attention seems to go to the more technocratic, 'politically neutral' ones, that is, those that reinforce the system.

Perhaps I was a hangover from the late sixties and seventies, fired by a new left radicalism untethered to the old conceptions of socialism. I don't believe the kind of countercultural radicalism I pursued at the Australia Institute would work any longer, which is perhaps why the Australia Institute, nowadays with more money and many more staff, operates more conventionally.

Given the circumstances of my departure, the farewell dinner at the Lobby restaurant in February 2018 was not for me quite the joyful and wistful event it should have been. I was carrying too much baggage into the room and so acted out the role of departing founder as best I could. Everyone else seemed to enjoy it. Bob Brown gave a humbling speech and David Marr was an acerbic and entertaining MC.

Over the years at the institute, with its intense emotions and stresses, I had forgotten why I was doing it. The state of clarity that led me to set it up had long since become jangled. My feelings were so complex and contradictory on leaving the institute that the best course was to suppress them and move on. I prefer clean breaks, anyway, and felt no obligations tying me down, so having said my farewells and thanked all those who played a part in the institute's success, I left that stage of my life behind.

Shortly afterwards, Farah Farouque, a senior writer for *The Age*, observed, 'He had to invent his own organisation to succeed,' which seemed about right.

§

After leaving the Australia Institute, in February 2008 I joined an eight-day walk into the Tarkine rainforest in Tasmania. I was at a crossroads, so it was a time, lost in the ancient forest, for reflection on where I had come to and where I was going. We carried everything we'd need. After I'd been loaded up with extra food, my pack weighed around sixteen kilos. Although I'd done some practice walks, I wasn't sure how I'd go. I found I had little in common with my fellow walkers. They were not enviros or even bush-lovers, and none seemed to have much interest in the world I came from. So I kept mostly to myself.

As a boy growing up in small-town Canberra, we would often wander down to the Molonglo River, roam around Red Hill or drive with the family out to the Cotter River to swim from the gibber-strewn shore under the casuarinas. The landscape shaped me. It shapes all who grow up in Australia. I think the uniqueness of Australians is the product less of the pioneering spirit of the settlers than of some indefinable emanation from the land itself. We are only beginning to accept that the mystery of that emanation was known to Indigenous people. Whether walking in the temperate rainforest of the Tarkine, the eucalypt woodlands of the Canberra region or the empty expanse of Lake Mungo, with each step in the silence one feels the vast pull of something uncanny, a lostness that washes away all of the distortions of civilisation. The feeling of the land's antiquity can catch in your throat because right then you know that your existence doesn't matter. To be truly Australian, it seems to me, is to learn to be unafraid of these feelings and to be at home with them.

After walking out of the Tarkine, dodging black snakes on the final fire trail, I made my way to Launceston airport for the return home. On a television screen mounted in the crowded coffee shop, I watched Kevin Rudd's 'Sorry' speech. It felt like a profoundly significant day for Australia. Tears came suddenly and I had to go outside.

§

A few weeks after I left the institute, I was invited to a reception at Government House in Yarralumla. The invitation took me by surprise. The world of receptions was foreign to me; I guessed my name was put on a list after I had been a finalist for ACT Australian of the Year for 2008. The last time I had been in the grounds of Government House was around 1963 to ride the flying fox and eat toffee apples at the Scouts' fête. Turning up to the reception on a sunny day, my life took a sharp turn. We were gathered on the lawns, a couple of hundred of us, under a large white marquee. I found myself chatting to a group of people including a tall, affable man. After a time, he said with surprise, 'Are you Clive Hamilton?' Yes. 'My name's Lawrie Willett. I'm the chancellor of Charles Sturt University. We are planning to create a position for a public intellectual. Are you interested in a job?'

The new position was designed to raise the profile of the university, but I wasn't interested. I'd decided to give myself more time to settle and then think about the next step. I felt, however, it would be impolite to say 'no, thanks'. We swapped cards and I didn't think much more about it. A couple of weeks later I received an email from Ross Chambers, a deputy vice-chancellor, asking if we could meet. Again, I thought it would be rude to decline, but I was also curious. We met perhaps a week later. Ross, a Russia specialist whom I would grow to like and admire, put an offer to me. They would make me a professor, pay me as such, and let me do whatever a public intellectual does. No teaching, no administration, and no obligation to raise research funds. Nice work, if you can get it.

Life is strange. We can do all the planning we like but often it is just serendipity that turns us from one path to another. If I hadn't been invited to the reception, decided to go and fallen into conversation with Lawrie Willett, my life would have taken another course. The major events of my working life have mostly been like this. I have sometimes advised young people in a rut to open themselves up to possibilities and see what happens, keeping in mind that adopting such an attitude is a privilege of the well-educated middle class.

Although the new position had no downsides, I had to overcome my academic elitism since CSU was towards the bottom of the university rankings. I phoned Rob Manne for his opinion. He said it's what I make of the opportunity that counts rather than the university that employs me. It was sound advice. I accepted the offer and began in June 2008.

My appointment would be attached to the Centre for Applied Philosophy and Public Ethics, a joint centre with the ANU and the University of Melbourne. My office would be at the ANU; however,

Ross Chambers soon told me that the university would like it if I also had an office at Charles Sturt's theology campus on Kings Avenue by the lake. Theologians! To cut a messy story short, after two or three years, I had shed the ANU connection and my only office was in George Browning House, a building I shared with a half-dozen theologians, a few doctoral students and some administration staff. After a while, I realised that the theologians were the best group of colleagues I'd ever had – deeply intellectual, broad-minded and, as Christians of the nicest kind, a pleasure to be around. They were much less dogmatic than most of the economists and philosophers I have known. Occasionally it felt as though I was destined to end up among theologians; years earlier, someone had described me as 'a cleric without the cloth'.

The position afforded me the luxury of time. I had long since stopped regarding myself as an economist and spent a large part of the next decade reading philosophy books. We never understand why we believe what we do unless we have a sense of the philosophical foundations of our worldview, although we have to reflect critically on those too. It was for this reason that I felt more simpatico with the theologians at George Browning House than the philosophers at ANU. The latter were afraid of theology. I once suggested to a committee of philosophers that a theologian be invited to a conference on the ethics of climate change. It was instantly dismissed, as if the presence of a theologian would somehow sully their conference.

I had in fact been reading philosophy quite intensely while running the Australia Institute, which led me to draft *The Freedom Paradox: Towards a post-secular ethics* in my last year there. The book, published by Allen & Unwin in August 2008, was an attempt to go more deeply into the intriguing fact that in affluent societies, many had attained the promise of freedom from want and oppression yet remained discontented, even trapped, which I characterised as the paradox of modern life. The idea of freedom had itself been captured and commodified. It was an unusual book. Nowadays, serious reflection on the human condition in Australia is more likely to attract puzzlement and mockery than considered responses, so it was bold of Allen & Unwin to publish it.

On publication, to the extent that mainstream philosophy noticed it at all, the book was met with indifference and probably disapproval. Of course, *The Australian* heaped derision on it several times over, describing me, inter alia, as 'the poster boy of the gloomy Left'. But the extensive correspondence I received from thoughtful people who, one way or another, had had to come to grips with things beyond the world of everyday experience was fascinating and heartwarming. For some, the book had a therapeutic effect because here was someone writing about deeper elements of experience that they'd kept to themselves. There is a whole world of experience out there in Australia that we do not speak of – who can be blamed for their discretion when Murdoch's jackals and Twitter trolls stand ready to pounce?

§

Although I retained the radical spirit, my views had shifted markedly from the everything-goes libertarianism of my political youth. The social revolutions of that time were culturally and politically inseparable from the sexual revolution. But in the pursuit of personal freedoms, the social revolutions morphed into an extreme form of individualism, one that was perfectly concordant with the spread of neoliberalism. Although disdained by the French left, the novels of Michel Houellebecq, when read sympathetically, are the most astringent critique of where the unfettered market has taken us. He was right: 'The sexual revolution was to destroy the last unit separating the individual from the market.' Yet the postmodernists still insisted it was somehow transgressive to take things ever further. To borrow from the Slovenian philosopher and critic Slavoj Žižek, perversion is not subversion.

So when, in May 2008, Sydney police arrived at the Roslyn Oxley9 Gallery and confiscated a number of works by photographic artist

Bill Henson, my interest was piqued. A complaint had been received that some of the images, including one featuring a naked thirteen-year-old girl, were child pornography. When the story broke there was uproar. Looking at the photos online, it seemed to me that the studies of the thirteen-year-old girl were confounding and discomforting, but she was not presented in a sexual way or as an object of normal sexual desire. However, to my mind that was not the end of the ethical dilemma. So I decided to buy into the controversy, writing an article for *Crikey*, one, it turned out, that would attract more responses than any other *Crikey* had published.

I argued that if the decision is simply 'art or pornography', the pictures are art. But sex and children are a highly combustible mix, one rendered even more volatile by the relentless sexualisation of children by advertisers and the media over the previous decade. The Henson exhibition cannot be isolated from a social milieu in which children's maturation is increasingly drenched with erotic imagery and controlled by a commercial culture that exploits children by imposing on them adult forms of sexual desire and behaviour. The eroticisation of childhood meant that we had been conditioned to see children as having adult sexual characteristics, urges and desires. In such a cultural environment, the naked body of a child, particularly a girl of thirteen showing the first signs of sexual development, could no longer be viewed 'innocently'. Henson's work was, I suggested, a provocation in bad taste, given the roiling public disquiet about the sexualisation of children. It was a mistake amplified by the gallery owner's decision to put those images on the internet, thereby relinquishing all control over how the images of the naked children were seen and consumed.

Bill Henson and his defenders reacted to the uproar as if the artistic merit of the work quarantined it from these tensions. The same blindness became apparent when artist Donald Friend was outed as a paedophile who'd preyed on boys in Bali. Artists and the artistic community love to transgress, but when crossing the boundaries attracts the anticipated reaction, they are outraged by it. It seemed to me that while much of the talkback chatter was crass and ill-informed, the moral panic from the punters was matched by the censorship panic from the aesthetes.

In June, a public debate was staged on 'art censorship' at the Museum of Contemporary Art. Given the museum's invitation list, and the excitement generated in the artistic community, the orientation of the audience was predictable. Chaired by David Marr, I was paired with Hetty Johnston, who had formed Bravehearts after her seven-year-old daughter disclosed she had been sexually abused. Against us were barrister Julian Burnside and curator Tony Bond. Hetty Johnston gave a calm and well-reasoned speech. When he rose to speak, Burnside heaped ridicule on her. From where I sat, it was an awful abuse of male power.

16
Requiem

O NE DAY IN August 2008, I was sitting in my office at the ANU, reading a scientific paper by climate scientists Kevin Anderson and Alice Bows. I had read hundreds of scientific papers over the years, but this was the most confronting by far. The simple numbers made it plain that it is too late to prevent the world warming by 3 or 4°C, sending the Earth into a different climatic regime, one much less sympathetic to human civilisation. It was an 'oh, shit' moment. It had such an emotional impact that I needed to go for a walk around the campus to settle down. I entered a long period of depression; not clinical depression but a deep despondency and alarm at where the world was now heading.

In one scenario, Anderson and Bows, from the United Kingdom's Tyndall Centre for Climate Change Research, set out the emission reduction task in a blunt way. The bottom line is that the future of the world depends on two numbers: the year in which global emissions reach a peak and the rate of emission reductions each year thereafter. These will determine the total amount of greenhouse gas emissions over this century, the resulting increase in the concentration of greenhouse gases in the atmosphere, and the global temperature rise that follows. The later the peak, the more quickly emissions must fall to keep within a given emissions budget.

Anderson and Bows made the optimistic assumptions that global emissions would peak in 2020 and then decline by 3 per cent a year thereafter. Three per cent is the required global average rate of decline; significantly higher rates would be required for rich countries to allow poor countries 'development space' to catch up. On this hopeful path, the concentration of greenhouse gases rises to a catastrophic 650 parts per million by the end of the century, meaning warming of 4°C and more.

Today, we are hoping global emissions might peak in 2030.

Until that day in 2008, I had beneath the surface been clinging to the hope that something would happen, some sharp shift in global sentiment and political resolve. I now understood that I could no longer cling to that hope, and that a grim future was no longer an expectation of what might happen if we do not act soon but the future that will unfold.

On one level, I felt relief at accepting what I feared might happen, relief at no longer having to spend energy on false hopes. I could allow myself to adapt emotionally to the facts. But it was not so simple. As I wrote *Requiem for a Species*, building on a presentation of the numbers and their inescapable implications, I daily had to fight off feelings of despondency, panic and rage. Still, the act of writing was a salve. Ploughing on was a way of sublimating the feelings that at times threatened to overwhelm me.

As usual, I asked a number of experts to read the draft, especially the chapters setting out the science, as I wanted it to be bulletproof. I had gnawing doubts about whether I should be writing the book, not because any of it was untrue but because it seemed cruel to be telling such truths so brutally. At times while I worked on it, an abyss would open up before me and I would have to pull myself back. I was afraid that if I fell into it, I would be unable to get myself out. I mentioned it to my friend Cordelia Fine, a psychologist and author at the University of Melbourne. She sent me a package containing a remedy she called

'Abyss-B-Gone' – some 'special' tea bags and biscuits, along with a delightful stick-figure diagram showing how to use the remedy. It was a funny and touching gesture.

§

In October 2007 I had travelled to Aspen, Colorado, to participate in a conference on 'creating a new ecological consciousness'. The thirty or so invitees included the leading environmental thinkers in the US. It was a seminal event for me, broadening my thinking and my community of interest, not least to the psychologist Tim Kasser, with whom I would soon write a paper on 'coping strategies' in the face of climate change. The intimate conference was the brainchild of Gus Speth, a renowned advocate responsible for founding the Natural Resources Defense Council as well as the World Resources Institute, and at the time serving as dean of the School of Forestry and Environmental Studies at Yale University. I suggested to Gus that an invitation to Yale would be welcome.

Janenne and I arrived in New Haven, Connecticut, in March 2009 for a three-month stay at Yale. We spent the first few days in an upmarket hotel on the edge of the town centre. On the first morning, the bellman said, 'When you go out the front door, make sure you turn right. Don't turn left.' A day or two later, in search of a pharmacy, we turned left and within minutes understood the warning. New Haven, we quickly learned, was blighted by crime, a social fracture based on a racial divide with deep historical roots. The impoverishment of much of New Haven's Black population contrasted sharply with the privilege of the elite white students at the university. Yale had built its own police force, supplementing the city's, to protect staff and students. Each day I walked the half-hour from our apartment to the School of Forestry and Environmental Studies down Prospect Street, along which were blue-lit emergency posts every hundred metres or so. Janenne was pretty much the only white resident of New Haven to catch the bus to a shopping district on the town's outskirts. Greeted with surprised but accepting looks, she said the bus trips were a glimpse into another world. At night we would sometimes hear gunshots echoing up from the rough part of town. We felt safer on the New York subway.

In April we took the train to Boston where I had a meeting with Noam Chomsky. Several years earlier I had sent him the page proofs of *Growth Fetish*. He emailed me saying 'right on target and badly needed'. The demands on Chomsky's time are enormous so it was a privilege to meet him in his modest MIT office piled high with wobbly columns of books, manuscripts and papers. Soft-spoken and polite, though with an intimidating intellect, Noam brings to any issue a stringent rationality. He told me he listens to talk radio, mainly Rush Limbaugh (similar to Alan Jones), whose audience is people with real grievances. What they say is internally consistent and powerful. They genuinely fear the liberal elites, whom they call 'the fly-over people', and the United Nations. He saw parallels with the late Weimar era in Germany and said the United States could go the same way.

Later that day, Janenne and I walked through Boston Common and came across a small and scrappy protest. We listened for a few minutes to some speeches about Washington elites but didn't take much notice. The next day there was a tiny item about the protest buried in the pages of *The Boston Globe* mentioning that the organisers called themselves the 'Tea Party'. That protest and several others around the country were the poisonous seed, vigorously cultivated by Murdoch's Fox News, that grew into the movement that put Donald Trump into the White House seven years later and invaded Congress in January 2021.

I was writing *Requiem* while at Yale and naturally took a close interest in the US climate debate. Obama was shirking his responsibilities on climate, doing nothing in his first term, so whatever he finally did could be undone by his successor. Environmental groups were split over the Waxman-Markey bill, which would establish an emissions trading scheme. It seemed that some of the bigger organisations had just crawled out of a cocoon and were having debates over climate change that had been resolved in the rest of the world a decade before. And a hegemonic attitude was discernible: whatever the United States decides, the world will follow.

Oddly, one of the worst to take this line was the renowned climate scientist James Hansen. I heard him speak at Columbia University. He was masterful on the science but his opinions on economics and policy were amateurish. His pontification on the merits and demerits of carbon taxes versus emissions trading, a highly complex question in the economics of the environment with no definitive answer, raised my hackles. I later emailed him, as politely as I could, expressing the view that some of us spend a lot of time insisting that only properly qualified scientists should be listened to on climate science, yet he speaks as if he were a qualified expert in economics and public policy. I received a haughty and dismissive reply.

While in New Haven, a letter arrived from the governor-general's office advising that I had been nominated as a Member of the Order of Australia and asking if I would accept the award for 'service to public debate and policy development'. It was a shock. Gongs belong to another world. Clearly, though, I had supporters out there. After giving it some thought, I decided it would be churlish to decline. When I turned up at Government House two months later in a suit, I felt distinctly out of place. Perhaps the several dozen other honours recipients felt the same way.

§

Throughout 2009, a fierce battle had been taking place in parliament and outside over the Rudd government's Carbon Pollution Reduction Scheme (CPRS). The scheme was a heavily watered-down version of Ross Garnaut's recommendations, corrupted by massive handouts to fossil fuel industries. I was disconcerted when a new grouping of NGOs called the Southern Cross Climate Coalition expressed its support for the scheme. I noticed that World Vision had joined the alliance, along with ACOSS, ACF, the ACTU and the organisation I had set up, the Climate Institute.

I had always shunned direct lobbying but this time I made an exception. In August 2009, I visited Tim Costello in his office at World Vision. I'd known Tim for a long time. He came to our house for dinner around 1995 and the three of us had a wonderful, warm conversation. I talked to Tim about how serious the climate situation is and how we are stuffed unless the world, including Australia, adopts strong mitigation measures. Tim jumped in to tell me that World Vision had broken with the others in the Southern Cross Climate Coalition. In solidarity with the poorest of the poor in Africa and the Pacific Islands, World Vision was demanding 40 per cent cuts for rich countries. I was relieved because Tim's voice carried enormous moral clout. The Southern Cross Climate Coalition soon began distancing itself from the CPRS proposal, asking for a much stronger target. The CPRS bill was defeated in the Senate in November 2009 after Rudd refused to negotiate with the Greens. In early 2011, the parliament enacted the much stronger Clean Energy Bill, negotiated between the Gillard government and the Greens.

At the end of September 2009 I travelled to Oxford to attend a scientific conference titled 'Four degrees and beyond'. Held at St Anne's College, it was the first time climate scientists had gathered to think the unthinkable, or rather to utter the unutterable. The world was firmly on a warming path to 4°C and we had to confront what that means. The last time the Earth was 4°C warmer was twenty-five million years ago. With *Requiem* mostly drafted, I was interested as much in how these savants coped emotionally with their special knowledge. It was a brutal two days, as one expert after another spoke of the likelihood of warming by 4°C and what would happen to ecosystems and human populations as it did. It was the kind of candid conclusion from the science that did not make it into the cautious IPCC reports.

As the meeting progressed, and the usual process of softening took place, scientists began admitting their deeper feelings. Some talked of being on an emotional roller-coaster, others of their despair.

Chairs began introducing sessions expressing hope that one of the speakers would bring some good news; each time they were disappointed. Nervous laughter greeted some of the blunter statements. Diana Liverman, one of the organisers, said she had spent the nights of the conference tossing and turning in bed. 'Part of me wanted to distance myself from what has been said and immerse myself in my academic work.'

A French population expert, François Gemenne from Sciences Po in Paris, speculated about how international law would treat citizens of nations that no longer exist. Many of those displaced in the Pacific will seek refuge in Australia, carrying passports from ghost nations. In 2002, during the Commonwealth Heads of Government Meeting in Coolum, I had pointed out that of the fifty-four members of the Commonwealth, twenty-seven are members of the Alliance of Small Island States. I was mocked for suggesting that the number of nations participating in CHOGM would decline to fifty-one in coming decades as some small island states disappear under rising sea levels due to climate change.

In addition to François, I met at St Anne's a number of people who would play a significant role in my future work, including population and migration expert Yadvinder Malhi of the Oxford Environmental Change Institute, and Kevin Anderson, whose paper had knocked me off centre and led to me write *Requiem*. David Karoly of the University of Melbourne gave a frightening account of the freakish fires that had devastated parts of Victoria earlier that year, in February 2009. For me, the most striking news story of that terrible heatwave was one describing possums falling dead from the trees as the temperature breached 46°C. I knew that days like that would no longer be so freakish in a decade or two. 'We are unleashing hell on Earth,' said Karoly.

§

When in early December 2009 I arrived in Copenhagen for COP 15, the fifteenth conference of the parties to the UN climate change convention, it was bitterly cold. The deniers always skited at that kind of thing, refusing to understand the difference between the weather and the climate. As always, the conference thronged with thousands of lobbyists, businesspeople and activists. After the first week, when a couple of hundred young activists paraded around the convention centre shouting slogans, the organisers overreacted and banned all but official delegates and the media. Over the next days, many half-frozen activists gathered outside the gates, trying to get in. Unwilling to remain cooped up in my hotel room, yet needing to stay warm, I decided to make use of the free travel pass we'd been issued. Each day I took the longest rail trips I could across Denmark, including one to Elsinore, or Helsingør, of *Hamlet* fame. I walked around for a bit, but the frigid weather sent me back to the train.

Climate campaigners and progressive governments had invested an enormous amount of hope in the success of COP 15, the most important since COP 3 in Kyoto in 1997. It was seen to be the last chance to reverse the trajectory of global emissions by 2020. The outcome was a fiasco, with a hard-fought agreement torpedoed at the last moment by China's intransigence, which refused to endorse rich countries' desire to adopt far-reaching emission reduction targets. It even opposed inclusion of the 1.5°C warming limit. As I wrote in an op-ed, there was a sense at the Copenhagen conference that we were witnessing not so much the making of history but the ending of it.

The global environment movement crashed into a deep despondency. When it finally dragged itself out, much of the optimism about a golden green future had evaporated. Since Copenhagen there have been ups and downs in global progress towards decarbonising energy systems. Positive signs like the 2015 Paris Agreement and China's apparent shift to taking climate change seriously have been countered by negative signs like post-Paris weakening and the new life given to denialism by Donald Trump. Beneath them all, two trends have been at war: the accelerating rollout of inexpensive and increasingly sophisticated renewable energy infrastructure, and enormous and continuing global coal consumption, driven by China.

The annual dump of some 35 billion tonnes of carbon dioxide into the atmosphere, and the evermore dire scientific warnings, govern the mood of the young people who have surged onto the streets since Greta Thunberg's lone school strike in 2018. Furious at the future bequeathed to them by previous generations, they are under no illusions about 'saving the world'. The best they can hope for is avoiding the worst. Beyond pandemics and wars in Europe, they know that the climate crisis will define their future.

17

The candidate

WHEN IN OCTOBER 2009 I was approached to put myself
forward as the Greens candidate for Higgins, I began making
diary notes each day, continuing over the next two months until the
election. The diary provides an immediate sense of what it was like to
be a candidate and the next two chapters are edited versions of it.

Thursday, 8 October 2009, Canberra
Brian Walters phoned. He's prominent in the Victorian Greens. Peter
Costello has announced his intention to leave politics, so there will be
a by-election for his seat of Higgins, covering the wealthy suburbs of
south-east Melbourne. The Victorian Greens know there is no time
to go through their lengthy selection processes, so they are looking
for a high-profile candidate. If I put myself forward for preselection,
Brian reckons I would almost certainly be chosen. The chances of
beating the Liberal candidate in the conservatives' blue-ribbon seat are
slim, he said, but it's not out of the question, given the disarray in the
Turnbull-led Opposition over climate change policy.

I wasn't interested. My life as an academic, with few responsibilities
and only self-imposed deadlines, was what I sought when I left the
Australia Institute twenty months ago. The hurly-burly of politics,

the tumult and indignities of campaigning – not to mention the possibility, however remote, of moving cities – held no appeal. I respect Brian and was not willing to reject the approach out of hand, so I said I'd think about it and get back to him in a day or two.

Sunday, 11 October

The more I thought about it the more I was put off by the idea. Janenne and I talked it over. I was a little taken aback at her willingness to consider the proposal, given how it would unsettle her life. In fact, in her gentle way she made it clear she thought it would be important for me to put myself forward. We have a deep emotional partnership in what I do, so perhaps she feels that by supporting the move she would be doing something for climate change and the future.

Thoughts of public exposure and the destabilisation of my life began working on my mind; I slept poorly. I woke this morning thinking there's no way I'm going to do this. But as the day passed, other thoughts arose. If running in Higgins could make a difference in the national debate over climate change, didn't I have an obligation to do it? Just how politically committed am I? Against this, the thought of becoming an MP was repellent – stuck in Parliament House dealing with all the idiocy or in an electoral office dealing with constituent worries. But what is all that against the obligation to make a difference if I can? Had I not just drafted a book on how dire the situation is? And the vital Copenhagen climate conference is in two months. Perhaps the by-election could be used to mobilise public sentiment.

By the time I phoned Brian on Sunday evening I was halfway there; three quarters by the end of the call.

Monday, 12 October

On Monday I went to Parliament House for the launch of the Greens' new climate policy. In the lift I bumped into Bob Brown and his chief of staff, Ben Oquist, along with a couple of parliamentary attendants. Ben looked at me and asked loudly, 'Well, are you going to run for

Higgins?' Momentarily stunned, I said, 'News travels fast.' We agreed to meet after the launch. I learned that Ben had been speaking with central office of the Victorian Greens and that I had Bob and Ben's backing. I knew Bob would not do any direct lobbying for me, as he keeps out of state branch affairs, but a quiet word here and there would help. As I left the office and made my way to the underground carpark, I knew I had committed myself and could not help saying, 'Clive, what the hell have you just done?'

Monday, 19 October, Melbourne
On the plane to Melbourne for the selection panel interview, I spied Peter Costello at the front leaving the aircraft. Another reason to have a go at Higgins, to take on the smirk. A long shot, but it would be a huge blow to the Liberals if they were to lose.

I found the Victorian Greens central office down a dingy lane in the CBD. I wondered how many other people had nominated for preselection. There were six of them on the selection panel, chaired by Bob Hale from the Stonnington Greens, the main branch in Higgins. The questioning was challenging. They asked about various statements from the past – like my comments on the constraints on the Greens as a third force in my *Quarterly Essay*. It was a sobering reminder of my political vulnerabilities in addition to the big one, a candidate swanning in from Canberra. I said I had developed a better understanding of the Greens' strengths since writing the *Quarterly Essay*, which seemed to satisfy them.

Tuesday, 20 October, Canberra
Bob Hale phoned to tell me I have been preselected as the Greens candidate for Higgins. Bob sounds like a sensible, committed bloke. The first congratulatory message came from Ben Oquist. I phoned Janenne to tell her the news. She's excited about it, but I'm sure some of the excitement will be the kind we can do without. All sorts of forces will be mobilised against me, quite apart from the Liberal Party.

Friday, 23 October, Melbourne

The announcement this morning outside Prahran Town Hall went smoothly. Plenty of media present. Bob Brown introduced me and spoke about what's at stake. My opening comments were not as articulate as I'd have liked, but I managed the questions well. Janenne phoned to say it is the lead item on ABC news. Before the launch, several Greens met up at a cafe with me and Bob, including Bob Hale, Richard di Natale and Sue Plowright, national convenor. The tabloid image of Greens as flaky dreamers could not be further from the truth. These people are hard-headed pros.

Bob Hale told me plenty of people are volunteering to help in the campaign; they're excited and inspired and want to pitch in. The Stonnington Greens are psyched but feeling a little overwhelmed as they have never had to run a campaign like this. We can't match the Liberals with funding, but we can outgun them with enthusiasm.

There's some concern that my views on censoring extreme porn from the internet to protect kids clash with Greens policy. There's a message to phone Scott Ludlum, the Greens spokesperson on the issue. He's a full-on libertarian. I'm not going to walk back too far because too many people have backed our call for treating the internet the same way as other media.

Sue told me the Greens office in Western Australia, Ludlum's home state, was on the phone panicking because members were resigning over my candidacy. I think it was only a handful. I said they must be fanatics and not too committed to the Greens. We might lose a few dogmatic libertarians but we'd pick up a swathe of supporters from the deeply concerned. The Victorian Greens office says they have already had quite a few joining the party in response to my candidacy. Janet Rice is to be my campaign manager. I have been impressed at the way the Greens machine has swung into action with a very capable campaign committee now buzzing.

The Liberals have chosen a financial exec, Kelly O'Dwyer, to run for Higgins. She's very close to Costello apparently. *The Age*'s Katharine Murphy asked if I expected a dirty campaign. 'I understand

Kelly O'Dwyer is an honourable person,' I replied, 'so I expect a clean campaign.' I have no idea what she's like. Her election flyer avoids all important matters and presents her as a nice, trustworthy local mother. Every photo features her wedding ring.

Monday, 26 October, Canberra
In an early interview at Parliament House on ABC TV *Breakfast*, Joe O'Brien asks if I'm concerned that running for the Greens could afterwards damage my credibility as an academic. It's a question I'd thought about. I replied that it probably would but if you believe strongly in something, you have to pursue it. Otherwise, what's the point? I've taken leave from CSU. The university seems unconcerned about my candidacy.

Then on to an 8.50 am interview with Jon Faine on ABC 774 Melbourne. This is an important one, but I am taken aback at his aggressive manner. He asks some silly questions about whether I want to deprive Toorak residents of their 4WDs. I'm becoming cranky. Then this question: 'How many primary schools can you name in Higgins?' I reply, 'Oh come on, Jon. I'm not going to play gotcha with you. Everyone knows I'm not from Melbourne. I'm asking Higgins residents to think of themselves as Australians.' Faine didn't like it; my reply made him seem petty. The rest of the interview was narky.

Bob Brown proposed dinner with the Greens senators in the Members' Dining Room at Parliament House. On the way in, I bumped into Labor communications minister Stephen Conroy, who made a point of congratulating me and saying, 'Hey, we can support you in Higgins, can't we, if we're not running a candidate?' I hadn't met him before but he was pretty grateful to me as a vocal supporter of mandatory filtering of extreme and violent porn.

At dinner, the conversation was mainly around the Higgins campaign, with several helpful ideas. Christine Milne suggested going to schools, asking the kids to give me messages to take to Copenhagen. Duncan Kerr, until recently Labor's minister for justice, stopped to shake my hand and congratulate me.

It's strange, I thought, as I returned to the basement carpark. It's as though I have become a member of a club. Not the Greens club but the politicians' club, as if the unspoken message of the congratulations is: 'Welcome aboard, you are in for a ride.'

Tuesday, 27 October, Sydney

I had a call from —— —— who said he does campaigning for the Labor Party and would like to help me in Higgins. He said he does demographic analysis. That's something we'd be interested in. He said he would do an analysis of Higgins. Then, after pausing to search for the right words, he told me he also 'runs interference, let us say, against opponents' and could help with that too. 'There's another world,' he said. Black ops, I assumed he meant. I didn't ask him to elaborate and said I don't want to go there. I want to keep my hands clean and my integrity intact. On the other hand, if the Liberals play dirty …

At a dinner following a meeting of a committee I'm on at the University of Technology Sydney, Margaret Simons, the media academic, persuaded me I must begin to use Twitter. She explained how it works. I'm resistant, until she produces the killer arguments: journalists read it, plus it's a very effective way to reply immediately to disinformation in the media.

I joined by phone a Greens campaign committee meeting convened by Janet Rice. They kept talking about 'corflutes'. What are they?

Monday, 2 November, Stratosphere

I'm on my way to Helsinki to participate in a conference on the future of social democracy. I was upfront with the preselection panel that I would be overseas for a week of the campaign. Fortunately, it's Melbourne Cup week, and the election is still five weeks away.

David Burchull, an old leftie who went over to the other side, has a crack at me in *The Australian* this morning. It's next to an anti-green rant by Brendan O'Neill, editor of the British online site *Spiked* and a favourite columnist in *The Australian*. It's amusing because *Spiked* is the successor to *Living Marxism*, the magazine of the Revolutionary Communist Party, a Trotskyist splinter group that hates environmentalism.

Wednesday, 4 November, Helsinki
God, it's cold in Helsinki. Maximum of 2°C today. It's snowing. I notice that the Finns don't jaywalk, which I am prone to do.

The conservatives have formed a coalition government with the Greens, which sticks in the craw a bit. Mind you, the conservatives are quite progressive in Finland, and the Finnish Green party is the most conservative in Europe. The Social Democrats were shocked when they lost the election and are looking for ways forward. I met with two Social Democratic MPs licking their wounds from the defeat. The new government plans to build another three nuclear power plants. The two have differing opinions on nuclear. The pro-nuclear one says she read that 'Tim Connolly' favours nuclear. I tell her that Tim Flannery did, but now he's changed his mind.

Thursday, 5 November
An email from Colin Smith, who is coordinating the volunteers in Higgins, saying volunteers are still flooding in. 'What I sense ... is that a lot of people who may or may not have voted for us before and who certainly have not joined the Greens are suddenly more interested and even ready to help the campaign. And that is on account of our candidate rather than the lack of a Labor candidate.'

A fascinating dinner put on by my hosts, the Kalevi Sorsa Foundation. There were six of us and much of the discussion was around European Union politics. The former foreign minister talks about Finland's financial disaster during the GFC, the world's worst because cowboys had been put in charge of the nation's finances. Future generations will be poorer as the country pays off the enormous debts they ran up. It was an act of criminal irresponsibility; the culprits all now live abroad. Voices that raised concern were patronisingly told they didn't understand the modern world of finance.

Friday, 6 November
An email comes through announcing that the Australian Democrats are putting up a candidate. Haven't they been dissolved? The announcement text is an unrestrained rant against me and my support for internet filtering. It's quite unhinged.

I see that Fiona Patten from the Sex Party is running in Higgins. The media release targets me. The Sex Party is a creation of the porn industry and was co-founded by Robbie Swan, Patten's husband. Some in the Greens see the Sex Party as a natural ally because it is libertarian on social issues.

I met the Finnish Green party's principal climate adviser, who is located in the conservative prime minister's office. He was scathing about the Social Democrats, who no longer know what they stand for. He knows I am a Green. I like being part of the international community of Greens. There's an easiness with those who identify similarly.

Saturday, 7 November
My speech to the conference went over well. Tomorrow I fly home. I'm feeling anxious about being away from the campaign but dreading the fact that I have to overnight in Sydney for a few hours, fly to Canberra at 6.45 am, unpack, repack and catch a plane to Melbourne at 3.30 pm. Purgatory, but no way around it.

On the web I read Prime Minister Rudd's speech ripping into climate sceptics and repeating his claim that global warming is the 'greatest moral challenge'. What a bloody hypocrite. Instead of negotiating with the Greens, he is pursuing a derisory target under the Carbon Pollution Reduction Scheme that ignores the science. Treasury modelling shows that under his CPRS, Australia's emissions wouldn't begin to fall until 2040! And he's handing out billions to the big polluters. It's a travesty.

Monday, 9 November, flying home
Another piece in *The Australian* going after me, this time by Ross Fitzgerald accusing me of being a 'social conservative'. Ross's views have not changed since 1972. He's just more splenetic.

Tuesday, 10 November, Canberra

Good to be home, if only for a few hours. Melbourne is in the grip of the longest November hot spell in a hundred years. Nick Minchin was on *Four Corners* last night saying global warming is an environmentalist plot to deindustrialise the West and that after 1989 communists had infiltrated the Greens. Unbelievable stuff. How does anyone with half a brain believe such rot? He also says that a majority of Coalition MPs are climate sceptics. Jesus. What's wrong with these people? So full of political prejudice and hatred of environmentalism that they're ready to reject overwhelming scientific evidence that Australia's future is grim. Ignorant, narrow-minded logs. I will go after them in my next speech.

Going through security at Canberra Airport I bump into Ben Oquist. He says we'd received polling results that are good for us. It seems most people believe the Rudd government should negotiate with the Greens rather than the Liberals on their Carbon Pollution Reduction Scheme.

Wednesday, 11 November, Melbourne

First full day on the campaign trail was a fairly quiet one. We had a win in *The Australian* this morning. They ran an opinion piece by me criticising the sceptics. It included a pointer and a photo on the front page. I have rarely missed an opportunity to flail the *Oz* for promoting denialism, but if I can exploit its desire to give the impression of balance, why not? Over the years, I have learned how to play *The Australian*. Fairfax papers are MIA on the by-election.

A poisonous email arrived this morning from someone claiming I had plagiarised the definition of 'affluenza' in our book. He demanded a response, threatening to go public. I never plagiarise but have no copy of *Affluenza* on hand to double-check. I forward the email to Elizabeth Weiss at Allen & Unwin.

Colin, the volunteer coordinator, calls by to deliver a bike. He tells me that my candidacy has been a shot in the arm for local Greens.

Thursday, 12 November

Elizabeth replies telling me she's checked the book. We had indeed acknowledged the source of the definition. She replied to our accuser, who turns out to be incompetent as well as malicious.

A quick trip to the Higgins office of the Australian Electoral Commission to lodge my nomination form turns into an hour-long hassle because of a technical screw-up. The AEC state manager and the deputy commissioner from Canberra happen to be in the office, so they get involved. I'm late for an appointment with a journo from *The Age* and starting to seethe. I say I'm leaving. A hundred metres down the street they phone me to say it's been resolved.

Days of leafleting ahead. Everyone elected to parliament has been through a long process of ritualised humiliation. One of the saddest sights I've seen was of a grinning Cheryl Kernot standing beside a busy road waving a sign saying, in effect, 'Vote for Me'. The indignity of it.

18

Election turmoil

Friday, 13 November

A big day ahead. Turned up at Malvern station at 6.50 am to hand out leaflets to commuters with the help of five volunteers. A terrific bunch. Our reception was pretty good and the experience not as unpleasant as I had expected.

Later, to the AEC office for the ballot draw. The room is hot and packed. Kelly O'Dwyer is there flanked by insufferable Young Liberals in blue. The returning officer says each candidate has the right to turn the handle of the wire basket holding the numbered balls. No one moved, so I leapt up and declared that this is the democratic process at work and turned the handle as three or four cameras appear from nowhere. Four or five other candidates follow suit but not Kelly, who sat looking as if she were there under sufferance.

Tonight, at the Glen Iris Uniting Church hall, was the official launch of my campaign. Robert Manne gave a wonderful introductory speech. The applause at the end of my speech was warm and prolonged and I understood for the first time how one person can take on the projections of a crowd, how one can embody the hopes of many.

1 High-school radical, with moratorium badge, Canberra, 1971.

2 The only item in my ASIO file, mugshots from an arrest at an anti-war demonstration in 1972. While some Australians go looking for their convict roots, others request their ASIO files.

3 Most of the graduate students at the Institute of Development Studies, University of Sussex, were from developing countries. So for the 1979 pantomime, I thought I'd give them a lesson in Australian culture.

4 With Nepalese villagers in the remote Sindhu Palchok district, 1985. ANU forestry professor David Griffin had asked me to do a cost-benefit analysis of his reforestation project, to keep the Department of Finance happy. The area was two days' walk from the nearest road. The hills were denuded of trees, cut down for firewood; in time, the project saw new forests flourish.

5 When the Australia Institute's research generated posters outside newsagencies, I collected them. For me, they were proof of our public impact. The buzzes, screeches and whistles of the fax machine (lower left) provided the aural landscape of the office. Today, it's the buzzes, screeches and whistles of social media.

6 With Michael Kirby and ANU Chancellor Peter Baume (a former Fraser government minister) at the opening of the Australia Institute's offices at University House, 1998. Michael introduced me to another High Court judge as 'a fellow stirrer'.

7 My reward from Barbeques Galore for stimulating sales of the Turbo Cosmopolitan with our 2002 report on 'Overconsumption in Australia: The rise of the middle-class battler'.

8 When Anna Fifield (on the right) of London's *Financial Times* and her friend Lucy Kebbell went on holiday in 2005, they took their copies of *Growth Fetish*.

9 Joining the Dalai Lama on a panel with Magda Szubanski, Sydney, 2007. I wondered why Buddhist monks keep their right arms bare. Apparently, for right-handers, it makes the robes sit more comfortably.

10 At a news conference with Bob Carr during the 2007 Sydney meeting of the Climate Change Taskforce; the media were interested in my views on the meeting's progress.

11 Crossing a river in the Tarkine, north-west Tasmania, 2008. After a long day of walking, I'd find a clearing on the forest floor away from the others, settle down in a little tent and allow myself to be engulfed by the towering trees and star-studded sky.

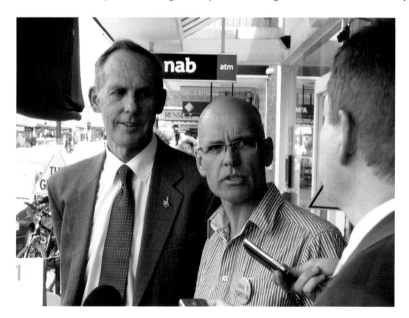

12 Campaigning with Bob Brown in the Higgins by-election, 2009. I have a theory that in parliament, extroverts are concentrated in the House and introverts in the Senate, because street campaigning is anathema to introverts.

13 Janenne (left) and my father's sister, Barbara Arnold, a librarian and historian, were there to see me gonged with an Order of Australia in 2009. Barbara, who died during the lockdowns, once told me that when she lived in Melbourne in the 1970s, an inebriated Bob Hawke propositioned her at a function. When she declined him, he turned ugly.

14 The Missing Bean in Oxford, a good place to think. Australians have opened coffee shops around the world, exporting our peerless coffee culture. Finding them is my first task in a new city.

15 This 1997 cartoon by Andrew Weldon captured perfectly how most of the world saw Australia at the Kyoto conference. For nineteen of the twenty-five years since then, Australia has had federal governments dominated by climate science deniers. Today in the United States, narcissistic billionaires are planning to get the hell out to Venus or something.

Courtesy Andrew Weldon

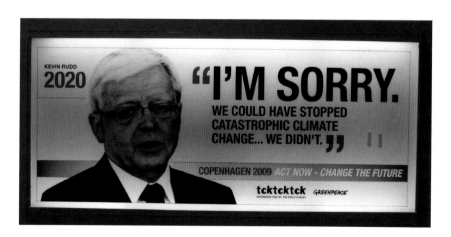

16 Perhaps this subway poster at the 2009 Copenhagen climate conference anticipated Kevin Rudd's later failure of nerve. Within the two major parties, any commitment to act on climate change has always been shallow.

17 At the 2015 climate conference in Paris, Australia demanded an extension of the infamous 'Australia clause', a gaping loophole in the 1997 Kyoto Protocol that allowed Australia to increase its 2020 emissions over 1990 levels by some 30 to 40 per cent. Greg Hunt celebrated with other Liberal 'moderates'.

Source: Fairfax, *Sydney Morning Herald*

18 When Putin walked in to the final session of the Valdai Discussion Club meeting in Sochi, 2017, I was a few metres away. He radiated menace and I felt a kind of dread. Powerful people, even repellent ones, have a magnetic effect.

Source: Reuters/Alamy

19 When, in November 2017, Allen & Unwin decided to drop *Silent Invasion*, exiled political cartoonist Rebel Pepper (Wang Liming) captured it this way. Although having my book spiked was a horrible experience, by attracting headlines around the world it was publicity gold. Who doesn't want to read a banned book?

Courtesy Rebel Pepper/Radio Free Asia

20 How the *Global Times* viewed *Silent Invasion*, 2018. The CCP's nationalist tabloid denounced me a number of times, quoting Australian critics such as Paul Keating. 'The Australian business community and academic institutions,' the newspaper declaimed, 'have criticised the book as inventing stories for malicious sensationalism, condemning the author for poisoning Australia-China relations for achieving fame.' Do these people know how their florid prose is read in the West?

21 Unveiling the honour board at Manuka Pool in March 2018. My youthful antipathy to all things military softened and matured years later when I learned about the suffering and sacrifice of my father's family from Tasmania. Two of his uncles were killed on the Western Front and his father, my grandfather, was gassed and spent months in a London hospital before being sent back. I'm sure the trauma he brought back to Australia affected my father and, one way or another, was passed on to me.

22 My accommodation in Dilsberg, a fortress village on a hill outside Heidelberg. The bells at the church next door tolled the hour and each quarter hour through the night. 'Tradition,' I was told. When Mark Twain visited in 1878, local children told him the village well was in fact the entrance to a secret tunnel that came out at the bottom of the hill, although no one knew where. It was said to have been built to smuggle in food during sieges.

23 An amphitheatre for Nazi rallies built in the 1930s in the forests above
Heidelberg. Inaugurating the theatre in 1935, Joseph Goebbels described it as
'National Socialism in stone'. It's not advertised and is hard to find. I am in awe of
what has been called 'the German genius', but my guess is that it will take another
century before the German consciousness is cleansed of the Nazi stain.

24 As the protests in Hong Kong reached a desperate peak in September 2019,
I was invited to join Hong Kong pop star and activist Denise Ho and dissident
Chinese Australian artist Badiucao at a fundraiser in Melbourne. Afraid of
angering Beijing, the National Gallery of Victory had declined to host the event. A
phalanx of police, some on horseback, guarded the event. That's Australia now.

25 How Britain's biggest-selling newspaper, the *Daily Mail*, began its coverage of *Hidden Hand* in July 2020. 'Useful idiots pages 12–15'! The tabloid published so many extracts that the publisher had to say 'enough'. Our book accelerated the transformation of British attitudes towards China.

26 The rest of Europe was mostly oblivious to CCP interference operations. When *Hidden Hand* appeared in mid-2020, it was translated into several languages and widely read (even more so in Asia). But not in insular France, which continues to fight old wars.

27 In January 2022, MI5 took the unprecedented step of issuing an alert, warning MPs to avoid Christine Lee, a united front operative with extensive links into the British elite. Mareike Ohlberg and I had exposed Christine Lee in *Hidden Hand* eighteen months earlier and I was often asked what took MI5 so long.

28 Two of the men with 'sniffer' phones, who made a point of sitting next to me at my regular cafe. After I began taking photos of these people, they stopped coming. A police counter-surveillance trainer told me that if you see someone once it means nothing, if you see them twice it's a coincidence, but if you see them three times they are following you.

29 In 2019, members of the Chinese community in Sydney launched the Chinese translation of *Silent Invasion*. Some had urged me to have it translated so their parents could read it. In Taiwan, when I told people the book had been denounced in Australia as racist and Sinophobic, they looked at me uncomprehendingly.

30 In Melbourne, February 2022, Murong Xuecun, recently arrived in Australia, holds his book, *Deadly Quiet City*, for the first time. A phone call from me prompted the famous author to go to Wuhan to investigate the lockdown. For several nervous months, I told myself that if he were arrested it was not my fault. If Murong were to return to China today, he would be incarcerated.

31 On a cool morning in March 2021, Janenne and I walked across the sand dunes behind Lake Mungo. The bush knows you are there. COVID lockdowns meant we had Mungo virtually to ourselves, deepening the uncanny sense of timelessness and the ancient pull of the land.

Courtesy Martin Maderthaner

After the speeches, one man marched up to the organisers and demanded his $10 donation back. Disconcerted, they gave it to him, at which point he wrote out a cheque for $500. I'd asked Elizabeth at Allen & Unwin to send four copies of my books. After I had signed them, they were auctioned. The top bid was $550 – amazing.

Exhausted at the end of the day.

Saturday, 14 November

Three hours of leafleting outside Prahran Town Hall with Janenne and three 'vollies'. It takes a lot of stamina to stand in the heat and be polite to passers-by. Talk about the crooked timber of humanity. Quite a few positive responses but the negative ones leave a deeper mark. Like the sleazebag who leans over the young woman volunteer. And the tough guy who blurts out, 'I hate all politicians.' I call after him, 'It's compulsory to vote, mate.' Along came the drug-addled nasty who told Janenne to 'fuck off' then cackled to his female companion. My immediate reaction was to look at Janenne and make a 'just shrug it off' gesture, but later I imagined thumping him.

Monday, 16 November

Two hours of leafleting at Windsor station this morning with Karin, a real old hand at the politics of the street. Getting to know her was a redeeming feature of the activity. She's terrific.

The papers are full of the Asia-Pacific Economic Cooperation meeting in Sydney trying to agree on a target in the lead-up to Copenhagen. It can't even agree on a weak 50 per cent cut in global emissions by 2050. Even with that we'll be toast.

Bob Brown rang to catch up on the campaign's progress. I tell him the organisation is great, the essentials of leafleting etc. are going well, but the campaign lacks flair.

Tuesday, 17 November

Yesterday, *Crikey* published my piece comparing climate science denial with Holocaust denial, arguing that any judgement depends on the type of ethical framework one adopts. I concluded that climate science deniers are not as culpable. However, just by posing the question I lump them together. Rob had said the analogy is unhelpful and I shouldn't publish. I didn't heed his advice, which was a mistake. The deniers are going berserk.

Spent three hours doorknocking this evening. It was my first experience of the campaigning activity I most dreaded. It's the introvert in me. I'd left my comfort zone back in Canberra and so forced myself through each gate to ring the bell or knock. Janet came along to hold my hand. Two vollies, Hugh and Barry, took the other side of the street. Although first-timers, they enjoy it. If a householder shows interest, they call me over for a chat. Most people are polite, but a few give us the brush-off.

Wednesday, 18 November
Leafleting at Prahran station this morning with Esther and Loris. Quite a few Australians of Indian heritage in the electorate and they are the most politically engaged. Generally, they are a pleasure to deal with.

Thursday, 19 November
The Higgins candidates gathered for the climate change community forum at Glen Iris Uniting Church last night. It had been 40°C that day. Peter Brohier, a vaguely green independent, wants to build a tunnel between Tasmania and the mainland. He sweated through a rambling speech tinged with messianic fervour. One Nation candidate Steve Raskovy is a bent-up old Hungarian ex-wrestler, now reliant on a walking stick. Contrary to One Nation policy, he believes in global warming, but he has his own theory to explain it after one day walking into his backyard and having a sudden flash of insight. Airplane contrails are breaking up the clouds allowing more sunlight to reach the Earth. The IPCC must have missed that one.

Stephen Murphy from the Climate Sceptics Party was affable but out of his depth. In response to any statement from the audience he would reply, 'There's no evidence for that.' On his right sat Joe Toscana, the independent anarchist, who mercilessly ridiculed Murphy as the mad uncle who just needed to be humoured. If I had a vote in Higgins, Joe would have been my second preference.

Although Fiona Patten of the Sex Party entered the race solely to oppose me and my nefarious plan to censor the internet, whenever the candidates assembled, she would naturally gravitate towards me and the Greens. Fiona's a likeable person. She admitted to the audience she was no expert on climate change before delivering an engaging and persuasive speech on why we need to act.

Kelly O'Dwyer's nameplate sat in front of an empty chair. She 'had another engagement', the organisers reported, adding that they had given her plenty of notice and had offered to change the date to suit her. O'Dwyer is avoiding any kind of public scrutiny, especially over climate change, which in her letter to voters she referred to, risibly, as 'global air pollution'. Global air pollution actually reduces the warming effect of increased greenhouse gases. 'Make me your representative in Canberra,' she seems to be saying, 'just don't ask me what I stand for.' It's the party system at its worst.

Friday, 20 November

Yesterday I hit a wall. Some candidates draw energy from campaigning; others have their energy sapped. I just want to sit in my office quietly working on the next book; instead, I have to *socialise*. Fortunately, it was a slow day. Janenne came with me this morning to leaflet at Carnegie station; her support has been way above and beyond the call of duty. Stalwart vollies Jeannie and Ana were there too.

In the south-eastern corner of the electorate, Carnegie is quite unlike the rest, looking and feeling like an ordinary Aussie suburb but with wide cultural diversity. Once again, we had a warm and engaged reception from voters from the Indian subcontinent, while those of Chinese heritage were mostly impassive. It must be the difference between growing up under democracy and dictatorship.

The Carnegie stationmistress (what's the official title?) is a gem, wishing a cheery 'good morning' to one and all and coming out of the station as each train approaches, hurrying along the stragglers like a mother duck. Ana reckons it must be the happiest station in Melbourne. What a marvellous asset to the community that woman is.

Wednesday night in Melbourne was the hottest on record for November. Lindsay Tanner compared Minchin and co. to the Montana militia, which was a steal from my stuff, but I'm glad to see them doing it. The stronger Labor's language, the more it allows me to be out in front.

I spent an hour today discussing politics and the environment with fifteen or so boys at Melbourne High, a selective public school not far from my flat. A very impressive bunch of young blokes; they knew so much. Sadly, none of them lives in the electorate.

Another round of doorknocking this evening. After Tuesday's initiation, dread of the unknown has been replaced by dread of the known.

Saturday, 21 November
Volunteer Jenny picked me up. I arrived at our stall in High Street, Ashburton, to hear a disturbing story told by a passer-by to Miriam, another vollie. The woman said she had been paid to join a focus group organised by Millward Brown, one of the world's largest market research companies, with an office on St Kilda Road. The focus group members were shown three ads for Kelly O'Dwyer and asked to comment on their preference. Then they were shown a mock-up of a fake website purporting to be an official Greens site, shaded green and with the party's triangular symbol. It featured a series of statements purportedly made by me and all chosen to show me in a negative light. The focus group members expressed their disapproval. Our informant said they'd been referred to a website address, but she had not written it down. Although it was not declared, she had the clear impression that the Liberal Party was behind the 'research'.

When I arrived back at the flat, I searched the internet but could find nothing. I talked it over with Brian. He advises doing nothing; if the Liberals are foolish enough to launch the website it would be good for us, especially as we know who is responsible. Remember what happened to Jackie Kelly at the last election after her supporters distributed false election material? Dirty tricks have a habit of backfiring.

Sunday, 22 November

The rain has been unrelenting last night and this morning. Not the ideal conditions for a street stall. But one of our volunteers, John, had set up one of those tents without walls across Armadale High Street. Even without the rain our reception in this blue-blood territory would have been cool. Liberal grandee Ron Walker and business favourite Graeme Samuel strolled by.

At 4.30 the doorknocking team – Sue, Matt, David, Hugh and Cameron – met up at the Orrong Hotel, perhaps the daggiest pub in the electorate. The rain eased and out we went.

I knocked on the door of a modest house needing repairs on a road filled with traffic. The woman who answered was around sixty and apprehensive, one of life's victims. Softening, I gave her the spiel and asked if she had anything she'd like to comment on. She told me her health was suffering because of the air pollution. The doctor said not much could be done. What could I say?

Australians can be an unforgiving mob. While waiting in the main bar for the other doorknockers to finish up, Andrew Symonds, the scandal-prone cricketer, appeared on the television, contritely telling the interviewer that he had 'made a few mistakes'. Propping up the bar, a grizzled old bloke with taped-together glasses jeered, 'That's a fuckin' understatement.'

Monday, 23 November

To Alamein station this morning with Janenne and vollies Margaret and Lorelei, a young woman who lives nearby and bounces with enthusiasm. You wouldn't pick any of us for Greens.

Spoke to fifty or sixty year 10 and 11 girls at Loreto Mandeville, a private Catholic school. They asked some very good questions, but shyly. The staff were pleased to have me there.

Tuesday, 24 November
Leafleting at East Malvern station this morning. I'd say it was the least friendly reception we've had to date. Who knows why? It's a big station; the area is solidly middle class. At the last federal election, the Labor candidate said Higgins is a diverse electorate and at the western end becomes 'Kath and Kim country'. She was flailed by *The Herald Sun*, which put it on page three. It was regarded as a major 'gaffe'.

I had a candid discussion with campaign manager Janet about the negativity with which various ideas to spice up the campaign are being met by our media people. Turns out, I'm not the only one to notice our media effort is bland.

Adam Kilgour, my marketing mate who helped set up the Climate Institute, was interested to hear about the focus groups with the 'push polling' directed against me. He consulted a former ALP heavyweight and phoned back to say it was almost certainly arranged by Crosby Textor, the Liberal Party–linked political strategy outfit, which would have commissioned Millward Brown to recruit participants according to specifications.

Adam said if he were being a really good friend, he'd be hoping I don't win because the life of a politician is one of pressing the flesh and ingratiating yourself with constituents. 'I know,' I replied. 'Maybe the best outcome would be to win 49 per cent of the two-party preferred vote.'

Wednesday, 25 November
Our timid media person said she'd been chewed out by the editor of the *Stonnington Leader*. The hard-bitten editor has had her feelings hurt because I referred to her paper as 'the local rag'. Instead of challenging her over the *Leader*'s pathetic coverage of the by-election, our media person apologised, explaining that I am an 'academic'

who doesn't understand these things. I bit my tongue, remembering my resolution to be a well-behaved candidate and not cause ructions within the party in the way other ring-ins had. As the Yoruba saying goes, 'He who shits on the road will meet flies on his return.' Interestingly, the *Progress Leader*, the local paper in the next district over, called to hear my views of Kelly O'Dwyer.

Our reception at Caulfield station this morning was the best we've had. For candidates, the temptation is to objectify the people who pass by, regarding them as no more than 'potential votes'. But I find myself regarding each person not as a potential vote but as a citizen whose vote counts as much as the next one and who, through that equality, acquires a certain dignity. Having a vote means having a bit of power, and it is somehow humbling when an elector indicates that he or she will be exercising that power in support of you.

After refusing to negotiate with the Greens, Kevin Rudd is 'gracious' in thanking the Opposition for its support for the CPRS 'in the interests of our kids and grandkids'. It's a shameless appropriation of the language of those who understand the seriousness of the situation and the utter inadequacy of the Rudd government's policy.

Thursday, 26 November
Some Toorak residents spend their lives apologising for their addresses, so it was not so surprising that Ana, Francesca and I received a pretty good reception at the station this morning.

I followed up morning leafleting with an interview at JOY FM, the gay radio station based in Bourke Street. We spent half the time on equal marriage, which allowed me to talk about the work I did with Michael Flood at the Australia Institute on 'mapping homophobia'. Surprisingly, among religious groupings, Catholics are the least homophobic.

Friday, 27 November
In Canberra, the Liberals are cannibalising themselves. Abbott, Minchin, Abetz and other denialists have resigned from the front

bench. Turnbull is sunk. This morning I thought for the first time: Cripes, I could win this. From our point of view, the sceptics' revolt in the Liberal Party could not be better. Pity about the planet.

The mood in the electorate seems to have undergone a distinct shift over the last day or so. At Armadale station this morning and in High Street, Ashburton, at lunchtime, the passers-by were noticeably more engaged and sympathetic. Are they existing Greens voters now more fired up, or people switching to us?

The extraordinary events of the last few days take us into unknown territory. Antony Green says on *PM* that before the last few days he expected the Liberals to hold Higgins comfortably; now he believes they are vulnerable. If Abbott instead of Hockey takes over from Turnbull, we'd expect a big reaction in our favour. So we should expect to score 28-plus per cent of primaries and perhaps 40 per cent of two-party preferred. We are hoping the Sex Party staffs their booths heavily because its how-to-vote card directs preferences to us.

Saturday, 28 November
A week to go until the election.

The disintegration of the Liberal Party dominates today's papers. *The Australian* reports a poll showing a 'massive majority' of Australians, and a strong majority of Liberal voters, support firm action on climate change. *The Age* has a nice article on how the Liberal collapse is helping me in Higgins. Below it is a photo of Kelly O'Dwyer giving a speech to no one save a baffled five-year-old girl, and one of me and Bob B laughing. Sometimes I think the nameless picture editors have more influence than the journalists.

Turned up at Prahran Market at 9 am for an hour of leafleting. Three or four Greens competed with three twenty-something Liberals sporting blue Kelly O'Dwyer t-shirts. It always puzzles me that young people can be conservatives. Maybe I'm old-fashioned but to be a political clone of your parents seems a repudiation of the freedom of youth. Anyway, I could see they were feeling dispirited, and the enthusiasm of our people compounded it.

The campaign team had organised a bicycle cavalcade, and around twenty supporters turned up. I had already expressed my reservations about it as a campaigning technique. It's such a Greens cliché, confirming all the stereotypes. Vollie Jenny is spot-on in suggesting there are many potential supporters in comfortable, middle-class suburbs who are turned off by scruffy Greens on bikes.

Yet it is a deep part of the culture of the party and the wider movement. All political parties have a distinctive culture among the membership, and nowadays it's the culture rather than the policies that attract members. At the front of the cavalcade, riding a tandem, I felt like a goose.

Sunday, 29 November
Australia All Over, ABC Radio's sop to rednecks, is on the air, with its usual mix of sentimental nationalism and conservative nostalgia. For all of Ian McNamara's eulogising of the Australian outback and the evocation of a sort of primitive bush mysticism, there is rarely any mention of Indigenous people. He's on now saying we should not worry about things that might happen in the future 'like global warming and Copenhagen and all that'; we should be worrying about doing things now. How do you respond to this sort of inanity? McNamara is a climate denier who for years has taken cracks at climate science. I once had an on-air stoush with him after I rang to object to some bloke who was bad-mouthing our data showing that Australians have the highest per capita emissions of industrialised countries.

Andrew Bolt is writing that Kelly O'Dwyer must be 'packing it' in Higgins because there is now a chance she will lose to that 'nutter'.

Monday, 30 November
Interesting conversation with a constituent in Carnegie while door-knocking yesterday evening. I asked about the origin of the unusual name of his house, 'Polygon Wood'. His grandfather was wounded in a battle at a place with that name in France in 1917. He told me that after he'd been going out with his partner for a while, they discovered

that her grandfather had been killed in the very same battle. Fate! I was pleased when he let on that he'd already voted for me in a pre-poll.

A few days later, I reach the page in *Good-Bye to All That* where Robert Graves mentions the battle at Polygon Wood. Synchronicity again. It's impossible for us to comprehend what those men went through. My grandfather was gassed and wounded in France, then sent back to the trenches. His two brothers were killed. Graves wrote that the conditions at Polygon Wood were more appalling than any they had yet known – 'three miles of morass, shell-holes, corpses, and dead horses'.

I'm captivated by an astonishing story Graves tells about an 'exchange of courtesies' between the British and German machine gunners.

> … by removing cartridges from the ammunition-belt one could rap out the rhythm of the familiar prostitutes' call: 'MEET me DOWN in PICC-a-DILLY', to which the Germans would reply, though in slower tempo, because our guns were faster than theirs: 'YES, with-OUT my DRAWERS ON!'

Ashburton station this morning leafleting with Margie (what a trouper she is) and Jonathan. Both are doctors. What a fascinating bunch.

In the Greens office in Little Bourke Street I met Ray, who, unprompted, had come up from Phillip Island with his daughter at 5.30 am to stretch a huge banner next to Toorak Road urging a Greens vote. 'I've got seven grandchildren,' he said by way of explanation. It was enough.

To Prahran Pool for a quick swim. It's a superb community resource – outdoors, accessible, well-managed and a pleasant atmosphere.

The index for *Requiem* arrived in the post. Allen & Unwin had their gun indexer prepare it and it's a ripper. A good index adds a lot to a book, and compiling them is an art. The publicists have also prepared a 'multimedia trailer' to go on the web. It's fabulous, I reckon.

Tuesday, 1 December

Early start to get to Malvern station by 7 am. Red Symons is on ABC 774 with his distinctive brand of weary nihilism, making it impossible for anyone to have a coherent conversation with him. 'I don't care about global warming,' he said. 'I'll be dead by then. Oh, there's the kids, I suppose.' Thanks, Dad.

Calls start coming in from 10 am with the stunning news that the Liberals have elected Tony Abbott as leader. How could they be so stupid? Joe Hockey lost because he foreshadowed a free vote on the emissions trading scheme. Abbott argued it is a policy issue rather than a conscience issue. Of course, it runs much deeper than a disagreement over how best to cut emissions. A worldview divides the sceptics like Abbott and Minchin from the moderates like Turnbull and Hockey. You would never hear the latter suggesting climate change is a communist plot. They think that's as unhinged as I do.

After the shock, the next thought is how much it helps us. It must make it a real contest in Higgins. Bob Brown rang to suggest some responses but essentially to calm everyone down. 'The Greens offer leadership on climate policy. We are a clear alternative to the Liberals. It's up to the voters of Higgins to make the decision.'

After lunch, to the pre-poll station in Spring Street, Malvern. Kelly O'Dwyer was already there. The media turned up for pre-arranged interviews with me – Channel 9, *The Australian*, *The Age*.

Doorknocking in South Yarra was encouraging, with a number of residents saying they could not vote Liberal again with Abbott as leader. Events seem to be falling into place perfectly in this by-election. We are planning a last-minute leafleting effort in key suburbs contrasting scientific opinion with Abbott's statement that 'climate change is crap'. But do enough people care?

Wednesday, 2 December

South Yarra station is an awful place for leafleting – constricted, teeming, chaotic. A *Stateline* camera crew wanted footage of me talking to a punter, but none were stopping. The crew were more

Frontline than ABC current affairs – tough, bluff and tabloid. The reporter sucked on a fag and kept his shades on through the interview. He asked me some Melbourne questions to see if I passed some sort of outsider's test. Best coffee? Which team? 'Carlton, I'm embarrassed to say,' signalling I have a team and know how my preference is seen. (As a fourteen-year-old in Canberra, it was the first Aussie Rules team I saw on TV.)

Doorknocking in Glen Iris and Burwood with a crack team of knockers – Linda, Barry, Hugh, Des and Jamie. I'm so impressed at the ability of these people to engage potential voters with such ease. After doing my first street I was despondent, wondering whether we'd been carried away with how well we might do. Then I hit Denman Avenue where the response was remarkable. We left feeling a little exhilarated.

After the session, I understood why I'm uncomfortable door-knocking. It's not just the feeling that I'm intruding as I step through the front gate. The power relationship shifts. When you are on their territory, instead of speaking as equals, supplication is part of the deal.

At Prahran pool to grab twenty laps on the way to doorknock-ing, Robbie the manager said, 'Aren't you …'. 'Yep, Clive Hamilton, the Greens candidate.' 'Gidday, mate, hope you do well.' Some local recognition.

Thursday, 3 December

Malcolm Mackerras is predicting a Greens victory in Higgins. A couple of people tell me it's the kiss of death, given his dismal record.

Leafleting at Burwood station, a woman strode past declaring, 'Anyone but Abbott.' The ABA factor is significant, like applying a squirt of WD-40 to rusted-on voters.

A volunteer at a pre-poll station says he was taken aside by a well-dressed woman who arrived in a supercharged Audi. She said she's a member of the Doctors' Wives Association. (There really is one?) They'd been discussing the election. They couldn't vote for

Kelly O'Dwyer because her heroes are Margaret Thatcher and Ronald Reagan. 'And she's only thirty-two.'

Albert Langer, the old Maoist ratbag, is in the front row of a public meeting in Fitzroy Town Hall. He's with a huge bloke with a camera who's fixated on me, taking a couple of hundred flash photos. It's designed to intimidate. Just before the start, I come down from the stage and crankily ask him to stop. 'It's a public place,' he says. 'Yes,' I reply, 'and you can be a prick in a public place.' He stops.

Speaking of fixations, at O'Dwyer's campaign launch, Costello told the Liberal faithful that he's received some loopy correspondence as treasurer, including one from Clive Hamilton claiming that the GST would result in an extra sixty-five deaths each year. The crowd duly chortled. He didn't mention that the claim was made in an Australia Institute submission to a Senate inquiry made jointly with the Australian Medical Association. And it was endorsed in the Senate committee's report. To this day, Costello is still mystified by it.

Friday, 4 December
One day to go. After leafleting at Prahran station, I make it to the ABC studios at Southbank for an interview on the Jon Faine program. Waleed Aly is filling in for Faine. We'd been told O'Dwyer had refused to debate, but Tony Nutt, Libs campaign director, would come instead. Nutt was a no-show, so it was just me with Antony Green providing comment down the line from Sydney. He said I had no chance of winning, which helped my underdog status. Waleed flayed O'Dwyer for not turning up, saying three times that she'd been invited but 'refused'. He did not give me an easy run, but I came out of it unscathed.

I heard from a journalist that Tony Abbott was planning a visit to Higgins today to support O'Dwyer. But he changed his mind. Damn.

Rob Manne has a fabulous opinion piece in today's *Australian* praising me to the skies and urging Higgins to vote Green. Copies of the paper were hard to find in the electorate. The newsagent at the bottom of my street told me a woman had come in early and bought the lot. The Libs probably rang around to members first thing.

Interview with Peter Mares on ABC's *National Interest*. Off air the producer told me that after O'Dwyer refused to participate they had asked Peter Costello, David Kemp (Lib state president), Tony Nutt and the Lib candidate for Bradfield. All declined.

Saturday, 5 December
Election day.

Miles (my son) is my driver and minder for the day. Myra (my daughter, down from Sydney) is also in town handing out how-to-vote cards. I have mapped out the day. At 8 am I visit the first polling booth, at Ashburton. Here and at every booth, the Liberals are out in large numbers. They arrived at 4 am, ahead of everyone else, to erect huge banners to dominate the streetscape. They must have spent a fortune on this campaign, including a Prius decked out in O'Dwyer propaganda. That's $40,000 alone, our entire budget. They are scared, and they should be. Losing Higgins would be crushing.

Plenty of media to film and interview me at Malvern Primary School booth. Later, at the Toorak Road booth, the spiritual home of the Liberal Party, three beautifully dressed older women from the area are handing out Greens how-to-vote cards with great élan. They confide that many older women had told them they'd always voted Liberal but this time it's Greens. So inspiring.

Melissa Fyfe of *The Age* phones to say the Liberals are claiming we are handing out material quoting the governor of Victoria, which is illegal. What rubbish. I check with Janet. It's a Climate Emergency Group leaflet and nothing to do with the Greens. And it's not unlawful anyway. Smacks of desperation.

I spend the day visiting booths all over the electorate. The vollies get a boost when the candidate turns up. Return to the flat with Janenne at day's end for a short rest.

I'm late getting to the afterparty at the beer garden of the Flying Duck pub in Prahran. About 150 have gathered, a mix of all ages. Such friendly, enthusiastic, down-to-earth people. The Greens' psephologist is in a corner hunched over a laptop tallying the real-time votes lodged with the AEC.

One of our scrutineers tells me he noticed that at his booth there were ten votes for the Climate Sceptics. Seven of the second preferences came to me. Go figure. Another vollie, Jamie, was at the Alamein booth where Peter Costello was handing out how-to-votes. He's left politics but has to do his duty on election day. Alamein is a very small, slow booth and Jamie reckons Costello was hiding there. Tim Costello phones to see how the counting is going. I'm touched by his interest.

Around 7.30 pm the trends are emerging and, as word spreads, a mood of disappointment falls over the crowd. It's strange because we performed at the upper end of expectations. It's the effect of the hype over the last week as various pundits said the Liberals could lose Higgins. Antony Green was right, though; it was never really on the cards. The hype sets you up for a crash.

After a time, a feeling of wistful satisfaction overtakes the crowd. We may not have pulled off a stunning upset but it was a great result for the Greens. (The final tally would be 32 per cent of primary votes and 40 per cent on a two-party preferred basis.) It's the highest vote ever for the Greens. Yes, there was no Labor candidate, but Higgins is the second safest Liberal seat in the country.

I give a speech expressing my gratitude to all of the volunteers and to the campaign committee and Janet Rice. They deserve it. I was sincere in my warm praise and appreciation to the Stonnington Greens, who were brilliant.

We didn't stay late. Messages came through expressing commiserations, others saying it was a fantastic result. Bob was full of praise for the campaign.

Sunday, 6 December
In the morning sun, Janenne and I are cruising up the Hume Highway on our way home to Canberra. I'm leaving behind life as a political candidate with feelings of satisfaction and relief. I do an ABC Radio interview in the car, reflecting on the campaign and the result. When

asked if I would be running again, I give a firm 'no'. I had no desire to do it again.

I was glad I would not be taking a seat in parliament but also pleased I had shown I could get out from behind my desk and have a go in the election. Comfort zones become too comfortable, and it did me good to meet, if only briefly, a couple of dozen new people every day for two months. Handing out leaflets at suburban train stations is where political spin meets authentic Australia. It's a great leveller, even if it's only a short interlude in the political cycle.

§

The loss to the conservatives sat dully with me for a few days, but I soon regained my equilibrium and prepared to fly out to the Copenhagen climate conference. A couple of days after the election, Bob Brown's director of strategy, Leanne Minshull, phoned. 'Would you be willing to put yourself forward as the Greens candidate for the Senate in the ACT at the next general election?' I was flattered to be asked. I probably would have won the preselection and my chances of defeating the sitting Liberal Gary Humphries would be much better than winning in Higgins. But I'd had a go at politics and once was enough.

My critics began referring to me as 'the failed Greens candidate', as if failing to win an election were a blot on my character. Of course, if Australian citizens were not willing to have a crack, we would not live in a democracy, so three cheers to all those failed candidates.

§

Two thousand and nine was not quite over. After Christmas, Janenne and I travelled to Queensland for the Woodford Folk Festival. Although I had been invited as a 'performer', I looked forward to a holiday after the intensity of the campaign.

There's been a bit of hippie in me since my teenage years. At high school I grew long hair, smoked dope and listened to John Mayall. When Jim Cairns, the Labor Party hero and deputy PM who went feral after politics, staged an alternative bush festival at Bredbo in 1977, we joined most others walking around naked. I still cringe when I think of it. Thank God there were no camera phones in those days.

So when the invitation came to be a guest speaker at the 2009 Woodford Folk Festival, it was like returning to my roots, clothes on. The festival site was hot but the patrons were chilled. *Requiem for a Species* would be published in three months. At Woodford, speaking to a few dozen people in a marquee, I got a sense of how the book would be received – even environmentalists would greet it with dull resistance. Later, though, a thousand people packed a huge tent for 'Kerry on the Couch', an event at which Kerry O'Brien would probe the thoughts and lives of prominent players. Bob Hawke was the star turn, with me and Christine Milne, then Greens deputy leader, also in armchairs on stage as support acts.

In the first part of the session, Bob expatiated to Kerry on how politics had become too adversarial. Opponents should come together and resolve differences in the spirit of conciliation. I soon made some pointed comments about the way the Hawke–Keating government implemented the economic rationalist agenda of free markets and deregulation, imposing severe social costs because of an obsession with economic growth. It was an argument to which the audience was naturally receptive, and Christine chimed in with support.

I could sense Bob beside me becoming agitated. When he responded, he was cranky, denouncing my views as 'crap' and ranting about 'professors in their chairs' abandoning the poor. When someone in the audience called out 'bullshit', Hawke savaged the heckler for engaging in personal attack, realising after a few seconds, as the audience had, that he had just launched a personal attack on me. It went downhill from there, or uphill if you like a good stoush. At laidback Woodford, conflict is rare, and the effect on the audience was electrifying.

Later, on ABC Radio, Kerry O'Brien reframed Hawke's bad behaviour as a welcome return of old-style political debate, while the gossip section of *The Courier-Mail* didn't exaggerate: 'A raging disagreement, hecklers and the odd four-letter word: just like old times for Bob Hawke.'

After the event, as Janenne and I sat quietly in the evening warmth at an outdoor eatery, on the other side of the deck a scowling Bob sat surrounded by his entourage. The festival organisers seemed to like the pinch of spice to Woodford's vegan stew, and for year after year, Bob received rock-star treatment from the festival organisers.

19

Cyberbullies

O N NEW YEAR'S Day 2010, Janenne asked, 'What adventures do you have in store for us this year?' 'I hate to think,' I replied. At the time, I was writing some twenty opinion pieces a year on aspects of climate change and giving dozens of public talks around the country, but the narrowness and nastiness of political debate in Australia was prompting me to widen my horizons. I began to look for opportunities to spend time overseas.

The last-minute breakdown of the Copenhagen conference in December 2009 threw environmentalists around the world down a long, dark tunnel of depression that would last a couple of years. So much emotional energy had been invested in a breakthrough that the collapse was crippling. Even so, they were not ready, by and large, to have the full implications laid out starkly in the way I had in *Requiem for a Species* when it appeared in March 2010.

I knew I would be accused of doom-mongering, so I'd done my best to set out the argument with utmost clarity and deal with all of the objections in advance. Yet heeding the message I was transmitting had less to do with the evidence and more to do with psychological preparedness, the willingness of the reader to let down their defences.

I devoted a large part of the book to exploring the 'coping mechanisms' we use to protect ourselves from discomforting truths.

In addition to an analysis of the various forms of denial, a substantial part of the book, building on the work of Tim Kasser among others, was taken up with the emotions that arise in response to the evidence – loss, grief, anger, helplessness, depression, betrayal. It would be another decade or so before people were willing to countenance these ideas, when a raft of books appeared dealing with climate grief and climate anxiety. Today, eco-anger, climate sadness, ecological grief and so on are part of everyday conversation among young climate activists, so much so that in early 2022 a scholarly article was published setting out a 'taxonomy' of climate emotions.

Requiem is an example of picking the zeitgeist too early. Although I was buoyed when some 350 people turned up to hear me talk at an event organised by Ove Hoegh-Guldberg, a coral reef expert at the University of Queensland, its reception felt muted. Some Australian reviewers simply missed the point, reading it through their familiar lenses. Overseas, some were more receptive. *The Times Higher Education Supplement* made it 'book of the week', but reviewers found it troubling. One began: 'Readers of a nervous disposition may wish to look away now.'

Word spread and over the next few years *Requiem* sold ten thousand copies in Australia. The book found its way into the hands of a few influential people abroad including Naomi Klein, whose breakthrough book, *No Logo*, had made her famous. A year or so later, while visiting their home in Toronto, Naomi Klein's husband, filmmaker Avi Lewis, told me that *Requiem* shocked Naomi and prompted her to write *This Changes Everything*. A few years later, while she was touring Australia, an email arrived inviting me to join 'an audience with Naomi Klein' in Melbourne. I thought only the Pope held audiences.

Some months later, after speaking to a subdued audience at the Byron Bay Writers Festival, an environmental scientist, a biologist, took me aside to berate me for painting such a gloomy picture. 'When you take away people's hope,' he told me, 'they give up.' 'So,' I replied, 'you think we should lie about the real situation?' I'm with Oswald Spengler on this: 'Optimism is cowardice.'

The research on hope and hopelessness and their effects on behaviour I had considered at length. People like the biologist were in truth acting out their own anxieties. I had become irritated at this deeply entrenched bit of pop psychology which everyone felt free to dispense. It's extraordinary how many scientists who rightly deride the inexpert for making pronouncements on climate science blithely make pronouncements on human psychological responses as if their opinions were as valid as the scholars who have studied it for years. It's the curse of the social sciences – everyone is an expert.

In September, *Requiem* won a Queensland Premier's Literary Award. It was judged the best work advancing public debate and carried a prize of $15,000. At drinks after the award ceremony, Premier Anna Bligh approached me, and we had a congenial chat. She told me her husband heads the state's climate change unit and he had said to her, 'We are fucked.' She put her hand over her mouth and said, 'Oh, I shouldn't say that, should I?' It was endearing.

The prize money was a windfall that I didn't need so, after consulting with my son, Miles, we donated it the Pakistan flood relief appeal.

The book went on to attract attention in Europe, and in October 2010 I arrived in Belgium to speak at a small conference on climate controversies at the Free University of Brussels. The next day, the speakers travelled to Paris where the conference resumed at Sciences Po. Located in the atmospheric sixth arrondissement, Sciences Po had traditionally been the training ground for France's political and bureaucratic elite but in more recent times had become a prestigious centre of political and social research. Before the session I was introduced to the chair, Bruno Latour. Described by *The New York Times* as 'France's most famous and misunderstood philosopher', Bruno's work has been hugely influential across the social sciences and humanities in the West. I was pretty starstruck, even more so when he expressed excitement at meeting the author of *Requiem for a Species*, which he described as 'a fabulous book'. (A couple of years later,

Bruno's wife, Chantal, told me that he went into a depression lasting six months after reading it.) From such an esteemed figure as Bruno, the praise was gratifying, although it has always felt perverse, even shameful, to be pleased at success in spreading a message like that.

§

For some time, I had been receiving abusive and threatening emails, mostly anonymous, a few out and proud, denouncing me for speaking in favour of taking action on climate change. Initially, I deleted them, not wanting them to pollute my hard drive. Occasionally, I broke the golden rule of 'don't feed the trolls', telling them if they kept it up they could expect a knock on the door from the police. After a while, I began storing them in their own folder.

Reading these early emails, and the occasional letter, was disconcerting, but they made me more incensed about denialism and determined not to be frightened off. It occurred to me that others like me must be receiving similar abuse and threats. I started phoning around to climate scientists, environmentalists and journalists. All said they too had been receiving them. Everyone felt that they alone had been picked out and were relieved when I told them others were in the same boat. I decided to name the beast, asking them to send me examples, though some said they routinely delete them.

In February 2010 I wrote a series of articles for the ABC's *The Drum* website titled 'Bullying, lies and the rise of right-wing climate denial'. I first pointed out that apart from the volume and viciousness of the emails received by climate scientists, the campaign has two features: it is mostly anonymous, and it appears to be orchestrated. I reproduced some examples. Professor Andy Pitman at the University of New South Wales had notified university security when he received threats like these: 'If we see you continue, we will get extremely organised and precise against you' and 'Fuck off mate, stop the personal attacks. Just do your science or you will end up collateral damage in the war, GET IT.' Pitman had to consider the safety of his staff. A University of Queensland scientist received a threat detailing the movements of his school-age children, including the bus stop they used.

Climate campaigners too had noticed a surge in the frequency and virulence of this new form of cyberbullying. The following message was received by a young woman: 'Did you want to offer your children to be brutally gang-raped and then horribly tortured before being reminded of their parents' socialist beliefs and actions? Burn in hell. Or in the main street, when the Australian public finally lynchs [sic] you.' Another campaigner opened her inbox to read this: 'Fuck off!!! Or you will be chased down the street with burning stakes and hung from your fucking neck, until you are dead, dead, dead!'

Today, vicious political harassment of this kind is a widely discussed social phenomenon, with women often targeted for the worst forms. In 2010, the targets felt alone and isolated, making the attacks more disturbing. This kind of online rage, fuelled by the Murdoch media, would give rise to Trumpian populism. It's worth remembering that the rage was first used as a political weapon against climate scientists and activists.

Few of those on the receiving end of this hatred doubted that the emails were being orchestrated. Scores of abusive emails over a few hours are unlikely to be the product of a large number of individuals spontaneously making the effort to track down an email address and pour forth their rage. The most effective enabler of this environment of hatred was *Herald Sun* columnist and blogger Andrew Bolt. His blog was the most popular meeting place for deniers in Australia. At the Murdoch tabloid, Bolt specialised in posts of angry ridicule directed at climate scientists and any others who publicly accepted the science. After each Bolt rant, those targeted would receive a deluge of hate-filled emails.

My exposé of how Australia's most distinguished climate scientists had become the target of a new form of cyberbullying aimed at driving them out of the public domain was immediately picked up in the United States where the phenomenon was even worse.

Scientific American gave it prominence, and in Britain, *Nature* did the same. Many more stories of intimidation emerged. Dr Kevin Trenberth, head of analysis at the National Center for Atmospheric Research in Colorado, turned over to university security nineteen pages of 'extremely foul, nasty, abusive' emails collected in the four months after the 'Climategate' storm broke in November 2009 – the release of emails between climate scientists stolen by Russian hackers from a University of East Anglia server. Another prominent climate scientist had a dead animal dumped on his doorstep and was forced to travel with bodyguards.

Stephen Schneider, an eminent climatologist at Stanford University, said that he had received hundreds of threatening emails. Exasperated, he asked: 'What do I do? Learn to shoot a magnum?' Schneider said he had observed an 'immediate, noticeable rise' in emails whenever climate scientists were attacked by prominent right-wing commentators, including those on Fox News.

Some writers write as a way of coping with life, and at times that's been true for me. Of course, being in a position to deal with one's anxieties by writing about them in major outlets is a privilege. Like others, I felt stronger after the beast had been named. Feeling alone as a victim of sinister forces can leave you carrying around a hollow fear, one immediately dissipated when you discover others being targeted in the same way. Nowadays, it's always pleasing, and a little inspiring, to see victims of cyberbullying, usually women, expose their cowardly abusers to public scorn.

§

While a raging battle was going on in the online underworld, above ground a grand political contest was taking place. In 2010, the mining companies were making money hand over fist and the Rudd government proposed taxing their super-profits. The industry went on the offensive in a well-funded campaign to kill the idea and undermine the government. It was organised and led by Mitch Hooke of the

Minerals Council, which was spending a 'war chest' on an advertising campaign that blanketed TV for weeks. Hooke said the government was acting like a communist dictatorship. A notoriously aggressive lobbyist who made no apology when accused of being a bully, Mitch Hooke was an obvious inclusion in my 2014 list for *Crikey* of those most responsible for blocking climate action, the 'dirty dozen'.

In June 2010, mining magnate Gina Rinehart decided to hold a demonstration against the tax in Perth. A couple of hundred turned up. A journalist described them as the best-dressed protesters he'd ever seen, unsurprising since Rinehart had given her employees time off to attend. She hired a flat-bed truck and harangued the crowd about how unfair and 'un-Australian' it would be to tax her super-profits. Another mining tycoon, Andrew Forrest, who had been warning that Australia was turning communist, stood by her and echoed the warnings.

Kevin Rudd backed down. Appalled at the ability of the mining industry to destroy a decision taken in the public interest by an elected government, I penned an op-ed that ran in *The Age*. 'There is something grotesque,' I wrote, 'about watching Australia's second richest person, Gina Rinehart with assets of $4.75 billion, and the fourth richest, Andrew Forrest with assets of $4.24 billion, pumping the air at an anti-tax rally and demanding justice.' I lamented the absence of public outrage at plutocrats claiming to be victims and undermining the democratic process, asking where the trade union movement was in all this.

Once in a while you write an op-ed that perfectly captures the mood of anger or anguish of half the population. This one did so and there was a huge reaction. It also led to the most bizarre phone call I have ever received.

The next day, Andrew Forrest's PA phoned. Mr Forrest would like to speak with me. Recalling that Forrest had whinged in public that the prime minister no longer took his calls, I said I was pretty busy, and he could try me in a couple of days. He phoned me two days later, at home after hours. I took notes throughout. In a whining voice, he told me he'd read my article and wanted to 'put the other side of the story'. He spent the next forty minutes trying to convince me that he is an ordinary bloke who started with nothing and worked hard. He had some failures before success and was a kind of accidental billionaire. He pays himself an annual salary of $110,000 and does not take more unless the share price of his company goes up. He's still the kid who grew up on a farm. Emphasising that since becoming rich he hadn't changed his lifestyle, he said, and I quote, 'I haven't changed my wife, my house or my car.' So he was wounded by what I had written and hated the idea of being lumped together with Clive Palmer, Rio Tinto and BHP. He's not like them; he's an ordinary bloke. He works at keeping the mining industry at arms-length and did not contribute a cent to the $100 million war chest to defeat the Rudd government's legislation.

I listened to all this then told him that, while he might think of himself as the same good bloke he was twenty years ago, now, with his wealth, power and responsibility, structurally (did I really use that word?) he is in a completely different position. He might consider himself to be unlike Rio Tinto, BHP and Clive Palmer, but from the outside he's just part of the mining industry. I told him that the billionaires' rally in Perth was terrible optics. He said he had to go, remarking that there is a 'lynch-mob mentality' in Australia, and he couldn't let the side down by not attending the rally.

Wow, I thought as he rang off, that's one insecure billionaire. 'Hey, Janenne, you will not believe what just happened …'

§

The Coalition won the most seats at the election in August 2010, although to form a government it needed the support of three independents in the House. It began negotiations. A few days later, I woke in the middle of the night with my heart pounding. I couldn't remember the dream, but immediately my mind was flooded with a series of thoughts for an opinion piece on why it would be unconscionable for the independents to install an Abbott-led government of climate science deniers. As soon as I arrived at work that day, a Friday, I wrote the piece that had come to me in the night. I sent it to *The Sydney Morning Herald*, to no response, and *The Age*, which said maybe next Tuesday. So I sent it to Nick Cater, *The Australian*'s opinion editor, who accepted it straight away, publishing in the Saturday edition in a prime spot. I was still publishing in *The Australian*, taking advantage of its pretence of balance by running a few articles from critics, though had a niggling feeling that I was being hypocritical.

Sometimes I can't help feeling that there is some kind of fate playing out. As Carl Jung once wrote, a person's life is a pattern that fits together and, as life proceeds, the pieces fall into place as if in accordance with a predestined design. Perhaps that's just how the mind works when looking back, like the person rendered a paraplegic who, decades later, says they would not have it any other way.

I'm not superstitious in the least, although occasionally I have premonitions. Sadly, they are about trivial matters. On one occasion, around this time, as I drove out of our street I passed the big conifer in a neighbour's yard and thought, if I were the owner of that tree, I'd have it taken out. Two days later, a team of men turned up and cut down the tree. And sometimes, something happens that feels inauspicious. One day in 2010, Janenne and I spent much of the day gardening, including heavily pruning the tall hedge at the edge of the backyard. We watched the blue-tongue lizard who lived in the hedge escape the disturbance by making his way around the side of the house into the front yard. 'Bluey', as we called him, had given us the privilege of making our yard his home and we felt affection for this beautiful creature. In the evening I took a load of cuttings out to the tip in the ute I had hired. Returning, I found Bluey dead on the road outside our house. I had run over him. His death and my role in it upset me for days. We buried him in the garden.

20

Roaming the world

I was unsettled in Australia, tired of the wearying, parochial politics and the anti-intellectualism of the culture. And I wanted to escape the role I had assumed in the public domain. It hemmed me in. I wanted to play in a bigger, more sophisticated arena, one more intellectually expansive.

In April 2011, I arrived in Oxford for a three-month visit attached to the Department of Philosophy and the Centre for Environment. I had wangled invitations on the back of publication of *Requiem for a Species*. The philosophy department seemed arid and uninteresting, scholastic in the unflattering sense of the word. The Uehiro Centre for Practical Ethics, directed by the Australian Julian Savulescu, where I had been allocated a shared office, was much more engaging. Most of the time I read philosophy books in the university library or in my cramped office. But it was also an opportunity to get to know some of the leading climate scientists and to travel to London, Cambridge, Edinburgh and Potsdam to give talks.

Over sandwiches in the lunchroom, a few of us casually discussed what are known as the cosmological arguments for the existence of God. One version of it is that if we take causation back in time, we must reach an initial cause, an uncaused cause, that is inexplicable except by the action of some divine being. Therefore, some deduce, God must exist. Remembering a question posed by Heidegger, I asked why God would debase himself to become the object of logical proofs. Across the table, someone replied, 'Why debased?' The gulf between those whose world is one of rationality and those who sense something more is unbridgeable. In my view, when Richard Dawkins began his book by declaring that the existence or otherwise of God is a *scientific* question, there is no point reading on – he's begun in the wrong ontological space.

In Oxford, I sought out the best place for coffee and quickly settled on The Missing Bean, nestled in quaint Turl Street and next door to a little jewellery shop that sold old suffragette rings set with amethysts, diamonds and peridot stones to represent the colours of the movement. I bought one for Janenne.

I would spend an hour of two each morning in The Missing Bean reading and writing, looking up to watch the world come and go. One day I fell into conversation with a man at the next table. It turned out he was a professor of economics at the University of Stockholm and one of those who decide each year who should receive the Nobel prize in economics, giving him a great deal of clout in the profession. Though amiable, his world was populated by 'rational economic man', so we avoided economic topics.

On another occasion, gazing onto Turl Street, I was thinking about how conservatives, including deniers, would respond when the world became much warmer and extreme events more frequent. It struck me that geoengineering would become an enormous public issue. I decided at that moment to write a book about it.

I had included a few pages concerning the Promethean dangers of geoengineering in *Requiem*. The term encompasses many kinds of technology, some benign, but includes grand schemes to counteract global warming by modifying the Earth system as a whole. The foremost scheme being researched was sulphate aerosol injection, that is, spraying sulphur dioxide into the upper atmosphere creating a layer of sulphate particles that would reduce the amount of solar radiation reaching the Earth's surface. In short, regulating sunlight. Allowing someone to have their hand on the global thermostat seemed a bad idea. The debate was being monopolised by a handful of people with a technocratic worldview that had little appreciation of the political and geostrategic risks of attempting to take control of the Earth's climate.

A couple of weeks later, in June 2011, I attended a workshop on geoengineering at the newly established Institute for Advanced Sustainability Studies in Potsdam. I was pleased the Europeans were getting involved because the debate had been dominated by Americans, who tend to be more gung-ho about technofixes. Dining one evening with a few of the other workshoppers, I sat next to Paul Crutzen, the legendary Dutch scientist who had warned the world about the hole in the ozone layer, winning a Nobel prize in chemistry for it. A few years earlier he had written a journal article advocating a major research program in stratospheric sulphur injections. The paper caused uproar because the subject had been taboo among climate scientists who feared that politicians unwilling to cut emissions would seize on geoengineering as a cheap and easy alternative, one that could go catastrophically wrong. I asked Crutzen why he had written it. 'Despair,' he said. Despair over the lack of effective mitigation measures and the hot world we were heading into to. He said he was surprised at the amount of criticism he had received, and I had the impression he had been shaken by it.

The book, *Earthmasters: The dawn of the age of climate engineering*, would not appear until early 2012, published by Yale University Press (prestigious but difficult). In the meantime, *Requiem* was attracting interest further afield. In August 2011, I found myself in La Plata, a rundown town about an hour from Buenos Aires, for a conference. I have always found that my hosts in developing countries treat me with the greatest respect and kindness, so much so, that I frequently feel like a fraud; I really am not so important. The Argentine publisher of *Requiem* told me that the book was being sold at street-side newsstands in Buenos Aires, an idea I could not get my head around.

When an opportunity arose to really join the world of global ideas, I wondered whether, at fifty-eight, I still had it in me. A phone call came through from an executive recruiter in the United States, testing my interest in a new position as CEO of a think tank being established in New York. The institute would promote the idea of a sustainable post-growth economy. I had been asked to comment on the think tank proposal some eighteen months previously. The institute was an initiative of Gus Speth, a master at raising funds. Though gratifying, the approach threw me into some turmoil. I seemed to have resigned myself to cruising through the rest of my working life. After the Australia Institute, summoning the surge of energy that would be needed seemed beyond me. Yet the idea of moving to New York to help develop an alternative to neoliberal capitalism had a certain glamour. Janenne was open to the possibility – bless her. In the end, the thought of establishing and running a new think tank, especially in another country, was too daunting.

§

In November 2012 I travelled to Milan to participate in a conference. To my puzzlement, some academics had arranged for an Italian translation of *The Mystic Economist*, a book near twenty years old with an embarrassing title, one I had left behind long ago. The conference was to celebrate the book's release. The venue was an ornate and graceful old theatre next door to La Scala opera house. 'Conference' did not seem to be the right description. Although there were some talks from me and a couple of heavy hitters from Paris and Rome, it was more of a cultural event, the highlight being a long performance from a very arty drumming ensemble. The event must have cost a packet and it was not hard to guess who paid, the diamond-encrusted dowager over whom the organisers fussed. She showed little interest in the proceedings and I guessed that, among Milan's cultural aristocracy, funding an event featuring various intellectuals was a means of building social capital.

Most of the proceedings were in Italian, so I sat in the gods with the interpreter hired for me. David, a personable young man, spoke quietly into my ear, too close for good hygiene. After an exhausting hour of concentration for both of us, he said the conversations on stage were in a high Italian that was hard to follow, and they were using intellectual terms that he couldn't understand. I suggested a break. David said he'd show me around Milan, so we took off on his Vespa with me riding pillion. I said I wanted to buy my wife a Milanese scarf. He knew the best shops, breezing through each one, rapidly appraising the offerings and, back on the Vespa, proposing a better one. When I commented admiringly on his decisive shopping style, he replied simply, 'I'm a gay man.'

From the back of a motor scooter ridden by a local is the most lively way to see a European city. With the scarf secured, David took me on a speed tour of churches and monuments, ending up at a quaint old square built around a bronze statue of a half-naked Napoleon whose buttocks shone after frequent rubs from Milanese hoping for good luck. I would remember Napoleon's bottom some years later when I came across the bronze guard dog in Moscow's Ploschad Revolyutsii metro station, whose nose was shining from thousands of lucky rubs each day. David and I returned reluctantly to the theatre next to La Scala.

§

I had been having an email correspondence with Bruno Latour and, while at Oxford in 2012, took the opportunity to visit him in Paris. Bruno had organised a kind of salon at his apartment in an old street close to Boulevard Saint-Michel. He had invited nine or ten younger academics and cultural types. I realised that I was expected to impress the group with brilliant observations. But I was not firing and had no profound insights to offer, stumbling my way through a conversation that left me feeling inadequate.

The intellectual culture in France puts Australia's to shame – even everyday people will have their favourite philosophers and poets. And the embarrassment of being monolingual is constant. My attempts to return to learning French were failing, despite my efforts. My brain is too literal to learn another language. My tutor told me I should copy the technique of the Italian manager of the Marseille football team. His French is clumsy but after a game he gets in front of a camera and just lets it flow out, however it comes. 'It sounds terrible, but we know what he means.'

In 2013 we spent three months in Paris after Bruno had arranged a visiting professorship at Sciences Po. With academics Christophe Bonneuil and François Gemenne, I had organised a conference, 'Thinking the Anthropocene'. François, an expert in migration at the University of Versailles, had that year became famous after he had used his expertise to humiliate a National Front leader in a television debate. A Belgian, he joked about his native land's reputation for beer, chocolate and Tintin. Christophe was a Marxist historian at the National Centre for Scientific Research. He lived near Belleville Park in the nineteenth arrondissement, the grittiest precinct of Paris inside the Périphérique. He and his friends were scathing of the fifth and sixth that we, and the tourists, preferred. 'A museum,' Christophe said. 'Who wants to live in a museum?' I saw his point, but what a museum! Besides, I liked living in a district where I didn't have to look over my shoulder while walking on the street at night as we did making our way to Stalingrad metro station from his flat.

One evening, Janenne and I went to Bruno's apartment for dinner, just around the corner from where we were staying in a university apartment building in rue Suger. Bruno and his wife, Chantal, a well-known musician, are gracious hosts. Uncertain about protocol, I arrived with a bottle of Bollinger, which I'd bought on special for €39. As he took it, Bruno said, 'Aha, this is one of ours,' referring to the winemaking family he comes from.

During the evening, Bruno and the other guest, Amy Dahan, a historian and mathematician, talked about the 1996 Sokal affair, an academic hoax aimed at ridiculing postmodernism. Alan Sokal, an American physicist, wrote a nonsense article stringing together various ideas from cultural studies that purported to show quantum gravity is a social construct. He submitted it to a cultural studies journal, *Social Text*, which published it. Sokal then revealed the hoax.

As French philosophy was the source of postmodernist studies, the affair was a scandal in France, evidentiary gold for the traditionalists. *Le Monde* carried a front-page story with photos of those it identified as the three principal postmodernist culprits – Jacques Derrida, Michel Foucault and Bruno Latour. Bruno was aggrieved to be bracketed with the other two because his essential argument cannot be equated with the postmodernists, who claim all truth is socially constructed. (The positions are different, although for most the difference is hard to grasp.) Bruno said it was Pierre Bourdieu who put *Le Monde* up to including him among the three, because Bourdieu hates him.

§

It was around this time that I first had contact with Graham Readfearn, a journalist whose concern about climate change had effectively seen him driven out of his job at *The Courier-Mail*. I encouraged him not to give up as only a couple of journalists were doing the kind of work he did, exposing the dirty tricks of the fossil fuel lobby. After two or three years freelancing, he was employed by *The Guardian*, edited by Lenore Taylor, one of the very first journalists to write seriously about climate change. I shared with Graham and a handful of others a real sense of dread. We were up against an enemy not just powerful and self-interested but evil, because it was willing to take down the world. It cast a pall over our lives, a sense that was slowly spreading across the environment movement, souring the buoyant spirit that had grown in previous decades when campaigning on easier problems.

In 2013, I was offered some respite when the National Library of Australia approached me to write a book on the history of protest in

Australia, drawing on its photo archives. Although attracted to the idea, I was committed to other things and initially suggested they ask someone else. But over the next three or four weeks, the idea nibbled away at me – it would be an escape to something light from the darkness of working on climate change – so I emailed to say that if no one else had been commissioned then I would do it.

I hired a research assistant, a talented young woman who'd come to me for advice on her honours thesis at ANU. Jemma Williams was a delight to work with because she injected so much enthusiasm into the project. More than that, I wanted to avoid the book being a memorial to baby boomer nostalgia, so Jemma's presence and advice helped me give it more appeal to young activists. I spent half of 2014 in the National Library's Petherick Reading Room for specialist writers, drawing often on the expertise of the research librarians, a fabulous resource too few people appreciate.

While others had written about protest movements, *What Do We Want?* is a book about the act of protest in all of its glorious variety, from the mass demonstrations of the moratorium movement, to the Knitting Nannas sitting atop tripods for climate action, to lone acts like that of Zelda D'Aprano chaining herself to a Commonwealth building in 1969 demanding equal pay for women. I had been a foot soldier at demonstrations in the 1970s, including an arrest for obstructing traffic at the 'Day of Rage' in Canberra in 1971. I admire citizens who get out onto the streets or into the forests intent on creating a better future.

To keep it manageable, I confined the protests to those of the main social movements. I wondered whether, as a hetero white man, I would cop some grief for presuming to tell the stories of the gay, women's and Indigenous rights movements. After it was published, no one expressed an objection. It may have helped that Germaine Greer agreed to write a foreword.

As the book progressed, the library managers became nervous. Conservative backbenchers had been denouncing the library for one of its exhibitions and the director-general was worried that my book, which would inevitably criticise conservatives, not least on climate change, would inflame them. I had included the infamous photo of Tony Abbott, by then the prime minister, standing in front of the 'Ditch the Witch' banner. When the library's board assigned a senior executive to review the draft text, a 'censorship' beacon was activated in my head. I asked my contact to send a message up the line saying that I would not agree to have my work bowdlerised in any way and hinted that a news story about the National Library of Australia, of all institutions, engaging in political censorship and historical revisionism would be damaging.

Good sense prevailed, but the process of getting the book from completed manuscript to boxes in a warehouse was extraordinarily slow. Working on the book provided a cheerful respite from my preoccupation with climate change, although when it finally appeared my hopes that it would make a splash quickly faded. It's true that the marketing of the book was minimal, but I had a strong expectation it would catch on, and to this day do not understand why that highly readable book didn't succeed. In 2021, five years after publication, I saw *What Do We Want?* remaindered in a display outside the NLA bookshop. What I had heard is true: it's dispiriting for an author to see their book remaindered.

Still, *What Do We Want?* was short-listed for non-fiction book of the year at the ACT Writers awards. The NLA's book promotions manager emailed to ask whether I'd be attending the awards night. 'So much happening that I thought I would skip it,' I replied guiltily. A few hours later, she emailed to tell me my book had won and she had accepted the award on my behalf. Serious guilt for not turning up. If I'm honest, I have a kind of local analogue of Australia's cultural cringe. At age eight, after a childhood in Canberra, I found myself on an ocean liner, P&O's *Arcadia*, spending eight weeks sailing dreamily to London via Colombo, Bombay, Aden and Gibraltar. We lived in London for two and a half years, twice touring the Continent. Canberra began to seem like a far-off and dull place. 'Still is,' I hear some readers thinking. But Canberra has changed enormously since then, and I can't imagine living anywhere else. Even so, the childhood prejudice remains.

§

In November 2015, I was in Paris for a conference on the Anthropocene held at the esteemed Collège de France and organised by the eminent anthropologist Philippe Descola, whose book *Beyond Nature and Culture* had caused a minor revolution in thinking. Although written with impressive scholarly detachment, I read it as reinforcing a romantic view of indigenous peoples whose uncorrupted reverence for nature holds the solution to our environmental problems. Too many progressive intellectuals want to characterise the Anthropocene concept as a product of Western colonial thinking. It drives me to despair. The Anthropocene is not a sociological concept but a *scientific* one, used by Earth scientists for a new epoch in the geological time scale. It represents a change in the way the Earth system itself functions, a change that will be visible in the rock record just like other divisions in the geological time scale.

Some of us have been defending the integrity of climate science against denialist claims that it is all politics and reflects the personal ambitions of a cabal of scientists, yet here people on the left are doing the same – treating a body of science as if it were a sociological or political category. One went so far as to tell the conference: 'The Anthropocene comes out of white supremacy.' Seriously. In the face of this epochal shift in human and Earth history, some are more interested in academic grandstanding. The problem is that some social science and humanities scholars find it impossible to separate the *fact* of human domination of the Earth – and there can be no better proof than the arrival of the Anthropocene – from the moral justification of human domination. Recognising humankind's extraordinary power over nature is not the same as defending it.

In one of the breaks, I conversed with Descola. He told me that my *Requiem* did not depress him because he believes in political activism.

'I am a militant,' he said, 'unlike Latour.' All of the scientific evidence shows that it's too late to undo much of the damage already done by carbon emissions. That is depressing for anyone who understands the implications, even if the worst damage can still be prevented by political activism. I took Descola's 'militant' stance as a coping strategy; it allows him to believe everything can be put back to where it was.

I had a newfound comrade-in-arms, Jacques Grinevald, a Swiss historian of science who was on my wavelength. We wrote a paper together debunking the argument that there is nothing new about the Anthropocene concept because the same idea was put forward in the nineteenth and early twentieth centuries. We showed that the predecessor concepts are simply not the same and could not have been because the Anthropocene concept was possible only after the development of Earth system science in the 1980s and 1990s. At the conference we had our first face-to-face meeting. Jacques was older than I imagined and in failing health. I suggested we go for dinner and took him to a magnificently decorated restaurant in the fifth arrondissement where we got a bit drunk and felt as if we had been close friends for decades.

On Saturday morning, the Collège de France conference was over and I sat in Les Editeurs, a café I frequented in the Odeon district. Sitting at a table beneath its giant Swiss railway clock, I was, as usual, being ignored by the waiters. I read that Obama had killed off the Keystone XL pipeline, interpreted as a means of building his credentials to broker a historical deal at the imminent climate change convention, COP 15 in Paris. A huge demonstration was being planned and Paris authorities were worried about 'black bloc' anarchists causing trouble, so they imposed border controls.

I had a well-placed contact working for the COP secretariat. He'd read *Growth Fetish*. We met for dinner at a bistro, Le Select on Boulevard du Montparnasse, which would become a favourite of mine. He gave me the secretariat gossip, including an internal debate over whether to invite Elon Musk to speak at the COP. Some were opposed because he was a threat to the European space industry. They prevailed. Around the world, the 'noise' created by the forthcoming conference was deafening. I was beginning to realise that, after years of wishful thinking, a decisive shift was occurring in the sentiment of global business. Instead of sticking their heads in the sand – or actively resisting the tide of science – corporates now saw that something historically profound is happening and they wanted to be a part of it.

From 30 November 2015, COP 15 was staged in a vast conference centre at Le Bourget on the outskirts of Paris. It was the fifth COP I had attended, and the mood was something new. Nations had already made commitments in advance that gave grounds for some optimism. But for me the real breakthrough of the conference was that big business had turned up for the first time, not the fossil fuel lobbyists but the biggest institutional investors, who were now engaged and worried.

A speech by Mark Carney, governor of the Bank of England, changed the way I thought. He said central bankers were now anxious that a rapid, structural shift in energy markets and the destruction of asset-value in some of the world's biggest companies would disrupt the global financial system. He called for an 'orderly transition' to a zero-carbon economy. As one business heavyweight put it, 'Investors are running ahead of governments.'

Yet the scientists were in another room tipping a bucket of cold water over us. Several of them, including Kevin Anderson and Hans Schellnhuber, calculated that country commitments brought to Paris were expected to limit warming to perhaps 3°C, which would be catastrophic.

I was torn. The Paris agreement was as good as could be hoped for. For the first time in years, I saw a glimmer of light, something to cling on to. Yet, the scientists were drawing a black curtain to shut out the light. I was suspended between emotional poles. Compared to the crushing 2009 conference in Copenhagen, Paris allowed us to breathe, if not too deeply.

The Paris agreement anticipated that the commitments made would be consolidated and extended when the parties reconvened after five years, at the Glasgow COP due in 2020. By the time COP 26 took place, in 2021, the IPCC's language had become much more urgent. Climate catastrophe could be avoided only through immediate, deep and sustained emission reductions. That would demand the rapid phase-out of fossil fuels. But the conference was plagued by foot-dragging and obstructionism, not least from Australia. The 'phase-out' of coal became a commitment to 'phase-down', and the major nations were unwilling to commit to the emission cuts needed to limit warming to 1.5°C or even 2°C.

The air was being sucked out of us. The thousands of young climate activists thronging the streets of Glasgow described the proceedings inside the conference hall as more 'blah, blah, blah' while the Earth burns. They feel as though they are suffocating.

21

Not a committee man

IN APRIL 2012, I received a phone call from Christine Milne, who had replaced Bob Brown as leader of the Greens. The Greens had reached an agreement with the Gillard government on a suite of climate policies built around a carbon pricing scheme. One element was the creation of the Climate Change Authority, modelled on the highly successful Climate Change Committee in the United Kingdom. The authority would advise the government on all climate policy measures, but particularly on the appropriate emission reduction targets for Australia. It would have nine members, including, ex officio, the chief scientist, at the time Ian Chubb. Christine told me that she had struck a confidential deal with the government according to which the Greens could choose three of the members. She wanted me to be one of them.

To be honest, I wasn't attracted to the idea. I didn't want the responsibility and I dreaded having to sit through meetings and agree to compromise positions on a subject I felt so strongly about. On policies I was flexible, but, as the author of *Requiem for a Species*, on the need to make deep cuts quickly I was unbending. Besides, I'm not good on committees – I'm impatient and I put people offside by being too vehement. Nevertheless, Christine was asking me, and I felt

I had an obligation to accept. To reject an opportunity to help shape Australia's climate policies merely because it would entail discomfort would be a serious ethical lapse. Had I known that, two prime ministers later, accepting would land me in an impossible ethical bind, I might have thought again.

For the Greens nominees, Christine wanted an ethicist, a climate scientist and an economist. When we met to choose the other two, she indicated her preference for individuals who are both expert and forceful so that they could carry the day in authority debates. It was not too hard to settle on John Quiggin, who was brilliant on the economics of climate change, willing to take on anyone and hard to beat in an argument. David Karoly, professor of atmospheric science at the University of Melbourne, was also an obvious candidate. David was highly regarded, completely on top of the science and forthright in his views, a rare combination. When Christine sent the three names to the minister for climate change, Greg Combet, he made it very clear that Clive Hamilton was unacceptable to the government. Christine asked why and Combet replied that I had said all kinds of outrageous things in public. Christine asked what they were, so at their next meeting Combet handed Christine a list of my outrageous statements, compiled by one of his staff. Christine read through the list and said, 'Well, I agree with all of those,' and reaffirmed her desire to have me appointed.

Combet was adamant, but Christine was not one for backing down. The appointments were discussed in cabinet. Some ministers were implacably opposed to my appointment, especially Martin Ferguson, the former ACTU president. He had participated in the launch of a denialist tract, and Andrew Bolt had called on him to come out of the 'closet' and join them. After politics, Ferguson would take up a position with the oil and gas lobby. He had denounced my work on climate change more than once and I had him among my 'dirty dozen' of those most responsible for preventing climate action. The impasse was resolved only when the decision landed on the desk of Prime Minister Gillard, who felt obliged to honour the deal Labor had made with the Greens.

In June a call came through from Steven Kennedy, deputy secretary of the Department of Climate Change, informing me of my appointment to the authority. The commitment would amount to two or three days' work each month and the remuneration was $25,000 a year. Christine phoned the next day to tell me that Greg Combet was worried about how *The Daily Telegraph* would greet my appointment. His office had asked Christine to prep me for the difficult questions, should they come. They didn't, although it was easy to see how the *Telegraph* could have manufactured a scandal out of it.

When the three of us – Karoly, Quiggin, Hamilton – turned up to the first meeting of the authority, held in a pleasant boardroom on the tenth floor of a Collins Street tower, it soon became apparent that we were the only appointees who knew anything about climate change. I heard later that the government had asked Ross Garnaut to join the authority, but he said he'd agree only if he were appointed to chair it. Garnaut was the author of the most important report on the subject in Australia, and I think his request (if he indeed made it) was fair enough. But the government wanted former Reserve Bank governor Bernie Fraser to chair it. Bernie has tremendous gravitas and, I would discover, is a superb chairperson when hard negotiations are underway. His disadvantage was that he knew virtually nothing about the subject. At the authority's first press conference, held at the Hyatt Hotel in Canberra, David Karoly and I winced when Bernie referred to the 'two per cent target' instead of the 'two degrees target'. However, Bernie was a true professional who took his commitments seriously and within a year or so had made himself an expert on climate policy.

It was an education for the other members too. Basic concepts like 'parts per million' and 'carbon dioxide equivalent' had to be explained. Early on, one member dismayed some of us by proposing we should 'hear the other side of the science'. She received a firm put-down and did not raise it again. On another occasion, one said: 'Explain it so that us girls can understand it.' One of the 'girls' was Labor favourite Heather Ridout, who'd recently stepped down as chief executive of the Australian Industry Group. She continued to act as an advocate for industry, sometimes interjecting with 'business will not accept that'. I reminded her that her duty was to act as an independent expert rather than as a lobbyist.

While some members of the authority were on training wheels, the secretariat was a racing machine. The CEO was Anthea Harris – savvy, professional, fully on top of climate policy and blessed with what one industry insider called 'disarming pleasantness'. With senior economist Kath Rowley providing much of the brainpower, every argument received careful, evidence-based scrutiny. The secretariat reminded me of the one at the Resource Assessment Commission, which attracted some of the very best and brightest. It's no great revelation that many of the smartest young people in Australia want to preserve the natural environment for the future.

§

The most important task given to the authority was to recommend to the government emission reduction targets over the short, medium and long term. The 'Targets and Progress Review' was a big and complex job that took up most of 2013. Board meetings were often tortuous, expertly handled by Bernie and Anthea as we wound our way through issue after issue, concept after concept, occasionally bringing in experts to drive home a point or a perspective. My interventions were sometimes unnecessarily adversarial or dismissive. It was a small comfort to recall a comment once made by a friend, 'Yes, but that's part of what drives you, isn't it?'

In deciding on emission targets, one first has to decide what is Australia's 'fair share' of global emissions. For that, you need an ethical principle. I had been arguing for the principle of 'contraction and convergence' since 1998, after I came across the idea at COP 3 in Kyoto. Under this scheme, global emissions would decline each year until the total reaches a safe level in, say, 2050 (the contraction). At the same time, every nation's share would be determined by its population, with each person's emissions converging on the same number, say, one tonne a year. Over time, every person in the world would have the same emission allocation. Ethically, it is the only defensible global principle. John and David backed it, as Bernie soon did, guided by the secretariat. It's a radical principle, but the more conservative members of the authority, knowing little about ethical principles, were unable to argue for an alternative.

Given my history of trying to alert Australians to the urgency of the task and the depth of the cuts needed, I knew I'd be reluctant to put my name to a report I could not defend. At every opportunity I pushed for more stringent targets. When we had to decide on a higher or lower probability of limiting warming to 2°C, I saw accepting a 67 per cent chance of limiting warming to 2°C as meaning a 33 per cent chance of screwing the world. To me, even a 75 per cent chance was too much of a risk. When it came to recommending medium-term targets, I favoured a 25 per cent rather than a 15 per cent cut in emissions by 2020 and much deeper cuts by 2030. And I was opposed to any recommendation that Australia should rely on buying emission reduction permits overseas, arguing we should not allow any delay to the transformation of our energy-intensive industries. All of these were argued out in the meetings and in email exchanges.

When the final draft of the report arrived, it did not go far enough for me. My view was closer to those in the submissions from some environmental groups, including the Climate Institute. I agonised over what to do and flagged that I was not sure I could sign on to the report. Bernie and I had some candid but respectful conversations. He's a masterful negotiator. In truth, Bernie reminds me strongly of my father, both men of calm disposition and great integrity, and I didn't want to disappoint him. In negotiations with Anthea and Bernie over several days, we agreed on some changes in emphasis and language that made it easier for me to go along with the majority.

The compromises on both sides were enough to allow me to defend the report in good conscience.

The most important recommendation was that Australia should reduce its carbon emissions by 40 to 60 per cent by 2030 (compared to 2000 levels). I argued we would need to reach the upper limit of that range if Australia were not to free ride on other countries, including poor ones. When the authority released its report in February 2014, the 'at least 40 per cent' number was widely reported and discussed in the media and the policy community. It quickly became the accepted benchmark for what Australia had to do, with the Labor Party soon promising to cut emissions by 45 per cent by 2030 (on 2005 levels). The Climate Change Authority had acquired a reputation for high-quality work and was broadly seen as independent, science-based and professional.

§

In September 2013, an Abbott-led Coalition won the election after a relentless scare campaign, amplified by the Murdoch press, against the Labor–Greens 'great big new tax', that is, the carbon pricing mechanism. An anti-science zealot, Abbott promised to abolish all of the emission reduction policies and agencies created by the Rudd and Gillard governments, including the Climate Change Authority. Several members of the authority resigned within weeks of the election, saying it no longer had the support of the government. I took the view that we had been appointed to a body created by the parliament and would stay on until the parliament decided otherwise. The authority had shown it could do high-quality, influential policy work, and I didn't want to see that go down the drain with the organisation.

Bernie Fraser, John Quiggin and David Karoly took the same view, and soon we were the only ones left except for Ian Chubb ex officio. Five was a quorum. Understandably, Anthea Harris and a number of other staff members began looking for more secure employment and departed within a few months.

One of Abbott's early moves was to set up a tame committee, headed by mining industry denier Dick Warburton and including ABARE's Brian Fisher (who appeared in forums side-by-side with fossil fuel lobbyists), to provide reasons to slash the Renewable Energy Target, reformed in 2010 by the Rudd government to set a target of 20 per cent of electricity supply to be provided by renewables by 2020. It duly recommended its abolition. The government also set up a review of Australia's targets to give it an excuse to reject the 40 to 60 per cent emission reductions in 2030 recommended by the Climate Change Authority (or 45 to 63 per cent relative to 2005 levels). In August 2015 Abbott announced that the government now aimed to reduce emissions by 26 to 28 per cent on 2005 levels by 2030, the same target as the Bush administration. That remains Coalition policy today, unchanged even after COP 26 in Glasgow in 2021. It's a do-nothing target, probably around what the market, with state government policies, was at that time on track to deliver anyway and well below those set by comparable countries. It was, of course, completely at odds with the science.

The government did not have the numbers in the Senate to abolish the carbon price scheme agreed between the Gillard government and the Greens. Nor could it scrap various other parts of the emission reduction machinery, at least not without the votes of the four Palmer United senators, including their leader, Clive Palmer, the billionaire mining magnate. The Palmer United senators were unsympathetic to climate policies, having campaigned to repeal the carbon price. But Palmer was in no hurry. After months of deadlock, Ben Oquist, now strategy director at the Australia Institute, began quietly talking to Palmer about saving the Renewable Energy Target, along with the Clean Energy Finance Corporation (another Gillard–Greens initiative to help fund clean energy) and the Climate Change Authority. In a bizarre twist, Don Henry, the executive director of the Australian Conservation Foundation, persuaded former US vice-president and climate change guru Al Gore to endorse Palmer's 'shift to the centre', and the pair of them staged a joint news conference at Parliament

House where Palmer looked out of his depth and Gore, after congratulating Palmer on his 'outstanding statement', looked like he was hoping no one back in the States would hear about it.

In October 2014, Palmer did a deal with the government endorsing Abbott's 'direct action' plan that would pay polluters to reduce emissions and scrapping the carbon price in exchange for the retention of the Climate Change Authority. The authority was given the task of conducting an inquiry into Palmer's proposal for an emissions trading scheme. Palmer also joined Labor and the Greens in refusing to vote for the dilution of the Renewable Energy Target.

In contrast to the Australia Institute's political deal-making, the Climate Institute argued for policy based on science. CEO John Connor had been lobbying senators not to vote for the Palmer–Abbott deal, arguing that it would be disastrous to pay the big polluters to keep polluting. The existing laws were working effectively to cut emissions and should be kept, he maintained, a view I supported. It was intriguing for me to watch the Australia Institute and the Climate Institute, two organisations I had created, at the heart of these events but taking sharply different positions.

While the authority had been reprieved, the government's hostility towards us was unabated. Abbott's environment minister, Greg Hunt – whose public commentary as shadow environment minister had led me to the opinion that he was the most mendacious minister ever to grace the front bench – continued his public sniping at the authority. The government refused to appoint replacement members and wound down the budget.

The authority had its work to do and we got on with it. Over time, however, the war of attrition proved too much for Bernie Fraser. He had been obliged to meet with Hunt periodically to report on the authority's activities. Bernie was always calm, considered and firm – he had, after all, been Treasury secretary and Reserve Bank governor under Paul Keating. At obligatory meetings in Hunt's office, the minister subjected him to a stream of abuse – accusing him of pursuing his own agendas, being a Labor Party stooge and suchlike – all in front of staff. Hunt is known for his abusive outbursts in private. Already semi-retired, by September 2015 Bernie had decided he did not have to cop it any longer and resigned.

§

A couple of weeks later, Malcolm Turnbull defeated Abbott to become prime minister. The atmospherics changed. Turnbull wanted policies that would facilitate Australia's transition to a new energy economy, but he was hamstrung by backbenchers hostile to any climate action, with some members quite willing to blow up the government. He and Hunt quietly hatched a plan to sneak some kind of disguised emissions trading scheme past the backbench. Part of the plan was to appoint a number of new members to the Climate Change Authority, which would recommend the scheme. And so in October 2015, five new Coalition appointees turned up, with Wendy Craik as the new chair. I knew Wendy a little; at Telopea Park High School she was a couple of years ahead of me, and I'd bumped into her once or twice when she headed the National Farmers' Federation and the Great Barrier Reef Marine Park Authority. She had an image of reasonableness and I hoped she was serious about climate change.

At board meetings, I now had sitting next to me former National Party politician John Sharp. As Howard's transport minister, he had been forced to step down after allegations he overstated his travel expenses. He had subsequently made a business career but remained close to the Nationals. I guessed he was picked for the authority position by National Party leader Warren Truss. He told me that he was there to make sure Turnbull never tried to introduce a price on carbon and that in his pocket he had a copy of the National Party's coalition agreement in which Turnbull promised not to do so.

Across the table was my adversary of earlier days Kate Carnell, now head of the Australian Chamber of Commerce and Industry and a Liberal Party favourite. At least Danny Price, an energy consultant, knew something about climate change; in fact, he was on a mission to see a 'baseline and credit' emissions trading system introduced, a version of emissions trading that enjoyed little expert support but which had been trialled, under Danny's guidance, in New South Wales. As opposition leader in 2008, Turnbull had invited Danny to address the Coalition party room on the benefits of emissions trading. He was the one to reveal to me that he and the others were appointed to carry out Hunt's cunning plan to come up with a disguised trading scheme. I know deniers can be thick, I thought to myself, but they are not so stupid that they would fail to notice an emissions trading scheme being slipped past them in the party room. Besides, it was not the authority's role to come up with tricky devices to help the prime minister out of a political jam.

Hunt soon made use of a provision in the legislation to appoint an additional 'associate member' of the authority, Andrew Macintosh. Andrew was the red-hot environmentalist I had recruited to the Australia Institute a decade earlier but who had since become a close adviser to Greg Hunt. He had switched sides.

§

When Ian Chubb's term as chief scientist expired in January 2016 he was replaced by Alan Finkel, who automatically became a member of the Climate Change Authority. As a neuroscientist, Chubb didn't know much about climate science, but he respected those who did, understood the basics and supported firm action. Finkel knew little about any kind of science as far as I could tell. At authority meetings he never expressed any concern about the impacts of climate change, gave no impression he understood the urgency of the need to cut emissions, and spent much of his first meetings pushing nuclear power. I was not surprised to read in March 2021 that energy minister and closet climate science denier Angus Taylor had appointed Finkel to embark on an international 'lobbying blitz' to persuade others that, despite all evidence to the contrary, the Morrison government took climate change seriously and Australia had a great record.

The vehicle for the realisation of the Turnbull–Hunt plan was a 'special review' into the feasibility of an emissions trading scheme that the government had promised to Clive Palmer. Hunt now commissioned the authority to conduct the review. At meetings, a pattern soon emerged in which the new appointees built a set of policies based more on political expediency than good science, let alone defensible ethical principles. In the early months, I believed that the strength of argument and the facts on the ground would see the direction of the board shift to a position closer to the one laid out so compellingly in the authority's first landmark report on Australia's targets. After a few meetings, it became clear that the new board members had not read that report, which some later admitted to without apology.

By early 2016, David Karoly and I had begun to swap notes on our growing disquiet about what the authority was going to recommend and whether we would feel comfortable putting our names to it. In our view, the internal draft of the special review was inconsistent with Australia's international obligations, essentially endorsed the Abbott government's failing climate change policies, and did not meet the legislated criteria for providing advice. We expressed our concerns at board meetings. In July 2016 we decided that we would each put our reservations in writing and in detail to the chair, but her response indicated little interest, and certainly not enough to modify the course the board was set on.

David and I considered our options. We could go along with the majority, we could resign, or we could write our own minority report (the options analysed in Albert Hirschman's classic *Exit, Voice, and Loyalty*). I wondered whether there was a precedent for a minority report from a statutory authority, but I could not find anything. I decided to phone Bernie, who was tending his horses on his property out past Queanbeyan. He understood our dilemma immediately and was sympathetic. He was unaware of any precedent for a minority report from a statutory body but could not think of a reason that would prevent us from doing it. Bernie did not give his explicit backing to our plan, but I came away from the call feeling that he was behind us. I asked John Quiggin if he would like to join us in a minority report, but he felt he could live with the majority one.

On 17 August, David and I wrote to Wendy telling her that, in our view, the final draft report was inconsistent with Australia's international obligations and that the recommended policies were inadequate to meet the emission reductions needed to stay within our carbon budget. We said we believed that our views had had little influence and we had therefore decided to write a minority report. We asked if we could call on the secretariat to provide a small amount of production assistance and requested that our minority report be bound into the majority report.

Wendy replied suggesting we discuss our concerns at the meeting due a couple of days later.

David and I met up beforehand to consider how best to approach the meeting. We avoided arriving early and when the meeting began it turned hostile quickly. David and I each took several minutes to explain our position. The members were furious with us and in no mood for compromise.

Wendy had come well prepared. She told us we should consider our positions and reminded us that if we published anything that drew on material that we were privileged to as members of the authority then we would be liable to legal action. Other members were jeering us. I was pretty fired up, of course, and suggested to the chair that, unlike the previous incumbent, she had shown little interest in accommodating other views and that perhaps she should consider her position. As we saw it, we were doing our job as members of the authority in good faith and were unwilling to go along with riding instructions given to the authority by Greg Hunt.

Although I knew we would lose, I asked for a formal vote on our requests for help from the secretariat and incorporation of a minority report into the main publication. I wanted it on the record. They were the first votes held at authority meetings.

The hostility directed at us only made David and me more determined and less likely to consider the sensitivities of the majority members when it came to expressing ourselves in our report and subsequent media. I wrote to Wendy a couple of days later expressing my dismay at what had transpired and her role in it. 'It is a fact of life in democratic societies,' I noted, 'that attempts at silencing dissent often make dissenters more determined.'

§

A few days after the meeting, David and I wrote to the new minister for environment and energy, Josh Frydenberg, informing him that we had decided to prepare a minority report. We told him that our requests for our report to be treated by the authority in a collaborative manner had been rebuffed. Frydenberg replied a week later, saying that if we intend to publish our own report, 'That is a decision for you,' adding that the Act 'makes it clear that the Authority can produce only one report'. Well, it would hardly endorse more than one.

We worked hard over the next two weeks to complete our report. On 5 September 2016, five days after the majority report was released, we published ours on the website of the Climate Council. We wrote an opinion piece for *The Sydney Morning Herald* explaining our decision, arguing that the majority report lacked credibility because it accepted the government's target of 26 to 28 per cent, which is inconsistent with the science and Australia's international commitments.

The 'unprecedented split' in the authority attracted extensive media attention. Our stance received strong support from progressive analysts and environment groups, but also some criticism from various pundits accusing us of wanting all or nothing and praising the majority for their 'clever' strategy to break the political deadlock. My successor at the Australia Institute, Richard Denniss, was among them, arguing that the majority were 'giving the Coalition a way out of the climate policy cul-de-sac'. I pointed out in a response a few days later that the political strategising was never more than wishful thinking constructed from a delicate series of hypotheticals. It assumed that sceptical backbenchers were too dopey to realise what's going on, that Turnbull was still the old Malcolm committed to taking action, that the prime minister had a lot of political capital, that he would spend it on climate change, and that Labor would go along with it all.

It made no sense. Yet it was on the basis of this particular reading of the political tea-leaves that David and I were expected to sign on to the report. When the 'pragmatic' path has zero chance of getting up, it becomes a delusional path. Moreover, while the pundits were free to advocate policies based on their judgements about what may or may not get the numbers in parliament, as members of a Commonwealth statutory authority with a legislated obligation to provide independent advice, we were not.

A couple of days after our report was published, Wendy Craik posted a brief response to recent claims in the media: 'I ... reject strongly any suggestion that the Authority has been politically influenced or motivated by political considerations in its work on the special review.' Any suggestion that the authority is not independent, she said, 'is both offensive and untrue'. And she vehemently rejected any suggestion that 'secretariat staff are inexpert or incompetent', which was weird because I wasn't aware of any such suggestions, and certainly not from David and myself.

I would have been happy to skip the next board meeting, but that would have been seen as a sign of weakness. When the meeting began, the bitterness spilled out, but we stood our ground. We were told we should resign, but that wasn't going to happen. It was ugly. In the lift on the way out of the meeting, one member of the authority threatened David Karoly with legal action, which sickened me. Afterwards, various members were emailing each other about taking legal advice and launching defamation action. I suggested a public debate instead, but there was no interest in that. When one member accused me of being an 'extremist', David replied that if I was an extremist then he must be one too. In my view, the chair should not have allowed it to get out of control like this.

Events went poorly for the majority. Even their modest 'pragmatic' suggestions for policy change were met dismissively by Minister

Frydenberg, and the main recommendations were soon rejected. The government shelved the report almost before it came out. Three months later, all hopes that Malcolm Turnbull would be the conservative leader who took serious action on climate change were crushed when he called for new, publicly subsidised coal-fired power plants to be built.

I had been refusing to resign as a matter of principle, but this was the last straw. Remaining on the authority was not just a waste of time but made me feel compromised. In my letter of resignation to Frydenberg in February 2017, I said that it was now 'crystal clear that the government has no interest in sensible climate policy'. My term was up in several months anyway. John Quiggin and even Danny Price resigned a month later, with John saying the government was beholden to right-wing extremists and Danny saying the government was immobilised by 'political panic'.

The authority secretariat had been shifted out of its flash offices in Melbourne into the environment department in Canberra, and its staffing was cut to only three or four. It never recovered, limping on in obscurity. The story of the Climate Change Authority went from tragedy to farce in 2021 when the minister for energy and emissions reduction, Angus Taylor, announced the appointment of former Origin Energy chief Grant King as the new chairman. King had been a paid-up member of the greenhouse mafia. Along with the appointment of other fossil fuel lobbyists as members, the authority, created with such high hopes, had become a dark joke of the Morrison government.

22

The China turn

IN THE WINTER of 2016, I was despondent about the future unfolding in a warming world. I was finishing the draft of *Defiant Earth*, the third in a 'trilogy' on climate change after *Requiem* and *Earthmasters*. Over two decades, I had written several books on climate change, penned hundreds of opinion articles, given two or three hundred public talks, and issued warnings through the media uncountable times. I had run for parliament, co-convened a high-level international taskforce, and fought for stronger recommendations out of the Climate Change Authority.

None of it had made any difference. The faint hope conjured by the arrival of Malcolm Turnbull as prime minister had been snuffed out by deniers on his backbench. The world was careening towards disaster with Australia leading the pack of carbon polluters.

I had done all I could. I had recited every argument. I had nothing more to say.

So now what was I going to do?

In August 2016, newspapers began reporting on large donations being made to the main political parties by wealthy Chinese or Chinese Australian businesspeople. The gifts were generous, to say the least. Why are they doing that, I wondered? What do they want?

It soon emerged that New South Wales Labor Party powerbroker Senator Sam Dastyari was at the centre of the donations. He took the money then fronted a media conference for Chinese-language journalists. Standing next to the most generous donor, Sydney property developer Huang Xiangmo, he contradicted his party's stance on the South China Sea and mouthed Chinese Communist Party (CCP) talking points. Along with revelations that a mysterious Chinese Australian businessman had paid off his personal debts, it was obvious to me that something very big and very dirty had wormed its way into Australia's political system, the more so when journalists began reporting the links of some of these wealthy donors to the CCP.

The implications of this are huge, I thought to myself. It's one thing for homegrown corporates and lobbyists to be corrupting our political system; it's quite another for an authoritarian foreign power to be doing it. It offended me. I decided that this would be my next book.

I had no expertise on China. As an undergraduate I had taken a course covering the Chinese Revolution, raising a metaphorical fist in solidarity with the oppressed people of China liberating themselves from the yoke of colonialism and feudalism under the bold leadership of Mao Zedong and the Chinese Communist Party. In other words, I had the standard leftist view that somehow managed to gloss over events like the famine caused by Mao's Great Leap Forward and the terror of the Cultural Revolution.

On the other hand, I was expert in Australian politics, and the main issue appeared to be the corruptibility of our political system. So three months later, after fulfilling other commitments, I immersed myself in the China influence question. It was a welcome distraction from my climate-induced despondency. If only I'd known what I was getting myself into.

Whenever one decides to work in an unfamiliar area, the strategy is twofold: read widely and talk to the experts. I needed to establish first up that no one else was writing the book I had in mind; if they were, I would probably have abandoned the project. Asking around, not only was no one else writing such a book but the experts I met over the next months were uniformly encouraging. Some were keen to see the China influence problem injected into the mainstream of public debate and they knew I had a track record of engaging the public.

In November 2016 I began research for what would be *Silent Invasion*. As soon as I had a clear outline of the book, I wrote a proposal to my publisher, Allen & Unwin, and sent it to Elizabeth Weiss. She was immediately enthusiastic and encouraging. Elizabeth too had been alarmed by the stories of CCP influence in Australia. She was a committed practitioner of Tibetan Buddhism so had an understanding of the repressive character of the regime. A contract was soon signed, with a substantial advance on royalties, and over the next months I felt reassured by the fact that Allen & Unwin, the company voted publisher of the year a dozen times, was strongly backing my work.

Over the first months, as I absorbed from the experts more and more about the nature, methods and ambitions of the Chinese Communist Party, my understanding of the world was transformed. The comforting belief that democracy and liberal principles, for all their faults, would prevail over authoritarianism was severely shaken. When I realised that the economic, technological and military power of China was on a trajectory soon to overtake that of the United States, and that an increasingly aggressive and totalitarian CCP regime was using its growing power to intimidate other nations into submission, I became afraid for the future in a new way.

§

For decades, the left has been able to exercise its anti-Americanism safe in the belief that the only alternative to an imperfect democracy is a better democracy. Those of us opening our eyes to the dramatic shift in global power into the hands of the ruthless men of the CCP began to worry less about the faults in the system of liberal democracy and more about the survival of the system itself.

Virtually all the well-informed academic experts and journalists I consulted and learned from were politically progressive, and their absence of ideological rigidity is precisely the trait that allowed them to see the changing world for what it is, rather than filter the truth through lenses of anti-Americanism, Mao-inspired romanticism or anti-racist virtue.

Over the months, I met with a broad range of people with experience and knowledge of the CCP's activities in Australia: Chinese Australians, public servants, academics, university executives, scientists, journalists – more than 150 meetings. One of the most felicitous occurred at the start, on 9 November 2016, the day of Donald Trump's election, when Alex Joske arrived in my office. I had read an article written by him in *Woroni*, the ANU student newspaper, about an incident on campus in which the head of the Chinese Students and Scholars Association barged into the campus pharmacy and aggressively demanded, on pain of a student boycott, that copies of the Falun Gong newspaper *Epoch Times* be removed. I tracked down the author and asked if we could meet. Alex was quietly spoken, composed and very young. I would later learn that his mother is Chinese, or rather of Chinese heritage, and that he had spent several years in Beijing as a child when his father, a Treasury official, was attached to the Australian embassy. He was fluent in Mandarin. Our conversation was fascinating; I could see immediately that here was a remarkable young man. As he was leaving, Alex said that if I were looking for a research assistant, he would be happy to help.

Within weeks I had Alex signed on as a part-time research assistant at Charles Sturt University, paid for from my research allocation. He developed an exceptional ability to ferret out vital information from Chinese-language sources and then provide an interpretation. Within a couple of years, this unknown second-year student at ANU would come to be seen by the community of CCP analysts as one of our most valuable assets. Everyone wanted him to work for them – and he was only twenty-one. Never in my career have I come across anyone with so much intellectual maturity at such a young age.

Looking back on the early months, I realise how crude was my understanding of the CCP. I had no idea how it operated in Australia, including the subtle and complex ways it insinuates itself into the Chinese Australian community. Outside China, there were only a couple of dozen people around the world who have studied the CCP's overseas influence operations, but a good proportion of them were in Australia (and New Zealand in the case of Anne-Marie Brady). One is Geoff Wade, a China scholar employed by the Parliamentary Library with an enormous depth of knowledge. Geoff provides an indispensable stream of tweets simply pointing out the activities of united front groups and individuals, that is, those who are part of the CCP's overseas influence operations. So valuable is his work that in 2021, a number of Beijing sympathisers attempted to have him fired from his job and published defamatory articles about him. Fortunately, in Parliament House there are many people who place a high value on his work.

Although not a CCP expert, the ABC's then political editor Chris Uhlmann had broken some important stories on CCP influence, so I was keen to meet him. I remembered him from years ago as a conservative candidate for the ACT Legislative Assembly and didn't expect to have too much in common politically. But on China we were as one, and it was a lesson in how, whatever the other differences, a commitment to the principles of liberal democracy ought to unite left and right. Chris was a fascinating source of insights into the more shadowy world of Canberra politics, including the politics of the intelligence community. It's the stuff that rarely makes its way into the media but which is essential for a deeper understanding of what's going on.

Arguably, no one has done more to expose and explain CCP influence in Australia than John Garnaut, first as a Fairfax correspondent in Beijing, then as an adviser to Prime Minister Turnbull and his department. I first met up with John early in my research at a cafe in Barton in Canberra's bureaucratic district. He seemed to know everything and everyone. His insights into China and the CCP were, for my purposes, unparalleled. As the son of Ross Garnaut, a Hawke government ambassador to China, he'd spent some years growing up in Beijing. I was relieved when he said he was delighted I was writing a book on CCP influence. John then said something wise: our problem in Australia is that we do not know how to think about China's interference. The comment struck me because, even at that early stage, I knew I didn't know how to think about China. I knew only enough to see that my accustomed ways of understanding the world had no slot into which this problem could be placed. I was beginning a process of remapping the world. As we parted, he made a comment whose significance I didn't really understand at the time. He said, 'You know, I am glad it's *you* writing this book, Clive.' 'Why?' I asked. 'Because you are from the left.'

Australians in general, and I had been as guilty as the next person, had all been swept along by the rhetoric of 'the Asian century', lulled by our self-congratulatory multicultural model, or reassured by our patronising view of societies to our north seemingly less sophisticated than ours. For those on the left of politics, the nostalgia of Gough Whitlam's early recognition of the People's Republic of China (PRC) in 1972 and the romance of a vast people 'liberating themselves' was like a whiff of chloroform that made us insensible to the true nature of the regime in Beijing. For some, the drug had such a powerful effect that even today, after all of the cruelties and bullying of the regime are plain to anyone, they cannot shake off their old beliefs.

I soon realised that for four decades, the most powerful people setting Australia's foreign policy all came out of that milieu, from Whitlam's decisive shift and then the Hawke–Keating government policy of resetting Australia's economic future in Asia, where 'Asia' morphed into China – Allan Gyngell, Peter Drysdale, Stephen FitzGerald, Dennis Richardson, Ross Garnaut, Gareth Evans, Geoff Raby, Ken Henry. They had drunk the Kool Aid of China's 'peaceful rise'. They were especially influential in the Labor Party, and they dominated the Department of Foreign Affairs and Trade (DFAT) and Treasury, where keeping Beijing happy became second nature. In DFAT's words, we must 'respect the differences in our political systems and values'; this was regarded as mature foreign policy. Tell that to the Uyghurs.

As I consulted more experts, and especially as I spoke with more Chinese Australians with direct experience, I began to appreciate the fanaticism and relentlessness of the CCP regime. It became clear that the CCP, as a matter of ideology, is not constrained by any respect for the rights or dignity of the individual. It was sinister, and the more I understood about the CCP's activities, the more uneasy I became. In November 2016 I was given an early warning by John Fitzgerald, probably Australia's most respected China scholar and at the time the president of the Australian Academy of the Humanities. With deep roots into the Chinese community, John had been almost alone in trying to alert Australians to the dangers of CCP interference. We first met in a cafe in Degraves Street in Melbourne. As I described my proposed book, John expressed his support; he knew me by reputation, and I guess he thought I was capable of pulling it off. His advice and backing throughout the saga of the book would prove invaluable to me.

As our meeting wound up, John told me I should assume 'they' are monitoring my communications. They may already be aware of my plans because I had been emailing him. 'Working in this area is dangerous,' he said. 'People have been killed.' As I left our meeting, I felt a dread inside. A number of very well-informed people would urge me to be careful about my personal safety. These warnings were more disconcerting because they alluded to a danger coming from a world that was opaque to me. At times I allayed my fears with an internal dialogue. I have been taking on powerful interests for quite a long time, I thought, I know how to do it and how to protect myself. What is different in this case? After all, I'm just an academic, so I can't be that threatening to the CCP. And I am in Australia where we have the rule of law and agencies whose job it is to protect citizens.

Still, it was troubling, and the more I learned about how the CCP operates, the more those protections started to seem flimsy. Looking back now, I can see that I did not really know *how* to be vigilant.

It would take two or three tumultuous years before I felt I knew what I was dealing with.

I was becoming more concerned about my safety, mainly my cyber safety but also my personal security. I began to wonder whether the microphones and cameras in my phone and computers were being hacked. Mixing with China analysts in Australia meant I learned about communicating through encrypted platforms, mainly Signal for phones and ProtonMail for emails. But I resented this cloak-and-dagger crap. I was an academic writing a book in a free country, yet the Chinese state seemed to have a presence everywhere. I saw it as sinister and it unsettled me in a way that was hard to escape. Still, I never considered giving up and filling my consciousness with something more benign.

§

One of my earliest links into the Chinese Australian community was John Hu (or Hugh), a former Liberal Party member of the Parramatta council who had helped set up a pro-democracy organisation of Chinese Australians. When we met in the cafe on the top floor of the Museum of Contemporary Art at Circular Quay, John and I hit it off immediately. He would prove to be an excellent source of information. I think he saw my book as a means to give vent to the concerns of many Chinese Australians about CCP influence in their adopted home. I was beginning to learn that almost all of the 'spokespersons for the Chinese community' that the media quoted and the politicians liked to be photographed with were, in fact, linked to CCP united front groups. Pro-Beijing people had over the years systematically taken over virtually all of the Chinese community and professional organisations, effectively silencing people like John.

I was also learning that most Chinese Australians who value living in a free country and hate Beijing's interference were too afraid to say so because the CCP had ways of punishing them. I heard story after story of businesses in Australia being boycotted, of advertising drying up under pressure from the consulate, of social ostracism, of anonymous threatening phone calls, and of ageing mothers in China being heavied by the security police. For me, this was another world I had no idea existed in Australia. It offended me deeply; no Australian ought to be intimidated and silenced this way. This is a free country – they have rights. But my Australia is not the Australia many Chinese Australians live in.

John Hu arranged a dinner with a few of his pro-democracy friends. One evening I stepped through a door off Ashfield's dingy shopping strip and mounted the stairs to a hidden Chinese restaurant. Ashfield has a long history as a suburb preferred by Sydney's Chinese immigrants, including the 1989 Tiananmen generation allowed to stay by Bob Hawke. Newer migrants have tended to concentrate in Ryde and Chatswood. As a result, Chinese-heritage residents of Ashfield tend to be more critical of the CCP compared to those north of the harbour.

It was a convivial dinner, and they soon opened up and shared their stories. Those who speak out against the CCP are not typical of the Chinese community, but they are the ones most alert to Beijing's intrusions. I'd been wondering how the Chinese community in Australia divides between those supportive of the Chinese government, those opposed to it and those indifferent or who want to avoid politics. I had no idea, so I asked my dinner companions. They offered a number of guesses, and I wrote in *Silent Invasion* that one of those present 'estimated those with strong pro-Beijing sentiments at twenty to thirty per cent'. I am accustomed to critics wilfully twisting my words, but I have to admit to being gobsmacked at Bob Carr's distortion when he characterised my reporting of the guesses by some Chinese Australians as 'Hamilton wrote that up to 40 percent of the Chinese in Australia are disloyal'.

At every meeting with an expert, Bob Carr's name would soon be mentioned. The former foreign minister had just been appointed, reportedly as the personal choice of Huang Xiangmo, to direct the Huang-funded Australia-China Relations Institute at the University of Technology Sydney, a think tank that took such 'an unabashedly positive and optimistic view of the Australia–China relationship' (in Carr's words) that it was already the butt of jokes. Everyone was watching Carr, wondering why he had become such a strident supporter of the Chinese government. Later, when I travelled to Beijing, the Australian journalists told me he was a frequent visitor. Clearly, 'Beijing Bob', as he was known, would feature prominently in the book.

I also became aware of the role of ANU academic Hugh White when he spoke at a conference put on by Bob Carr. His argument, made over and over, is simple: China will soon be the biggest economic power, it wants dominance in the region and is much more determined to achieve dominance than the US is to retain its place, and Beijing is more willing to use nuclear weapons than Washington. It's therefore inevitable that Washington will abandon the Asia-Pacific, leaving Australia no option but to align itself with China. I was appalled at this, not so much for its intellectual crudity and lack of historical understanding (White would argue that it is not necessary to understand the CCP, only GDP and nukes matter) but for its moral bankruptcy. He has argued we must capitulate to the CCP regime, suggesting it wouldn't be so bad to be a client state and maybe our system isn't that great. We might value our democratic society and independence as a nation, he's written, but 'alas' (it's his favourite word), that's not how it's going to turn out. So it's better if we just accept it.

Frankly, this capitulationism dismayed me. I think of all of the people throughout history – the dissidents, the freedom fighters, the anti-colonial resistance, the small nations next to overbearing neighbours, like Ukraine – who have bravely defended independence and freedoms against a big power. Then I look at this comfortable academic who says that, alas, the more powerful always prevail so we too must accede, sacrificing our independence and, if necessary, giving up some of our everyday freedoms.

23

Spies and informants

As I immersed myself more deeply into the shadowy world of CCP influence activities in Australia, the shape of the planned book emerged. It corresponded to the remapping of the world going on in my mind, geopolitically and with much more emphasis on the fragility of democratic institutions.

By early 2017, I was starting to develop a framework for making sense of the organisation of CCP interference in Australia, focused on the individuals who served as vectors for CCP influence. It seemed that the most important thing to understand was the way the CCP uses personal relationships to advance its objectives. Not surprisingly, the name Huang Xiangmo kept coming up. Early on I drew a rough map of his connections, on one side with Beijing's operatives in Australia and on the other with 'useful idiots' among politicians, ex-politicians and university executives.

It was apparent that there were other agents of influence like Huang who were more careful about attracting attention. It was also becoming clear that Australia hosted a dense network of CCP-guided united front organisations embedded in the Chinese Australian community and that hundreds of operatives were actively working away to influence the centres of power and subvert the nation's democracy.

Understanding these networks and amassing information on the backgrounds and CCP links of the operatives became essential to my work. It would have been impossible for me to trace the connections without Alex's deep dives into Chinese-language sources here and in China. A couple of other Chinese Australians with the requisite skills, who must remain nameless, also helped out. Two factors made the task much easier than it might have been. The first was that, odd as it may sound, many agents of influence seem to regard the Chinese language as some kind of encryption, so in Chinese-language publications here and in China they often speak quite frankly about their activities. The second was that united front operatives like to brag about their achievements and influence. They want the Party to appreciate their efforts and reward them and the Chinese community to see how well-connected and powerful they are. After publication of *Silent Invasion*, some united front agents became more circumspect, taking down incriminating web links.

§

I didn't know any spies. And I didn't know whether they knew me. My friend David McKnight, who wrote a history of ASIO, had sent me the transcript of a tapped phone call to me from a socialist activist inviting me to attend a summer camp, but that was the extent of my ASIO links. Throughout the research and writing of *Silent Invasion* I entertained the hope that one day I would open my PO box to find an anonymous brown envelope stuffed with secret intelligence documents. No such luck. So, I thought, if the mountain won't come to Muhammad … I wrote a letter about my research, now at the first complete draft stage, to the top dog, requesting a meeting, and posted it to ASIO's Canberra monolith at 70 Constitution Avenue.

It was a long shot, so I was surprised to find myself a few weeks later walking a little anxiously into the ASIO building. I was hoping I was still beneath the radar of China's spy networks but expected them to be watching the comings and goings of this building.

Hadn't *Financial Review* journalist Primrose Riordan broken a story about a company controlled by a Chinese billionaire linked to the People's Liberation Army that had just built an apartment block directly across the road from ASIO?

Entering the building, security was tight, but in a relaxed Australian way. I didn't know what to expect, though I knew that ASIO had been transformed from the paranoid bunch of spooks that tapped the phones of priests opposed to the Vietnam War and compiled a dossier on film critic David Stratton from 1969 because he went to a film festival in Russia. The person I met struck me as sensible, well-informed and mildly conservative politically. Perhaps remembering the traumatic events of the 1973 'ASIO raid' by Labor attorney-general Lionel Murphy, the organisation aims for bipartisanship. The most valuable thing I learned from that meeting was that the picture of the world I had put together from all of my sources was consistent with the one held by ASIO, including many of the individuals of concern. I even knew some things they didn't. Remarkably, as they themselves noted, I was relying solely on open-source information, available to anyone who knows where to look and how to interpret what they find. Nowadays, tapping phones and surveilling suspects matters less to spying than knowing how to use the internet effectively.

Soon after, at a cafe in Brunswick East, I first met up with a Chinese Australian researcher I will call Amy Cheng. As we built trust over the next year, she would become a close collaborator and source of high-quality information. Amy spoke at length about united front work in Melbourne and Sydney, and the various politicians who had been drawn into their networks. Her mother would say, 'If you eat other's food, your words become softer. If you accept gifts from another, your hands become weaker,' which pretty much sums up the CCP foreign influence strategy. When I later expressed my misgivings over whether the information in the near-finished book would be used by racists to vilify all people of Chinese heritage, Amy told me that Chinese people in Australia *want* me to write it. 'We're in the same boat.' It was reassuring. Others expressed a similar view, although they were not perhaps typical of the diaspora. Even so, I knew from the start that the 'racism' accusation was inevitable.

Speaking of those who eat others' food, in the course of my research I came across the disturbing case of Joel Fitzgibbon and his friendship with Helen Liu, a Chinese Australian 'businesswoman' linked to China's military intelligence. When Kevin Rudd appointed Fitzgibbon defence minister after the 2007 election win, some defence intelligence people were deeply concerned. But people at the top didn't want to look into it, and certainly no one in the Labor government. Liu had donated substantial sums to the Labor Party and she knew Kevin Rudd, among other Labor luminaries. Liu was also close to Bob Carr and his wife. Even ASIO appears to have been unwilling to push it too hard, perhaps not wanting to open a can of worms.

Renegade defence intelligence officers carried out their own investigation into Fitzgibbon's relationship with Liu, off the books, as it were. In 2009, their report found its way into the Fairfax papers, courtesy of Nick McKenzie, Richard Baker and Phil Dorling. It ought to have been a gigantic scandal, but everyone seemed to want to cover it up. Phil Dorling told me that the press gallery in Canberra just didn't believe it; that kind of spying doesn't happen in little Australia. A top intelligence official told me that the Liu–Fitzgibbon affair didn't go anywhere because 'News Ltd wasn't interested'. While the Americans and Canadians were uncovering Chinese spy networks, in Australia the consensus was that Beijing had no interest here. There is so much more to the scandal that has never seen the light of day and which I could not report in the absence of hard evidence. Sometime after *Silent Invasion* was published, I was told that some ALP figures would not forgive me because of 'what you wrote about Joel Fitzgibbon'.

§.

It was difficult to arrange a meeting with Chen Yonglin. I wasn't so surprised as he is Australia's most high-profile Chinese defector.

When he walked out of the Sydney consulate in 2005, Beijing put him under enormous pressure. He knew his life was in danger, and that of his family. And he was shocked to discover that he was not welcomed by the Australian government, which put smooth relations with Beijing first. While the Australian government was deciding whether to allow him to stay or send him back to China (and an almost certain death), the consulate tried desperately to track down Yonglin and his young family. Sydney was too dangerous so they quietly rented a house in Gosford, a town an hour north of Sydney. Within days, consulate security people turned up in his street. How did they find him? He thinks they asked a Chinese real estate agent to consult the register shared within the real estate industry to keep track of good and bad tenants.

I was nervous and watchful as I waited for Chen Yonglin outside Ashfield station on a sunny weekday. I thought it likely both of us were being followed. Yonglin, or 'Andy', was smooth-faced and personable and seemed relaxed. We walked to a busy Chinese restaurant, which struck me as an odd place to discuss CCP spying. We sat down, and I immediately began asking direct questions. Yonglin became nervous; other diners were a metre from us. He proposed we go somewhere else. We left and crossed the street to enter a daggy Aussie pub, all Tooheys and pies and old blokes araldited to their stools at the bar. It was so incongruous to be sitting in this setting talking to a Chinese defector eating a steak, but what I heard over the next hour or two could only have come from someone who worked for years inside the CCP's system of foreign interference and repression.

Yonglin's task at the consulate had been to closely monitor and harass Falun Gong exiles from China. Names spilled forth – the informant in the Supreme Court judge's chambers, the New South Wales minister supplying information to the Sydney consulate, the united front agent working for a federal politician. When I asked about the use by Chinese intelligence agencies of honey traps – sending attractive young women to lure men into blackmail situations or to access their computers – he said they are reserved only for top-level delegations to China. Lower-level Australian officials are more likely to find prostitutes in their camera-laced hotel rooms, a blunter tactic. I have often wondered just how many of the 'friends of China' among our political and university elites are being blackmailed. A senior intelligence person told me that there had been 'numerous cases' of Australians caught in honey traps in China. 'It's standard practice. We don't do it in Australia because of the risks to the women.'

§

After some months I began to realise how CCP influence work is enmeshed with China's espionage activity. One encounter that stands out was a meeting I had with one of Australia's leading cybersecurity academics, who told me how a post-doctoral researcher from China came to collaborate. Together they developed software to test forensic cyber-tools. They went to Beijing for a conference, but the post-doc disappeared with a laptop containing all of their work. Australia's world-class centres for cybersecurity training, where our military experts are educated, are high-value targets for infiltration and technology theft. At the time, and still in some cases, the universities were oblivious; for institutions committed to seeking knowledge, our universities are skilled at not wanting to know.

A top Australian intelligence official, not long retired, told me the starting point for understanding China is the social and business culture of favours and gifts used as a means of building networks and relationships. He talked about how a wealthy Chinese Australian businessman had established himself as a person of credibility and stature by making gifts to political parties and universities. China, he said, does not want to subjugate other countries per se but to get them to serve China's interests.

The senior China people I talked to in the Department of Foreign Affairs and Trade had a schizoid attitude. One moment they would anxiously acknowledge the scale and danger of the PRC threat, the next they would remember themselves and begin to emphasise engagement and building harmony, as if their role were to counter-balance the alarums being sounded by the security agencies. As we discussed the threats from interference operations and cyber, one said, in a moment of weakness, 'It's much, much more sinister than it might appear,' before reassuring me that our institutions are robust and quite able to handle the threats.

Another contact was a political officer from the US embassy, whom I met at the Maple & Clove cafe in Barton. She was extremely well-informed about CCP influence activities in federal parliament and at one point remarked that the US was asking itself whether Australia was too far gone, whether it had been captured irrevocably by China. Having spent months closely studying the networks of influence, including with powerful former politicians, it was an anxiety I shared. One day, a senior Labor Party figure phoned me. He was apoplectic about the penetration of the CCP into the New South Wales right, the most powerful faction of the party, where it was making 'friends' like Tony Burke, Chris Bowen, Sam Dastyari, Bob Carr and Paul Keating.

§

If I was unsettled in Australia, I knew that going to China would be even more intense and I prayed my work had not crossed the radar of the CCP's secret police. I took the first of two research trips to China at the end of 2016. I had little idea what to expect. It was around midnight when the taxi from Beijing airport came to a stop, disgorging me and my suitcase into a very dark lane. I had booked accommodation on Airbnb and it was in one of Beijing's last hutongs, the old residential districts that had mostly been bulldozed. The Australians I later met up with looked at me with a kind of admiration when I told them I was staying in an Airbnb in a hutong; no one in their world does that. I squinted to make out a number on a door, which opened into a tiny passageway. In the pitch black it took me ten minutes to feel my way up and down and along the walls, suppressing my rising anxiety, before my hand found a keypad, one that accepted the number I'd been sent. The apartment was modern and pleasant, with a couple of appliances that I later identified as air purifiers. It turned out the apartment was owned by an urbane, fortyish Chinese woman who had left her high-stress job to run a yoga studio. In the morning, I was a novelty out in the hutong's laneways, but I felt quite safe among the locals. My host later took me on a walking tour, explaining how a nearby Buddhist temple was controlled by monks loyal to the Party.

Apart from encounters with Australian journalists and my well-informed Beijing friends Philippa Jones and David Kelly, who run a research and strategic advice company, meetings were hard to arrange. I was an unknown foreign academic, so why would Chinese academics and experts take time out for me? Rowan Callick, Phil Wen and Angus Grigg – China correspondents for *The Australian*, Fairfax and the *Financial Review* – were extremely helpful, especially concerning the Australians coming and going and how they were treated in China. They roll out the red carpet for Bob Carr. 'They love him in Beijing.' Keating was a regular visitor too. I learned about the grooming of senior business figures. The main business cheerleaders for China were seen to be mining magnate Andrew Forrest, media proprietor Kerry Stokes and James Packer, although Packer's relationship was complicated after the arrest of Crown Casino employees in China.

One day, while speaking with a thirty-something Chinese journalist who'd worked with Western news organisations, I mentioned the activities of Chinese students in Australia. 'Brainwashed, totally,' she snorted. Someone else later pointed out that young people admit they have been brainwashed, but they mostly aren't interested in exploring different views.

A couple of days into my Beijing visit, an 'airpocalypse' event descended on the city. A yellow poisonous haze obscured buildings and drove Beijingers inside. I walked along an empty Chang'an Boulevard in the freezing night air, struggling to breathe. I'd heard about these events but the intensity of it left me reeling, and I had lived in Jakarta. Back in my Airbnb, even with the air purifiers running (powered by the coal-fired power plants that were responsible for the smog), the sulphurous stink wafted through the bedroom as I slept.

A week later in Shanghai, I met up with a Chinese journalist who worked with a Western news outlet, a tricky position because she's expected to spy on her employers. She's regularly called in by the secret police for a 'cup of tea'. She told me about the red lines, the three Ts – Tibet, Taiwan, Tiananmen. Stay away from them and you should be okay. That was then; the red lines have now multiplied so that any kind of public comment needs vigilance. She described how officials who have become wealthy through corruption send their children and money overseas, hoping their children can obtain a foreign passport and give the parents a bolthole when things turn sour in China. Australia is a popular choice.

Australia cops a lot of criticism in the Chinese media and from officials because we have made a lot of money from China yet ally ourselves with the United States. It's widely believed that China 'saved' Australia from the 2008 global financial crisis and we should be grateful, as if paying the going rate for our minerals was somehow an act of charity. To me it's bizarre, but the sentiment, the expectation of our gratitude, is strong at all levels in China.

I met a couple of academics who sat across a big shiny table and bored me with the Party line on everything. But there was one academic who left a mark on my thinking. When I knocked on his door, he'd forgotten our appointment and was in the middle of scoffing his lunch. A bluff man, he waved me to a chair and kept on munching. He is a prolific and prominent defender of the Party, and he knows Australia well. So I was incredulous when, in response to my questions, he launched into a searing critique of the Party and the Chinese people, one that confirmed most of my impressions, except for the racial stereotypes he threw around. I knew many intellectuals didn't believe the Party's BS, but I could hardly believe my ears as I filled page after page of my notebook with his pungent remarks. Before leaving, I checked with him that it was all on the record. 'Yes, yes,' he assured me. A couple of weeks later, back in Australia,

I typed it all up and emailed it to him, telling him I planned to put it in my book and asking him to check it. I think he was shocked to see his words written down and replied quickly. He did not want the comments attributed to him, and he had edited the text, heavily watering down the criticisms he had made and changing the tone radically. Well, I thought, you can't have it both ways. So I disguised his identity and included the transcribed text, with a few corrections and clarifications, in the book.

My conversations with people who had long and deep experience in China were rewiring my brain as I tried to come to grips with the problem. When I met up in Beijing with *New York Times* correspondent Chris Buckley – an Australian of legendary status among foreign correspondents – he observed, 'Chinese people are not robotic.' Those who parrot the Party line, he said, do not necessarily believe it, and Party critics may still have strong nationalist feelings towards China.

A few days later, on a pleasant night in Shanghai, I left a restaurant on the Bund to stroll the two kilometres back to my hotel. As I passed the bar next door, an attractive woman emerged and made a beeline for me. She struck up a conversation in very good English, asking me the usual questions. In such situations, an answer leads to more questions. I was relaxed, but also guarded. I wondered whether I had really been picked at random as a well-heeled Westerner who could be shaken down one way or another. She was persistent and my instinctual politeness meant I was not willing to give her the brush off. After ten minutes she was asking me to take her to a bar. I stopped and said to her:

'I couldn't do that. I'm married.'

'Why does that matter? Your wife wouldn't know,' she replied, puzzled.

'But then I would need to lie to her.'

'Chinese men never care about that.'

Excusing myself, I made my way through the crowds towards the hotel, alert for a tail.

§

Four months later, I was back for a second trip to China. Rubbing shoulders with ordinary Beijingers in a hutong is a tourist delight, but this time work requirements came first so I stayed at the upmarket St Regis. It's assumed the hotel is riddled with listening devices, so foreigners often arrange their meetings at the Starbucks across the road. It seems likely, though, that state security eavesdrops at Starbucks too.

I arranged to meet ABC correspondent Bill Birtles on a corner in the busy shopping district Chaoyang. He arrived on a motorbike. Telling me to hop on, he took off fast, going the wrong way down a one-way street, past a policeman or two, turned onto the main road, wove through the traffic and after several minutes stopped at a bustling restaurant. Over Jing-A beer and Thai food, Bill was a font of insights and colourful stories. He was at home in Beijing, with an easy familiarity with the locals. Bob Carr had been in Beijing again a couple of months ago, telling Bill that Huang Xiangmo means no harm and is the target of a witch-hunt. (In 2019, Huang was banned from re-entering Australia on ASIO advice.) I heard from a couple of journalists the rumour that Bob Hawke was gifted a villa on Hainan Island as a reward for joining the board of the Bo'ao Forum, the CCP's 'Davos' (the meeting place of the global elite for the World Economic Forum). He was a frequent honoured guest in China.

Geoff Raby is an urbane man, fully at home in Beijing, who can spin a highly plausible story to justify the CCP regime and its achievements. We spent a boozy evening at a tapas bar in Sanlitun, very boozy in his case, although he can hold it far better than I can. The former diplomat, and our man in Beijing from 2007 to 2011, led the charmed life of a well-heeled expatriate smiled on by the regime. He has been a favoured guest explaining China on Geraldine Doogue's *Saturday Extra* radio program – awkwardly favoured in the eyes of some ABC staff. Perhaps Geraldine was beguiled by Geoff's stories at tipsy dinners in Sanlitun's best restaurants. Even I wanted to believe the spin. 'Look at all these middle-class Chinese,' he said, gesturing to the clientele clinking wine glasses in the soft light. 'They're happy, they're not complaining.' It was true, yet I couldn't help popping the cosy bubble by asking him about human rights abuses. He said he didn't know much about them.

That was in April 2017. Since then, Beijing's bullying and the sharp rise in tensions has forced Geoff to navigate a narrow path between remaining in the regime's good books and avoiding the ridicule heaped on the likes of Bob Carr and former Liberal Party trade minister Andrew Robb who went to work for Landbridge, the Chinese company with a lease on the Port of Darwin.

One of my most fascinating encounters was with a young Beijing political scientist who, over an hour or two, provided an extraordinarily insightful analysis of the conflicting tendencies within the regime and Chinese society. Ye Fei was around twenty-five and remarkably well read, telling me how intellectuals have ways of accessing all kinds of Western books and journals despite tight censorship. As he saw it, the fault line in China was between the pragmatists or liberals, who want China to minimise conflict in the world, and the nationalists, who want a global system with Xi Jinping as emperor. The difference is reflected in a fierce debate among academics, between those who see China as another nation-state and those who see it as a superior civilisational state entitled to dominate the Asia-Pacific region and even the world. Australia, 'to put it bluntly', may continue to enjoy the benefits of being white for another decade or two, but that's it; after that we can expect China to talk down to Australia in the same condescending way it does to Asian countries.

Even as he spoke, I worried about Ye Fei's safety; he was so frank, I guessed he must be watched by the CCP's thought police. A few months later, I was distressed to learn that at a party with friends, Ye Fei had suddenly become ill, collapsing on the kitchen floor. He died in hospital a few hours later. Perhaps he was just unlucky, but I could not fend off the lurking feeling that he had been killed.

Ye Fei's characterisation of the nationalists was a helpful introduction to my meeting with one of China's most famous and powerful intellectuals, Zha Daojiong, professor of international political economy at Peking University. David Kelly, a China scholar who'd brokered the meeting, came too and was as astonished as I was at the aggressive stance Professor Zha adopted towards the two Australians sitting opposite him. Australia doesn't have to choose between China and the United States, he told us in very good English, it has to choose between 'stupidity and less stupidity'. Stupidity means trying to punch above our weight as our foreign minister, Julie Bishop, was attempting to do. In a recent Singapore speech, she urged China to move closer to democracy. 'Fuck off,' Zha exclaimed, 'who are you to tell us what to do?'

Whoa, I thought, scribbling in my notebook.

Zha is credited with the idea of the One Belt, One Road Initiative, adopted by Xi and now indistinguishable from Beijing's foreign policy. He said if Australia doesn't want to join, that's fine. 'Perhaps you folks think China wants to take over Australia,' he laughed, naming a number of Australians advocating a tougher stance. Then he mentioned Hugh White. Chinese professors loyal to the Party are full of praise for White, interpreting his book *China Choice* as 'we choose China'. Zha, however, suggested his argument could be interpreted as saying the only answer is for the United States to nuke China. 'Don't imagine you can terrorise us again,' he said. 'We've been here five thousand years.'

'Phew,' I said to David as we left, 'and this guy says he's not like the hawks but wants China to use its power in a cooperative way. The hawks must be scary.'

David Kelly and Philippa Jones took me to a dinner with a few members of Beijing's literary-intellectual scene. Rowan Callick joined us. We gathered at a stylish restaurant in Chaoyang. We could speak freely because we were in a private room, although the conversation returned to safe subjects when the waiters entered. These intellectuals had a sophisticated understanding of the Party and the state and how China is seen in the rest of the world. They could name and discuss the Western apologists for the CCP, the 'useful idiots' who appeared on the Party-controlled television station CCTV praising the regime, like John Ross, who had been London mayor Ken Livingstone's business director. A well-known novelist explained to me that urban professionals live in a 'golden cage', enjoying many 'lifestyle freedoms' but none of the other kind. On home visits, their children studying in Hong Kong complain about being embarrassed at not knowing Chinese history, like the Tiananmen Square massacre, which was familiar to their Hong Kong counterparts. And the parents are disappointed when their children studying in Australia return home to tell them they didn't make friends with any Australians, only with other Chinese students.

By this stage I was nervous about being in China. The authorities probably know what I am doing, I thought. I had met too many people in China and in Australia who must have been on their watch lists. I'd heard the stories about hidden cameras in hotel rooms. ASIO warns Australians about complimentary phone chargers that download your data. I had taken a burner phone and was using a VPN on my laptop, from which I had removed anything that might offend the authorities. The government was undertaking a campaign calling on citizens to watch out for foreigners engaged in spying or attempting to recruit Chinese people to their side. Cartoon posters were appearing, showing a suave white man chatting up an innocent young Chinese woman. Racism and paranoia go hand in hand in China under the CCP, as they do elsewhere. One day, drinking coffee alone in a cafe, I looked around to see a young woman furtively filming me and my laptop screen with her phone camera.

§

As I learned more about what the CCP was doing in Australia, an unfamiliar sentiment began welling up inside me: CCP, get the hell out of my country. Patriotism gets a bad rap on the left and for good reason. It has been owned by the right, especially the uglier elements of the right. Yet around the world, allowing the right to own love of country has been a disastrous political miscalculation by the left. Of course, people like me tend to express in public only our criticisms of Australia, and there is plenty to criticise. Yet, for the first time, I found my inner patriot coming to the surface. Isn't it the source of that powerful feeling of joy and relief when we fly back into Australia after an extended absence?

Patriotism is not nationalism, even if elements on the right elide the two. When in January 2020 Labor's deputy leader Tanya Plibersek sent out a Twitter thread defending patriotism as an expression of solidarity and reminding us of the palpable truth that 'To love your country is not to assume it's better than others', she was monstered, accused of speaking 'the language of white supremacy'. What bullshit. The left makes me despair sometimes. Do they think Korean people are not patriotic? Do they believe that Chileans or Samoans do not love their country? For God's sake, why allow the right to annex such a powerful and understandable sentiment and turn it into something noxious? As Tanya Plibersek wrote: 'You can cherish this nation and want to make it better.' It's so obvious, yet many on the left allow the strategy of the right to shape their opinions.

§

In October 2017, as the book approached completion, I took a detour. I'd been invited to join the annual meeting of the Valdai Discussion Club, 'Russia's Davos', to appear on a panel about climate change. It was my first visit to Russia. When the plane landed at Moscow airport, the Russian passengers clapped. I'd heard about this custom, a hangover from the days when the national carrier was nicknamed 'Aeroflop'. Before catching the plane to Sochi, I spent a couple of days in Moscow. The Moscow metro is worth taking just for the amazing 'socialist classicist' architecture of the stations, built as palaces for the people during Stalin's time. On a walking tour, the guide explained that, for the benefit of blind people, a male voice is used to announce the arrival of trains heading to the town centre and a female voice is used for trains heading for the suburbs. Muscovites who forget the rule have a mnemonic: your boss's voice calls you in to work and your wife's voice calls you home.

The conference was staged at a grand resort hotel in the snow-capped mountains behind Sochi, a few hours' flight south from Moscow. The Russian experts – political scientists and strategic thinkers – were intellectually impressive, although their worldview struck me as twenty years out of date. They still lived in old Europe. Charmingly, they referred to Australians as 'antipods'. Foreign minister Sergei Lavrov gave a longwinded opening address. A wily politician, he spoke of Trump's 'strategic frivolity', a nice phrase. In an alliance of convenience, Russia had been growing closer to China, although the Russians seemed to regard 'the Chinese' with suspicion, if not historical disdain. Madam Fu Ying, a senior foreign affairs official and former ambassador to Australia, spoke about the One Belt, One Road Initiative (OBOR), telling a disbelieving audience that China simply wants to share its benevolence with the world and has no intention of interfering. Later at drinks, when I asked the head of Shanghai's OBOR Security Centre whether OBOR was aimed at enhancing China's strategic influence in the world, he replied: 'Of course, what would you expect?'

One night I got chatting to two experienced German journalists at the bar. One had written a biography of Vladimir Putin. He told me that he had once been interviewing Putin on a plane flying high over Africa. At one point, Putin looked out of the window and, with a sweeping gesture, said, 'This is all China's now.'

Walking through the foyer on the last day, a sudden shift in the atmosphere was palpable, one of those moments you walk into a room and, just from the vibe, think, 'Huh? What's going on?' I soon learned that the large men in suits with intimidating scowls and ear-pieces were the advance security detail for the unscheduled arrival of President Putin. Late that afternoon, we filed through body scanners into the little lecture theatre for the big event, around sixty conference participants plus a ruck of media, who'd appeared from nowhere, at the back. We took our seats, with a heavy in a suit stationed at the end of each row, I guessed to prevent anyone rushing the stage.

Ostensibly, Putin was joining a panel event with Jack Ma, billionaire owner of Alibaba (China's Amazon), and Afghanistan president Hamid Karzai. When Putin walked into the room, I felt a sinister frisson. From my seat, my only thought was 'This man kills people'. After the introductions, the impeccably dressed Karzai spoke for ten minutes about Afghanistan. Jack Ma was banal, mouthing marketing slogans, a lightweight. Then Putin spoke. He was mesmerising, for me at least, because of the menace he radiated. His words were compelling, but his presence repellent. There followed more than an hour of close questioning of Putin. The Russian academics were respectful but not afraid to fire challenging questions at him on all of the difficult geopolitical problems facing Russia. Putin was masterful, giving well-informed and coherent answers to them all. The contrast with the bumbling US president could not have been sharper.

§

By the end of October, I had a complete draft of the book. Eleven months from start to finish was fast. Such a short turnaround was possible because I had over the years become a book-writing machine; I knew how to do it. And, of course, I had plenty of help. There was something else though. Prior to shifting my attention to China, I had been in the doldrums, my enthusiasm had slumped, my productivity had halved. Now, I was fired up each day, the machine was in overdrive. The manuscript had been revised in response to commentaries from three expert readers. It had been copyedited and amended in response to a review by a defamation lawyer. In early November, it was ready to be sent to the typesetter, with a publication and publicity schedule mapped out in detail. It was all systems go. Nothing could stop me now.

24

Censored

A T 2 PM ON Thursday, 2 November 2017, Elizabeth Weiss phoned to tell me that Allen & Unwin had decided it would not publish my book, *Silent Invasion*. They had had a meeting with an expert who had described the retaliatory measures Beijing might take, including vexatious litigation by CCP-aligned billionaires – 'whales', she called them. The CEO, Robert Gorman, had decided to pull the plug.

It was a thunderbolt. I felt betrayed. The company had backed me from the start and expressed enthusiasm throughout, and now they were telling me they were so frightened of Beijing's shadow that they would not publish a book criticising the Chinese Communist Party. Allen & Unwin had dramatically confirmed, in a way even I could not have anticipated, the argument of the book.

I told Elizabeth that this was the end of my relationship with the company and asked for the paperwork revoking the contract to be sent. I went for a walk to calm down and process what had just happened. I'd never been censored before; it was galling. And I felt the book contained a message Australians urgently needed to hear: that our democracy was being undermined. I had a head of steam, yet now the whole thing was about be derailed. It was unthinkable.

I knew I had to find another publisher right away. Returning to my office, I made a list of people to contact.

That evening I phoned John Garnaut. Here was the irony: John was the expert whose advice had so frightened Allen & Unwin, and I had recommended him! John was as stunned as I was; the news seemed to floor him. He was being sued for defamation by Chinese Australian billionaire Chau Chak Wing over a story he wrote in *The Sydney Morning Herald* linking Chau to a UN bribery scandal, so John was an experienced whale watcher. I heard later that Allen & Unwin were 'gun-shy' following a big payout to members of Schapelle Corby's family after publishing a book allegedly defaming them.

On Friday, I phoned Chris Feik at Black Inc. I'd known Chris for some years. In 2006 I wrote a popular *Quarterly Essay* for them on social democracy, and Black Inc. had published *Scorcher* in 2007. I explained the situation and pitched the book. Chris said he'd have a look but cautioned me that they had published a lot on China, including Hugh White. I was uneasy. Along with a new journal they were publishing, *Australian Foreign Affairs*, Black Inc. seemed to be taking a position that was, in its effect, sympathetic to Beijing. I posted a hard copy of the manuscript.

I decided to email Robert Gorman to put my feelings on the record. You have abandoned me, I wrote, and 'your decision is a landmark victory for the CCP's campaign to suppress critical voices around the world'. I suggested the decision would eat away at the soul of the company. Looking back, my anger with Allen & Unwin was partly due to the fact that the company had always taken pride in publishing books on important causes, yet now they were acting like the big commercial outfits. I knew there would be staff members appalled by the decision.

The following week I met up with Chris Uhlmann. I wanted his advice on the best way to break the story. Chris had not long moved from the ABC to become the new Laurie Oakes at Channel 9 and was struggling with the culture shock. He too was incredulous and immediately saw the significance of the story.

The next day, Robert Gorman replied to my email, opining that 'Silent Invasion is an extremely significant book' but they were worried by 'the very high chance of a vexatious defamation action', adding that Beijing may also retaliate by crashing their website and blocking Allen & Unwin from having their books printed in China. (Most Western publishers have their books printed in China, which has inexpensive, good-quality printing.)

Robert wrote that they did not want to drop the book completely, only delay it until after the current defamation cases had been finalised and the new foreign interference laws were passed. It was an impossible position to put me in: shelve the book to gather dust then reassess in two or three years. No author could go along with that, and certainly not this one.

I decided to give the story to Nick McKenzie at Fairfax. I first got to know Nick when he was researching his sensational Four Corners program on China's influence, which had aired five months before. I'd spoken with him on and off through the course of writing the book so he knew its significance and the implications of a publisher being frightened out of publishing. He asked for proof that Allen & Unwin had canned the book because it was afraid of Beijing's retribution. Robert had done me a favour by putting it in writing.

Chris Feik emailed saying Black Inc. was not interested. He caricatured the argument, saying it would stoke prejudice, even though I had gone to great pains to distinguish between the CCP and Chinese people. I was fighting the Chinese Communist Party and he was fighting Pauline Hanson. It was a warning to me about how many on the left would see the book, that is, through old lenses that blur and distort the new world. After Robert Manne read an early draft, he urged me not to publish it. It was the first time we had had a major disagreement. I realised I was going to lose friends.

On Friday, Louise Adler, CEO of Melbourne University Press, phoned. Nick knows her and I'd asked him to tip her off about the forthcoming story. Louise had taken MUP downmarket by chasing sensationalist political books, but as the country's foremost university press, MUP had to be taken seriously. She was super keen and put a compelling case for me to sign a contract with MUP. She pushed me hard to agree there and then. I indicated strong interest and said I would let her know soon. I posted her a hardcopy.

§

Over the weekend I was apprehensive; I knew Nick McKenzie's story (written with Richard Baker) was about to break. On Monday morning, on the way to work I swung past the newsagency at Kingston shops to buy the papers and sat in the car to read them. The story of my book dominated the front pages of *The Sydney Morning Herald* and, especially, *The Age*, which carried the banner headline 'Silenced: Decorated author fears for free speech after publisher pulls China book'. Brilliant. The story spilled onto page ten, taking up the whole page. They had written that it was 'exceptionally rare that a perceived threat from a foreign power prevents or delays publication. It raises serious questions about academic freedom and free speech in Australia.'

As I got to work, things were exploding. Over the next hours, requests for interviews poured in, and it was back-to-back all day. ABC Radio was soon leading its news bulletins with it. The international media began calling – *The New York Times*, BBC, CNN, *The Washington Post*, Deutsche Welle, *The Japan Times*, *The Straits Times*, and more.

It was overwhelming. Journalists the world over despise censorship, and they had been sensitised by the Cambridge University Press row, in which CUP had deleted certain articles from its academic journals sold into China.

Over the next days, supportive emails flooded in, including from numerous Chinese Australians. Anger was directed at Allen & Unwin, with some calling for a boycott. In emails and social media, people suggested crowdfunding the book's publication. A Sydney businessman who operates a printing company phoned to tell me he was so incensed about what had happened, and so worried about China, that he would publish the book himself and damn the consequences. The investigative journalist Phil Dorling suggested tabling the manuscript in the Senate, thereby receiving the protection of parliamentary privilege.

On Monday, 13 November, Louise Adler emailed to say that MUP would be honoured to publish the book. She set out terms for the contract and said she would ask their defamation lawyer, Nic Pullen, to read the manuscript and advise on any changes needed. Then she asked me to seek interviews with Bob Carr and Sam Dastyari to give them a chance to respond to my claims. Really? She had published Dastyari's bid for rehabilitation, *One Halal of a Story*, and felt she should give him a chance to respond.

Her request irritated me. I had already sought Carr's response. He initially agreed to an in-person interview then changed it to a phone interview, pulling out at the last moment and asking me to email my questions. He took several weeks to supply answers. When he finally did, he vigorously defended his benefactor Huang Xiangmo and said he would happily take money from him again. And I saw no reason why I should ask Sam Dastyari. Louise pressured me to sign a contract straight away, but I didn't want to be railroaded. I wanted a few days to test interest among other publishers.

Louise needed to run the book proposal past her board. But I shouldn't worry, she said, the board had always respected editorial independence and took pride in their tagline 'we publish books with spine'. I checked online to see who was on the MUP board. You must be joking – Bob Carr! Louise later assured me Carr would recuse himself from any decision about *Silent Invasion*. Okay, I thought, and what about behind the scenes?

At seven that evening I found myself in Sky News Australia's Parliament House studio. A couple of senior political figures had facilitated an invitation to appear on *The Bolt Report* and urged me to accept. How could I agree after Bolt's long history of climate science denial and vicious attacks on me? I loathed the man. At times, I told myself, we have to swallow our feelings and put the issue first. At least, that was the high-minded explanation. In truth, I felt extremely vulnerable. I was exposing the clandestine activities of the CCP, and I knew how ruthless it could be. I was worried about my safety and that of my family. A Bolt interview would generate support in high places, which I needed. So I found myself crossing an ideological boundary in a way I never thought I would.

I assumed we'd stick to the topic, but Bolt broke the unspoken contract by bookending the interview with cracks at me over climate change. I suppose he wanted to signal to his loyal audience that he was not embracing Clive Hamilton, but it chafed me. Even so, his lead-in was highly sympathetic, and he otherwise gave me a good run. I did what I had to do, I thought, as I walked into the underground carpark.

Back at home, I watched ABC *7.30*'s long lead story about the book by Dylan Welch. It was perfect. At my office early the next day, I saw that *The New York Times* had published an extended story about the scandal written by Phil Wen, who had become the Reuters correspondent in Beijing. I'd given Phil advance warning about the book's scotching.

Outraged letters had flooded into *The Age* and *The Sydney Morning Herald*, beating up on Allen & Unwin. Only Bob Carr was defending the decision not to publish, writing, 'The recent "China panic" stories fall woefully short of an evidentiary base.' He was sweating; he knew he was in for a caning in the book.

Mary Kelly, deputy vice-chancellor at Charles Sturt University and my supervisor, was asked about the book. She said she supported my academic freedom. As I'd soon discover, when things soured, Mary would be my only staunch supporter in the senior ranks of the university administration.

The next day, I had a difficult conversation with the head of the university's legal office, who told me that the university's insurance policy may not cover defamation actions against me. It was as if a big flood were about to wash away my house and I'd received a call from my insurance company, telling me, 'You know that flood insurance policy you've faithfully kept up? You need to read the fine print.' It was clear she did not understand the legalities of book contracts or how much reputational damage would be done to the university if it became known they had hung me out to dry. It was the first shot in a painful dispute. Emails arrived pointing me to 'the obligation of staff to avoid defamatory and libellous communications', as if I wasn't doing my best to stay out of court.

§

Soon after, our office manager, Hazel, told me that she'd noticed a young woman of Chinese heritage – well-dressed in black, perhaps twenty – loitering around our office building on the university's theology campus. For some hours she sat on a bench twenty metres from the door, playing with her phone. At lunchtime, she came inside and asked Hazel if she could wash her hands and was shown the bathroom. Afterwards she was seen hanging around on the deck. It was all very odd, and Hazel thought she should alert security. I agreed. It was quite possible she had been sent by the embassy to do some surveillance of my workplace. It was unnerving.

Security had always been relaxed at our building. Now, the alarm was turned on outside business hours and swipe cards were needed to enter. Soon, security cameras would be installed. The building is close to the headquarters of the Australian Federal Police (AFP) so the area is well covered by CCTV. Hazel and centre director Stephen Pickard were endlessly supportive. A top policing and security expert arrived to offer advice. The young woman's phone may well have been a 'sniffer' device, he said, capable of picking up all wi-fi and mobile communications in the building. He said the embassy was probably monitoring me and compiling a dossier. He urged me to change my travel routines.

A week or so later, the fiancé of a colleague arrived to give me a lesson in counter-surveillance techniques. They were the kind of thing he taught to undercover police, like how to spot someone tailing me. Staff were asked to keep a lookout for anything suspicious. A break-in to my office was considered a possibility; after all, that is what happened to Anne-Marie Brady at the University of Canterbury in Christchurch, after she exposed CCP influence activities in New Zealand. I began hiding copies of the manuscript and especially the notebooks from my visits to China containing names of people who would be in trouble. I bought an external hard drive and changed my passwords. I drove out to a cybersecurity company in Fyshwick where, at the request of a cyber expert I knew, the boss had agreed to check my devices for free.

I was bewildered by all this, and angry. 'Why must I do all this?' I fumed. 'I'm just an academic who wrote a book. I live in a democracy where people like me can write books without having to fear for my safety.' I was naïve then, even though I was the bloke who literally wrote the book on CCP interference in Australia.

John Garnaut had arranged for me to meet Justin Bassi, Prime Minister Turnbull's national security adviser. I was keen to get to know Justin for a number of reasons, not least because the link would give me more protection. We met at 8.30 am at ONA, a busy cafe in Manuka. It was cool and crisp when the three of us sat down outside. I was surprised we were being so public about it, but it was in my interests to be seen with the PM's national security adviser.

Justin was urbane, quietly spoken and fully switched on to the China influence problem. The story of the book's spiking broke while Turnbull was in Vietnam at the Asian leaders' summit and was the subject of informal discussions among the leaders. I put forward the idea of tabling parts of my book in parliament as a means of giving protection against defamation actions. Justin asked if I'd like to meet the PM to discuss the situation. I left our meeting feeling reassured, figuring there must be agencies watching out for my security.

§

All kinds of people were making contact to lend support, and I spent much of my days replying to their emails or hearing their stories on the phone. They included many Chinese Australians. One call that stayed with me came from a businessman in Melbourne, retired but well connected. For years, he and his wife had been taking in Chinese students as lodgers. Recently, he had been walking through the CBD with one of those students. They came upon a Falun Gong practitioner collecting signatures on a petition. When he said, 'Let's go over,' she begged him not to. She kept walking while he signed the petition. Two weeks later, the student's parents back in China had a knock on the door from Ministry of State Security heavies. They were warned to keep an eye on their daughter who was creating trouble in Australia. It sickened me to think that we allow PRC spies to operate on our streets.

A Labor Party heavyweight phoned to say he was stunned by what had happened and offered to assist if he could. He was no longer in parliament but remained an influential figure in the party. It was reassuring to hear that in the Labor Party there was a strong pushback against the likes of Bob Carr and Sam Dastyari. Over the following months, I spoke to several Labor people alarmed about CCP interference, especially within the New South Wales branch of the party.

At the end of November, two months earlier, the Dastyari affair had blown up again. The *Herald* reported that Sam Dastyari had visited Huang Xiangmo at his Mosman home. The senator told Huang to leave his phone inside while they talked outside because ASIO was probably monitoring him. The government accused Dastyari of giving intelligence advice to a foreign agent. Bill Shorten sacked him from the shadow cabinet, but there was pressure on him to resign from parliament. Of course, it played straight to the themes of the forthcoming book so I was in demand by the media, including Fran Kelly on ABC Radio National (the pressure was getting to me and it was not my best interview by any stretch). A couple of days later, I did an interview with Ben Fordham on 2GB. If I can do Bolt, I can do

Ben Fordham, I thought. (There was one red line I would not cross: I declined several requests to appear on Alan Jones's show.) At the end, he asked me when my book would be published. I said I was in discussions, so let's see. 'Well, to publishers out there,' he said, 'publish this book. I can assure you we will promote the living daylights out of it.' Marketing gold. Ben Fordham would prove true to his word.

§

At her request, I had sent Louise Adler three reports on the book from peer reviewers. She needed them to keep her board happy. She had run the idea of publishing the book past Glyn Davies, the University of Melbourne's vice-chancellor; he was fine with it, although I picked up a hint of nerves. The fact that an editorial decision was being made by the board and the vice-chancellor was ringing alarm bells for me. Louise was confident MUP would publish. She sent me the defamation lawyer's advice; Nic Pullen had raised a number of general concerns then listed specific ones by page number. I studied the advice carefully and couldn't see anything that was not easily fixed. I had learned enough about defamation to know that the question is not whether a statement is defamatory but whether the claims are true and demonstrably so.

The draft contract from MUP required me to indemnify the publisher against the costs of any defamation action. I was shocked to read that, but a later clause stipulated that the publisher would provide me with defamation insurance. I wasn't sure that would be enough.

A few days later, I received a text message from Louise with 'disappointing news'. They were abandoning the book. In light of the legal concerns, 'MUP doesn't have the necessary resources to make the project viable in a very busy 2018 publishing programme.' In a very busy 2018 publishing program – really? They'd already offered me a contract. I would later hear from two people close to MUP that the university was worried about the effect of publishing my book on the flow of revenue from Chinese students. So Beijing can set

MUP's publishing criteria. It was a real kick in the guts. I thought no publisher in Australia would go near the book now. I felt exhausted and defeated, and that night I slept fitfully.

Over the next days I considered my options. I was determined to get the book out one way or another. Since the Australian publishing industry, despite its big talk about free speech, was jumping at the shadow of the CCP, I explored the possibility of publishing overseas. I phoned Brian Walters SC, my go-to mate on defamation matters. He told me overseas publication wouldn't work because distributing and promoting the book in Australia is captured by the defamation law. But he liked the Hansard option; it would provide unqualified protection.

Louise Adler did make a useful suggestion after pulling the book from the MUP schedule – try Sandy Grant at Hardie Grant Books, based in Melbourne. He had spoken out against censorship on the ABC *7.30* program's segment on Allen & Unwin's withdrawal, although his cameo had not registered on me. Not expecting much, I put a call through; he was busy, and a week later I had heard nothing back. So I decided to put the pressure on. I emailed him, praising his intervention on *7.30*, and said that I wanted to talk to him about Hardie Grant publishing my book.

Four hours later, Sandy came back to me. He proposed a meeting and asked to see the manuscript. Could this be the breakthrough I so badly need, I wondered. But I had been burned a few times and wasn't going to invest too much hope in it.

A day later, I had a phone hook-up with Sandy and Hardie Grant's managing director, Julie Pinkham. I explained the situation and events of the previous month. They were very interested in the book. It was a relief to hear them both looking for arguments that played down the risks rather than being freaked out by them. They'd heard about MUP's decision (Australian publishing is a small world). I mentioned MUP's weighing of publication against the risks of a lawsuit and a hit to its Chinese student income. Sandy said, gnomically, he understood there were other factors at play.

While at Heinemann in 1987, Sandy was, famously, the publisher of *Spycatcher*, the book by former British spy Peter Wright exposing the activities of MI5 and MI6, publication of which the British government tried to stop. The case went to the High Court. Acting for the company was a young gun barrister, Malcolm Turnbull. I loved the synchronicity here. Heinemann won the case and the book went on to sell like the proverbial. Sandy asked if it would be helpful if he phoned 'Malcolm'.

As I hung up, a wave of relief washed over me. 'I think I have found my publisher!' A few days later, Julie emailed me a contract in which Hardie Grant undertook to indemnify me against all damages and costs that may arise from a defamation action. I was full of admiration for Hardie Grant, the only publisher in Australia, it seemed, willing to put its money where its mouth is.

§

From the vice-chancellor down, Charles Sturt University had taken a strong interest in my moves from the day the story broke about Allen & Unwin dropping the book. Sadly, my employer, which had always treated me well, was more interested in protecting its assets than my academic freedom.

I had always got on well with Andy Vann, the vice-chancellor. Andy told me he wanted to back me but they had to get the approval of their insurance company, Unimutual. I was pretty scathing: I suggested they don't wait for the accountants at the insurer to decide whether academic freedom is worth defending. Just back me. I said my book was the product of the work I was employed to do and I *expected* my employer to support me. Andy let on that the vice-chancellor of a university criticised in *Silent Invasion* (I had interviewed two of its deputy vice-chancellors for the book) had pressured him about my book, saying his researchers were being unfairly targeted.

The university was scared and out of its depth, and over the next few weeks, as the pressure mounted, the relationship reached breaking point. Andy told me that if I wanted the university to cover me against legal actions then I must have any publication contract vetted. I must also submit the manuscript to CSU lawyers for review and agree to have the whole thing approved by Unimutual, which may refuse cover or charge a 'retention amount'. I found this set of demands barely believable. They meant that the normal protections for my academic freedom now depended on the calculations of the actuaries at an insurance company. Exactly where did the principle of academic freedom enter into Unimutual's risk algorithm? I was seriously pissed off at the university. I asked Andy how much the university was willing to pay to defend the academic freedom of one of its professors if a retention amount needs to be paid? Ten thousand dollars? Two hundred thousand?

I heard later that on two occasions when my work made the headlines, CSU executives were en route to China to meet university partners there. They were worried about being arrested. In the end, none of their Chinese partners asked about my work.

Although Hardie Grant would indemnify me for anything in the book, it didn't cover anything I might say in public. I decided to go over Andy's head and appeal to the University Council to force its hand. The book had been vetted for defamation already and I wanted unconditional public backing, with or without insurance cover, including protection from any costs arising from litigation, vexatious or otherwise. I wrote to the chancellor, arguing that CSU had an opportunity to be a beacon to all those who believe in free speech, asking her to put it to the council. She did not acknowledge receipt of my letter. Months later, the council passed a resolution supporting free speech. By then it was irrelevant and no one even notified me.

In response to Andy's instructions – reinforced with references to various university policies and regulations – I had resolved that I would discuss the issue no longer. The hell with it, I thought. Let them sack me and see how that plays out in the media – and in parliament.

§

In early December, John Garnaut and I had gone up to Parliament House to hear the PM's speech introducing the new foreign interference bill, world-leading legislation that would outlaw interference activity by the CCP (and any other foreign power). The law was in direct response to a secret report prepared by John, the existence of which had leaked out. The PM's speech was scheduled immediately after the final vote on the marriage equality bill. Parliament House was packed with activists bubbling with excitement. We managed to find standing room in the House of Reps public gallery. The marriage equality vote was held and celebrations erupted. The chamber soon emptied except for around twenty MPs on the government side and one lone MP on Labor's. I think it was Anthony Byrne, deputy chair of the Parliamentary Joint Committee on Intelligence and Security.

The PM gave a powerful speech in which he mentioned the significance of the report he commissioned that was the motivation for the legislation. I whispered congratulations to John. Ever the pro, he said nothing as he couldn't admit it was his report. It was a watershed day in Australia's history, both for the marriage equality vote and for the beginning of the pushback against CCP attempts to subdue the nation.

A week later, Primrose Riordan, now at *The Australian*, reported that universities were expressing anxiety about the new legislation. The peak body, Universities Australia (formerly the AVCC), said it was concerned about 'academic freedom'. What hypocrisy. Where were they when an Australian scholar could not find a publisher because publishers were afraid of retribution from an authoritarian foreign power? They said nothing. Most universities had decided that academic freedom was not an inviolable principle but a factor to be 'balanced' against other interests (as the two deputy vice-chancellors put it to me). In good neoliberal style, they had put a price on it. To this day, Universities Australia continues to ingratiate itself with Beijing.

The same day, ABC Radio morning news led with a story by Tom Iggulden concerning the Department of Defence turning a blind eye to Australian military technology being siphoned off to the People's Liberation Army, a problem that had been exposed a few months earlier in an article by Alex Joske and me. It was followed by a segment on *AM* featuring interviews with me and Peter Jennings. 'God. That's my husband,' Janenne exclaimed as the segment finished. 'He takes on David Jones, then the coal lobby, and now it's the frigging Communist Party of China.' She puts up with a lot but, hey, at least it's not boring.

§

On 20 December 2017, I flew to Melbourne to meet Nic Pullen, Hardie Grant's defamation lawyer and, handily, MUP's too, so he had already read the manuscript. Sandy Grant and Julie Pinkham arrived for the meeting in Nic's Collins Street office. I trusted these people. We all wanted to get the book out. I revealed the live option of securing parliamentary privilege, an idea that was getting support. Nic liked it, legally. However, we decided to proceed as if it would not happen, making all necessary revisions to the text to minimise risk. Publication by parliament would make the text available free on parliament's website but was unlikely to have much effect on sales. I guessed maybe a few hundred people would read it there, but the publicity over such an unprecedented intervention would be huge. As far as I could discover, no parliament anywhere had ever done such a thing.

After Sandy and Julie left, Nic and I got down to business. A former journalist, Nic began by saying that his job is not to stop publication but to facilitate it. He was genial, professional and on my side. We spent two hours going through the manuscript, with me pointing to the extensive changes I had already made in response to his advice to MUP. Only a few small additional changes were needed.

After making my way to Hardie Grant's Richmond offices, I had lunch with Sandy, Julie and Arwen Summers, who would be my 'publisher'. Their enthusiasm was a tonic to me. To avoid

Beijing-inspired injunctions, we agreed to keep publication by Hardie Grant secret, even within the company, until the book was on the shelves in bookshops. Sandy said he would have it printed in Australia to protect his usual Hong Kong printery.

§

While taking a short holiday with family in northern New South Wales, the promised contract with Hardie Grant was the best Christmas present I could imagine. As 2018 got underway, my mood shifted to one of excitement infused with apprehension. So much could still go wrong. And my security anxieties were undiminished.

On 11 January, I met with my supervisor, CSU deputy vice-chancellor Mary Kelly. Mary understood academic freedom and backed me in my dispute with the vice-chancellor. I learned that after the article in the *Herald* by Alex Joske and myself revealing that the Australian Research Council was funding Chinese military scientists to do research in our universities, the ARC wrote to all universities telling them to clean up their act. At a meeting of deputy vice-chancellors in Tasmania that Mary had attended, officials from the defence department had walked in unannounced to make sure the universities had got the message about what they must do to comply with regulations. The other DVCs looked daggers at Mary. The University of Technology Sydney and the University of New South Wales were particularly annoyed because the regulator subjected them to a full audit, much more onerous than the more casual ones they were used to.

Excellent, I thought, that's exactly what should have happened, at least as a start. Those universities had been selling out Australia for years. Now they had been exposed, they were engaging in denial, deflection and blame-shifting.

When the contract from Hardie Grant arrived in the post, I notified Andy Vann and informed him I planned to sign it the next day. Within hours, I received a long email detailing the various rules and regulations I must abide by. In effect, he instructed me not to sign it until the university had assessed it and the wider situation. It was a Sunday.

Over the next few days, it was clear to me that Andy was receiving advice that was ill-informed, to say the least. He had been told that the university might be sued, which was ridiculous. The university didn't know what it was doing. On Thursday, going directly against the vice-chancellor's instructions, I signed the contract and posted it back to Hardie Grant. I felt there were larger forces at play than CSU over in Bathurst. Besides, I had powerful backers. The university could do what it liked.

§

I made two submissions to parliament's national security committee inquiry into the proposed foreign interference laws. The first was a detailed exposé, written with Alex, on the structure and operations of the CCP's united front in Australia. It highlighted the role of the Australian Council for the Promotion of Peaceful Reunification of China (ACPPRC), Huang Xiangmo's outfit and the central CCP influence agency in Australia. That submission became a frequent reference source for journalists and other researchers.

The second was the manuscript of *Silent Invasion*. On 22 January I took a copy to the marbled entrance hall of Parliament House and handed it to the committee secretary, Anna Dacre, one of those highly professional and discreet public servants who keep the place running smoothly. She knew I was handing her a hot potato. Later that day she phoned to tell me she had received some legal advice. While publication on the committee's site would attract privilege, publication of the same words by a commercial publisher would not. I indicated I had different advice. She suggested a couple of academic experts in parliamentary law that I might like to talk to.

That night, Andrew Hastie, who chaired the committee, phoned me from Perth. He was fully supportive of publication by the committee. 'I support free speech and I don't like bullies,' he said. My sentiments exactly. There's no reason why the left and the right cannot both be committed to protecting democratic freedoms and Australia's sovereignty.

The MUP story was bursting to get out, so I phoned Nick McKenzie to tell him what had transpired. Nick has an uncanny ability to make you tell him things against your better judgement and I found myself unloading the whole story about trying to secure parliamentary privilege. Feeling guilty, I had him swear to keep the confidences, as the situation was delicate. He saw the significance immediately. He phoned the next day to tell me that there was a split in the committee, and he passed on some strictly confidential information about what was happening.

On Monday afternoon, 29 January, Anna Dacre phoned to tell me the committee had decided to publish my submission with Alex but had decided to accept the manuscript only as an 'exhibit' and not as a submission. It would therefore not be publishing *Silent Invasion* on its website. I was surprised; I had thought it was a slam dunk. I probed for reasons, but her job was to communicate the committee's decision.

Nick's story the next day was the page-one lead in both *The Age* and the *Herald*. But it didn't mention the moves to publish my manuscript in Hansard. Instead, its focus was on a joint ASIO–AFP collaboration to implement the new laws and on our united front submission, 'the most detailed exposé of Chinese government influence operations to ever be published'. Nice one, Nick; it was true.

I was due to appear before the national security committee on Wednesday but slipped into the hearing on Tuesday to listen to testimony by Peter Jennings of the Australian Strategic Policy Institute and to get a feel for the proceedings. I was feeling conspicuous as there were only two others in the audience when who should walk in and sit next to me but Andy Vann, there to represent Universities Australia. It was awkward for me, but he was breezy and didn't appear to be holding a grudge. In the tea-break I managed to grab a couple of minutes with chair Andrew Hastie and Labor's deputy chair, Anthony Byrne, my strongest supporters. I learned that negotiations about publication were continuing.

Meanwhile, I had been speaking to Brendan Gogarty, a parliamentary law expert from the University of Tasmania, who raised a new obstacle. Documents published by parliament are subject to Crown copyright, so Hardie Grant would need to obtain a licence if the committee were to publish the manuscript. The rules are murky, though. The Yirrkala Bark Petition of 1963 comes into it somewhere: would the Yolngu people need to obtain a licence to publish their own petition?

On Wednesday, my half-hour slot giving evidence to the committee extended to just over an hour. There was no hostile questioning and plenty of opportunity to explain my position. Among other things, members were interested in the difficulties I was having publishing. Chairman Hastie concluded the session by quoting into the record the last two rip-roaring paragraphs of my book. After the session, Neil James of the Australia Defence Association approached, handed me his card and congratulated me. Bedfellows.

§

Monday, 5 February 2018 was the start of a big week. Nick phoned to tell me that the next day, the *Herald* and *The Age* would be running his story about the committee considering publication of the manuscript. The story would put pressure on Mark Dreyfus, Labor's shadow attorney-general, who was standing in the way of publication.

Early on Tuesday, I detoured to Kingston shops to buy copies of *The Age* and *The Sydney Morning Herald*. Nick's story, written with Richard Baker, was on the front page of both with the headline 'Controversial China book may get parliamentary protection'. It began: 'Key members of Federal Parliament's national security committee are backing a move to use the committee's powers to publish an explosive book on Chinese Communist Party influence in

Australia.' Turnbull had been briefed and was happy for it to happen, they reported, although diplomatic fallout was inevitable. The story went on to talk about MUP. 'It's understood that at least one senior Melbourne University official raised concerns about Beijing's ability to dissuade students from attending the university if MUP published the book.'

That day I was inside another media whirlwind, including several overseas outlets, all following up on Nick's story. They could see the significance of such a gambit by a parliament. My contact in the US embassy told me the State Department was watching events closely. Support flowed in by email and text.

On Wednesday, I arrived at the ABC's Northbourne Avenue studios at 7.55 am for an interview with Fran Kelly on Radio National's *Breakfast* about the book's possible publication by parliament. She blindsided me with a question about Sydney University vice-chancellor Michael Spence denying to her that anything untoward happens on his campus. Spence claimed that when ASIO briefed a meeting of vice-chancellors about CCP activities, one of those present asked if ASIO had hard evidence. Spence alleged that ASIO had said no. I said I knew that to be untrue. I described the activities of the Chinese Students and Scholars Association at Sydney University and Spence's own actions in kicking the Dalai Lama off campus under Chinese consulate pressure. Fran said, 'So are you saying he's lying?' Whoa, careful, Clive. I suggested he spend less time down at the Chinese consulate and more time taking note of what happens on his campus. Bang!

Leaving the studio, I was fretting that I had gone over the top. Nick texted saying, 'You nailed it,' which calmed me down.

That same morning, I received a call to tell me the committee would publish the book at midday. I was on tenterhooks. By early afternoon nothing had happened; something was amiss. The ABC's Dylan Welch, whom I'd notified of impending publication, phoned to say some Labor members were resisting. A message a bit later told me to wait another day.

In Beijing, a foreign ministry spokesperson was asked about my book at a regular press conference. He spouted the usual guff about Sinophobia and China's desire to live in peace and harmony.

On Friday I was in Melbourne to meet the Hardie Grant crew. After Nick McKenzie's story on Tuesday, all the staff now knew. The receptionist couldn't wait to tell me about the flood of support the company had received from the public. There was a buzz of excitement around the office because Hardie Grant had picked up the book no other publisher would touch. They were pumped.

At a two-hour meeting in the boardroom with seven senior staff, I heard about the enormous interest in the book, with 6000 pre-orders already, a month out from publication. I said I'd be very surprised if we didn't sell at least 20,000. There was general agreement. In the end, *Silent Invasion* would sell 30,000 copies in Australia and be published in several languages, including Chinese, Korean, Vietnamese and Japanese. (The Japanese publisher later said it sold an astonishing 60,000 copies.) WHSmith wanted to put the book on their advertising screens at airports. They asked Hardie Grant to prepare a short video and suggested it be modelled on their current one promoting E. L. James's latest book. Just the thing, *Fifty Shades of Red*. In our discussion of the media strategy, a publicist said Geraldine Doogue seemed very pro-Beijing. I was glad it was not just me who thought so.

A few days later, Julie Pinkham emailed to say that Hardie Grant's distributor, Penguin Random House (which takes orders from bookshops then dispatches books from its warehouse), was refusing to distribute *Silent Invasion* unless Hardie Grant indemnified it against legal action, agreed to pay for a barrister and sent a copy of the manuscript forthwith. It was totally unprecedented and absurd. 'Piss-weak bastards,' was all I could write back. After a stiff letter from Sandy, Penguin backed down, probably when they realised they were one day away from being the villains on the front page of *The Age*. It was all getting crazy.

On Wednesday, 14 February, Nick McKenzie phoned to say he had heard there was a problem to do with Chinese interference within the national security committee. An alarm bell rang loudly in my head; I had alerted a committee member to a possible agent of influence close to the committee, but I was not willing to say anything except to confirm there was a potential problem. Nick phoned later that night to tell me a third party had independently alerted him to the issue. It was explosive.

§

Progress stalled on parliamentary publication. While I waited, some very disturbing news came through from Geoff Wade at the Parliamentary Library. Anne-Marie Brady, my counterpart in New Zealand, had now had her home in Christchurch burgled after her university office had been broken into a few months earlier. They stole laptops and her passport but left cash and jewellery. The police were sweeping her home for bugs and taking prints. It sounded sinister. I emailed Anne-Marie with support. She replied saying she'd received a warning letter. It's one thing to be burgled by crooks, quite another to suspect state actors have been in your house snooping around and thieving. Prime Minister Ardern would soon call in the secret service to investigate.

The burglary prompted me to again review my security at work and at home. I let Hazel, our office manager, know and suggested we step up our vigilance. We had a meeting at which a senior security expert advised me to be very careful to protect any sensitive materials. I could expect cyber intrusions and it was likely the Chinese embassy had mounted an intelligence operation against me, and it would become more intense. Okay, I thought, now I'm scared. The next day a pair of AFP officers arrived; they knew about the burglary in New Zealand. We discussed measures to protect my safety, including placing my work and home addresses on a police watchlist, meaning any call would receive an immediate response. We talked quite a bit about my safety at public events like book launches and writers' festivals. They gave me their cards that read 'Federal Agent' with addresses across the road and invited me to call anytime. They were downbeat and professional, and pretty impressive.

At the same time, I was coming under a barrage of cyberattacks. Google was messaging me about unusual activity. I changed passwords again and took my laptop and desktop out to the experts in Fyshwick. A couple of days later they told me they had found malware in 'every nook and cranny' of the laptop, some of it recently planted and possibly by 'state actors'. We talked about wiping the hard drive clean and rebuilding from the operating system up, but even that contained risks. It was safer to buy a new one.

Through this whole period, each day I carried around a low-level feeling of dread, looking over my shoulder and never knowing what might be coming. I thought I might better understand it if I re-read *1984*, but a quarter of the way in I found the evocation of life under surveillance by a sinister force so disturbing that I had to put the book aside. Gerry Groot, perhaps Australia's leading academic expert on the united front, was quoted saying that the Brady burglaries could have been outsourced by the Chinese embassy to triads. Great – now I had to worry about organised criminals.

§

By mid-February I had given up hope that the book would receive the protection of parliament. News out of the national security committee's internal wrangling indicated that one or two Labor members were 'going mad', with Mark Dreyfus the main roadblock. I wanted to put pressure on him over his obstructionism – he was now threatening to 'blow up the inquiry'. And I wanted to get my retaliation in first because I had been told he was going to accuse me of 'making stuff up' in the book.

So, on 19 February, *The Sydney Morning Herald* carried an op-ed by me entitled 'Labor has a cancer growing in it that must be cut out'. I wrote that Labor, urged on by Dreyfus, was gearing up to oppose the foreign interference legislation and that apologists for China in the party had been entrenching the CCP's structure of influence. It was strong stuff, but I thought it had to be said and I knew it would be welcomed by some in the ALP.

Not Paul Keating, though, judging by the raging letter in the *Herald* a day later. It was so abusive I was surprised they published it. Bizarrely, he dredged up my criticisms of the Hawke–Keating economic reforms, a subject on which I had written nothing for years. He finished the letter by calling me a 'nincompoop'. Weird. Bob Carr was out there promoting Keating's letter and calling me 'a Green party zealot'. I was told by a senior ALP source that Rudd was 'cranky' too, and soon enough he had a letter in the *Herald* fulminating against my op-ed and calling me 'a third-rate academic'.

Now I had two ex-PMs and an ex-foreign minister after my blood. Fuck 'em, I thought. Fortunately, *The Australian* published a feature article about me and the book, written by Rowan Callick, one of the good guys writing for the Murdoch broadsheet whom I'd met in Beijing. I came out of it looking intrepid and determined. When you're feeling under siege, boosts like that are especially heartening.

On 22 February, with publication four days away, a box containing copies of *Silent Invasion* arrived at my office. Hardie Grant had moved so fast that the book was due to appear a few days before the original Allen & Unwin publication date. Holding a copy of a new book for the first time is always a milestone moment, and never more so than in this case. *Yes*, I said to myself, this is the definitive up-yours to all those who stood in the way of this book's publication. It was surely unstoppable now. Julie Pinkham emailed to tell me *Silent Invasion* had reached sixth on the Amazon Australia bestseller list, and it wasn't even out yet. A few days later, the Saturday editions of *The Age* and the *Herald* carried two long extracts. We were finally out in the world. With the newspapers spread over the kitchen bench, I felt relief and exhilaration in every cell.

25

The reception

O N PUBLICATION DAY there was a buzz among China watchers across Australia about *Silent Invasion*. Inevitably, the critics were now coming out. On that very day, the *Australian Book Review* carried a long review attacking the book, written by David Brophy, a Trotskyist from the University of Sydney. It was driven by an old left stance in which the real enemy is US imperialism. Any trouble between China and Australia, he argued, must be all our fault because of our history of anti-Chinese racism. He didn't ask why the same concern about CCP interference was being played out in Taiwan, Singapore, Canada, New Zealand and elsewhere. Ostensibly a review of a book about China under the CCP, it was mostly about the United States and Australian racism. It was classic 'whataboutism', a debating trick rather than an argument. (In marriage therapy, she says, 'You never talk to me,' and he replies, 'What about all the money you spend?')

Some of the social media reaction was hysterical, not least the tweets of Su-Lin Tan, a journalist at the *Australian Financial Review*. She branded me 'racist in chief', wanted to send me to China to 'learn a few things', and said she'd like to hit me with a wok and ladle. A day or two later, race discrimination commissioner Tim Soutphommasane joined the pile on in the *Herald*, referencing 'yellow hordes', 'white

Australia' and the like. Without any evidence, he wrote off *Silent Invasion* as anti-China and promoting Sinophobia. It was so superficial that he couldn't have read the book. I replied a few days later lambasting him for trashing the views of Chinese Australians who strongly support my argument and helped provide evidence for the book. Like the CCP, Soutphommasane was silencing the victims.

On cue, the Chinese embassy issued a statement about *Silent Invasion*:

> The author of the book has been recklessly playing up the 'China Threat' for quite some time, trying to defame and smear China by all means. His allegations, which are imbued with disinformation and racist bigotry, fully reveal his malicious anti-China mentality. His vicious intention is doomed to fall flat on its face.

In Beijing, when a foreign ministry spokesperson was asked about the book, he launched into a pre-prepared broadside, repeating Keating's attacks but ramping up the insults in that hysterical CCP way. The *Global Times*, a party tabloid, published a photo of *Silent Invasion* being flushed down a toilet. And a few days later, the PRC foreign ministry attacked me for my 'rumour-mongering and racial prejudice, fully exposing his own anti-China dark side'. It was theatre, but also disconcerting for the message it sent to red-hot patriots in Australia.

§

Experts had advised me on the risks of public appearances, so I was nervous when I travelled to Adelaide for my first public event at Adelaide Writers' Week. An incident that night didn't help. I was in my pyjamas ready for bed in my room at the Stamford Plaza hotel when there was a loud knock on the door. Peering through the spyhole I saw a man of Chinese appearance, apparently room service. I had ordered nothing. I opened the door a bit and he said, 'Bucket of ice, sir?' 'No, thanks,' I replied and closed the door. It was unsettling.

I phoned reception and described what happened. 'Is that usual?' I asked. 'Sorry, sir,' came the reply. 'A woman came to reception and asked for a bucket of ice to be delivered to your room.'

The next day, a bright Sunday morning, I walked down to the festival site on the lawns by the River Torrens. All talks were free and on open-air stages. At noon, as I made my way through the crowds to the green room, I bumped into the Hardie Grant crew. As we chatted, an ALP elder stopped and congratulated me. His wife, who had already read the book, leaned in to say conspiratorially, 'It's spot-on.' In the green room (well, the green tent), I chatted awkwardly with Damien Cave, Australia correspondent for *The New York Times*, who didn't believe this China threat stuff and had tweeted that, as the session chair, he would be giving me a hard time. I was ready for that. The festival director, Laura Kroetsch, arrived to tell us that Crime Stoppers had had a tip-off that a protest against me was planned. Laura said they'd stepped up security and the police were on hand. My disquiet rose a couple of notches, although I knew how sensational it would be if Chinese students tried to stop me speaking.

Recalling the police advice that I would be most vulnerable when making my way to and from events, we warily walked out of the green room to see a huge crowd waiting in the outdoor setting, filling the seats in the central arena with hundreds more sitting on the grassy rise on the far side and on extra chairs on this side. There were maybe seven or eight hundred people. I scanned for any troublemakers but could see nothing. Two policemen were prominently placed at the entrance, arms crossed, chests out. We approached from behind the stage and took our seats. I studied the audience for any potential dangers, spotting Sandy Grant towards the rear. Damien introduced me, briefly as requested. I began by outlining the difficulty of finding a publisher, praising Hardie Grant for picking it up and Sandy Grant in particular.

I then responded to those who accused me of xenophobia by describing the measures I took from day one to avoid any such accusation and the prominence of Chinese voices in the book. I devoted most of my words to the silencing of Chinese Australians. The crowd listened attentively. My opening rebuttal of the xenophobia charge and the sympathy of the crowd seemed to have taken the wind out of Damien's sails, and his questions were probing but without aggro.

The session wrapped up to generous applause. Laura did her job of dragging me away from buttonholers and leading me to the book-signing table. The queue was daunting; Sandy estimated that two hundred people had lined up. I picked up a lot from dozens of brief chats. The most frequent comment was 'You're very brave', which made me nervous because it implied I had a lot to be brave about. The takeaway message from that hour or two was that there was widespread anxiety from all kinds of people. Many commented on something they'd observed or read that had unsettled them. I didn't pick up any racist views, such as generalisations about 'the Chinese'.

The deepest expressions of gratitude came from those in the queue of Chinese heritage. One woman, fifty or so, had migrated from Xinjiang (so probably a Uyghur) and spoke to me of the concentration camps recently built to take those caught in the crackdown. Her daughter, who looked to be in her twenties, said the session had allowed her finally to understand how her mother feels living in Australia. They both radiated a beautiful inner composure. I could see we were each moved by our brief meeting.

As I signed the last book, I breathed a deep sigh of relief; the first public event was over and I was in one piece. It all augured well. The Hardie Grant team could not have been happier. As we chatted at a table in the sun, Sandy checked his phone to see that *Silent Invasion* was an Amazon bestseller in Australia and the USA. We were flushed with success. 'We haven't received the first legal letter yet,' Sandy mused.

§

Back in Canberra, I met up with my US embassy contact. There was strong interest in my book in the State Department; they saw Australia as a laboratory for CCP influence and worried that our politics would shift to a pro-China position, given Beijing's influential supporters among our elites. I learned from her that Mark Dreyfus had become 'hysterical' in his opposition to publication. Around Parliament House, some Labor people were saying my aim in writing the book was to harm Labor and help the Greens. My God, I thought, is that really how these people see the world?

I'd arranged to meet Børge Bakken, an expert in China's police and criminal justice system who had taught for years in Hong Kong. He relayed a story from another regular researcher at the National Library, a China expert who, like me, works in the Petherick Reading Room, a place reserved for registered researchers. She'd noticed a couple of 'Chinese students' snooping around the pigeonholes. When she challenged them, they left quickly. She then asked the front desk staff who owns the pigeonhole they were taking items from and was told 'Clive Hamilton'. Whoa! How could they know the number of my pigeonhole, other than from an insider? I notified my AFP contact so that it would be on the record.

ANU historian Frank Bongiorno wrote a thoughtful review of *Silent Invasion*. It was quite critical on some fronts, including the title, but finished by writing that the book 'is, without question, one of the really important Australian publishing events of recent years and a truly significant contribution to debate about Australia's future relationship with China'. On reflection, although the attacks on me and the book got under my skin, taken together with the expressions of appreciation, they signalled that *Silent Invasion* was a book that *mattered*. In the end, that's what every public intellectual hopes for.

§

In March 2018, I jumped briefly out of the stream of China events. One day, a Monday, I oversaw the unveiling of a restored honour board at Manuka Pool. The plaque had been installed in 1947 to commemorate the deaths of nine young men who frequented the pool in the 1930s before going off to war, never to return. Friends of Manuka

Pool, of which I was president, had had the decaying and forlorn honour board repaired and spruced up. For a small event put on by a little community group at a local pool, the turnout was extraordinary. Top brass and department secretaries had accepted our invitations.

When proceedings began, I explained why we had restored the board. Rebecca Scouller, our vice-president, introduced our oldest member, Merv Knowles, who was ninety-five and present on the day the pool opened in 1931. An air commodore representing the chief of the Australian Defence Force then spoke of the sacrifice of the nine young men whose names are recorded on the plaque and whose bodies are buried in far-off places. He then performed the unveiling.

We moved to the pool's concourse, which is enclosed on four sides. The pool had been cleared and all was still under the heat of the late afternoon sun. A bugler from the Royal Military College band stood alone at attention at the other end of the shimmering water. On the signal, he performed an emotion-charged rendition of the Last Post. As the final note faded and stillness descended, we bowed our heads for a minute's silence. At the sides of the pool stood a few families in swimming costumes, including one heavily pregnant woman in a bikini holding her belly in two hands. The cries of the crows over-head only deepened the silence. It's hard to imagine a moment more intimately Australian.

§

Chinese Australians from the pro-democracy Australian Values Alliance decided to hold a launch of *Silent Invasion* in Sydney. John Hu suggested I ask a Greens MP to book a room at New South Wales Parliament House. David Shoebridge, a member of the upper house, readily agreed but soon pulled out, pressured by a couple of people from the 'anti-racist left' in the Greens. I told him I was dismayed that a Greens MP should actively join the silencing of these Chinese Australians, already under pressure from an authoritarian state. Christine Milne in Hobart soon heard of my 'deplatforming' and phoned me aghast. Christine and Bob Brown had for years despaired at the wrecking influence of the hard left faction in the New South Wales Greens, built up around Lee Rhiannon and Shoebridge. Luckily, a more courageous Greens MP, Justin Field, stepped in and booked the room for the Australian Values Alliance to hold the launch.

Despite a deep split in the Greens and a ferocious social media campaign organised by a fanatical activist who openly praised CCP rule, Justin held his ground, and on 14 March the event went ahead. New South Wales police had been put on alert by the AFP in Canberra and security was tight. As I approached the room, I was surrounded by people shaking my hand, thanking me, asking me to sign copies of the book and getting their friends to take photos with me. Of the 130 or so people packed into the room, well over a hundred were Chinese Australians, Tibetans or Uyghurs.

John Hu welcomed everyone and spoke of AVA's support for the book, as did AVA official Albert Fan and Associate Professor Feng Chongyi of UTS. Chongyi lent me strong support throughout. Introduced by China scholar Kevin Carrico, I told the gathering I wrote the book firstly for them and spoke of the silencing of Chinese Australian critics of the CCP. The mood in the room was one of excitement, solidarity and gratitude. At last, someone 'respectable' in mainstream society had taken seriously what they knew and feared about the CCP in Australia.

A week later, John Hu phoned in an agitated state. He'd just been deported from China after landing in Shanghai with his eighty-year-old mother and carrying his father's ashes to be scattered. As the plane docked, security police came on board, picked out John and took him off the plane. They held him for some hours then put him on a plane bound for Sydney. He soon learned that his name had been added to a watchlist with explicit mention of his role in the launch of *Silent Invasion*.

By mid-March, more than 20,000 copies of the book had been printed and I was replying to a constant stream of emails from a wide variety of people concerned about CCP influence. Hundreds of them.

An unusual one was from a Canberra woman telling me about her father-in-law, a former brigadier, now ninety-four and stuck in a nursing home. He's a big fan of *Silent Invasion* and *Defiant Earth*, she wrote, and it would be such a boon if I could possibly visit him for a chat. It's hard to say no to a plea like that, so I called in on Saturday afternoon. He was trapped by his failing body in a place he hated. 'You can go mad in here,' he told me, and I could immediately see why for a man of his intellect. It was the only building I've ever been in where you have to punch in two codes to get *out*. Please God, don't let me end up in a place like that. I'll take the fentanyl first.

§

A Canberra book launch was organised at the ANU for early April. I was worried about it as my alma mater was a hotbed of patriotic activity by Chinese students. Organised by Colin Steele, the former university librarian, and Rory Medcalf of the National Security College, the event would be held at the Molonglo Theatre. Within a couple of days, registrations had exceeded the theatre's capacity. Rory and the organisers were taking my security seriously – pre-registration was required, rapid exit routes were scoped out, door checks would be in place, and additional security guards would be present. I'd begun to wonder, though, whether the Chinese embassy, conscious of the likely backlash, had instructed its supporters to stay away.

On the evening of the event, the lecture theatre was packed out, with people standing at the back and sitting in the aisles. Security was conspicuous. I chatted with a burly AFP officer whose brief was to monitor anti-CCP groups and CCP intimidation of them.

The atmosphere in the theatre was charged but I didn't detect any hostility. Rory's questions were mostly foreseeable, but he threw at me a couple of tricky ones. When he said, 'Now I turn to the chief accusation …' I interrupted: 'Did you say the *cheap* accusation?' which got a laugh. Of course, it was the racism charge. I replied that I knew from the start it was a risk and described the series of measures

I took in the research and writing to head off the accusation. And when I put it to a group of Chinese Australians, they replied, 'We're more afraid of the CCP than of Australian racists.' Most in the audience seemed persuaded. I'd been around ANU for many years and my politics were well known.

After doing hundreds of events over the years, I'd learned to be attuned to the quality of the applause at the end; it's the best guide to how things went. That night it was warm and prolonged. A prominent professor later emailed describing the event as 'an electric occasion'. With that event out of the way, I was ready to withdraw to my office, out of the public eye.

§

When *Silent Invasion* was published, only a handful of us were warning of the dangers of the CCP. Throughout 2018, the media reported more and more stories about China, Xi Jinping's ambitions and CCP influence in Australia. Editors knew that Australians had become concerned and wanted to read China stories. On 10 April, David Wroe broke an important story in the *Herald* about the PRC's secret plans to acquire a naval base in Vanuatu. I had flagged it as a possibility in my book, but even I was shocked by how quickly Beijing had moved.

Beijing's apologists were out in force. The *AFR* was positioning itself as the voice of pro-Beijing business. Paul Keating, paid to advise the state-owned China Development Bank, used his rhetorical skills to laud the Chinese government and savage Australia's pushback. Australia's most naïve businessman, Andrew Forrest, was trying to pressure Turnbull to bow to Beijing. He truly believed China is our greatest friend and mouthed CCP talking points. At the high-profile, Beijing-backed Bo'ao Forum in Hainan, Forrest actually spoke of 'our shared humanity in the coming century', a favourite Xi slogan. Joining him on the platform, Bob Carr praised Xi Jinping as 'a truly far-sighted and eminently wise leader'. (What do they have on him?)

Later, at an event in Sydney put on by Carr's China-funded Australia-China Relations Institute, Professor John Keane of the University of Sydney argued that, despite appearances, China is in fact a democratic country. We should stop worrying, he said, and finished with words you have to hear to believe: 'China is the future of democracy.' It was fascist talk – totalitarianism is democracy, aggression is peace, the people and the leader are one.

Silent Invasion was also being read and discussed among Canberra diplomats. I was invited to intimate lunches at expensive restaurants and embassy residences. They told me they all had the same problem. A diplomat from one Asian country said of China's spreading influence: 'If nothing's done to stop it, we'll no longer be a sovereign nation.'

§

I had been invited to testify before a US congressional committee and to speak at the State Department, and it was a relief to fly out of Australia in late April. I'd been too caught up in the febrile atmosphere; time away would allow me to regain composure and reflect on what had happened. I travelled via Canada, with the first event organised by the Canadian Security Intelligence Service in Ottawa, ASIO's counterpart but much more open to the world. People from several civil service departments were invited and it was standing room only. They were all grappling with the problem of CCP interference.

Arriving that evening in Toronto from Ottawa, I read on my phone that near the city centre a van had deliberately mounted a kerb and killed twelve people. On the streets walking to my hotel, the atmosphere around Union Station seemed unchanged, with excited crowds making their way to a Maple Leafs ice hockey game. The massacre was of course all over the papers in the morning, but there was no discernible change in the public mood. I'd been in cities after terrible events – Paris after Bataclan, Sydney after the Lindt Cafe, London after the knife-wielding attack at Borough Market.

A miasma of shock and grief settles over the city. In Toronto, I picked up nothing. A couple of others I asked had noticed the same thing. Perhaps it hadn't yet sunk in.

At the University of Waterloo, I gave a lecture and a seminar on the Anthropocene, then flew to Washington, DC. As the aircraft approached Ronald Reagan airport, the flight attendant announced that we would be landing 'momentarily'. I hoped we would have enough time to get off. The next day I arrived at the Russell Senate Office for my appearance before the Congressional-Executive Committee on China. Two others were testifying in the same session, both from human rights groups.

In my statement, I outlined the story of my book, linking Allen & Unwin's pull-out to the intimidatory effect of defamation actions by Chau Chak Wing. I made a point of mentioning John Hu's travails in the hope that exposure before the US Congress would give him a bit of protection. And I took the opportunity to respond to a couple of my critics, including Kevin Rudd, well known in Washington.

The chair and co-chair asked me a few straightforward questions. I realised that the hearings were not aimed at eliciting new information (they have staff to do that) but to give exposure and congressional imprimatur to the views of well-informed critics of the CCP.

I excused myself early to make my way to the Department of State. As I was leaving, a public servant from the Australian Department of Home Affairs introduced himself; secretary Michael Pezzullo had asked for a report on my appearance. I arrived at the state department at Foggy Bottom, now understanding what journalists mean when they say 'over at Foggy Bottom'. It's the name of a neighbourhood.

I had been invited to give a lecture at the Bunche Library, deep in the bowels of 'State'. I concentrated on united front activity in Australia and the way elites are subverted to serve Beijing's interests. The questions were pointed and well informed. It was already clear that some people in Washington were watching events in Australia very closely indeed. After the lecture, I met with people from various parts of the state department. The last was with seven or eight people in a nondescript meeting room in a remote corner of the huge complex. On the wall hung portraits of Donald Trump and Mike Pence. One of them remarked that, as far as he was aware, they were the only photographs of the president and vice-president in the entire building. Everyone understood the point.

It had been a huge day, and over dinner alone that night I reflected on some of the impressions I had formed. Although Russia still hogged the headlines, many analysts and officials were focusing more on PRC influence and how to deal with it. But they lagged Australia in their grasp of what the CCP was up to, and they knew it, which was why they were so keen to hear from me and, more so, John Garnaut, whose views have been very influential in Washington. One mystified senior State official said to me: 'Bob Carr was an American history buff, an Americophile. What happened to him?' I offered an opinion or two. They were all puzzled by Kevin Rudd and where he stands on China. They couldn't work him out because he's all over the shop, so I obliged with a bit of history.

Although it had not been published in the US, *Silent Invasion*, or at least the story of it, was well known in DC. The following day, Friday, was filled with interviews and talks at Beltway think tanks. Monday was my main public event in Washington, a lecture at the Center for Strategic and Budgetary Assessments on K Street, ground zero for Washington lobbyists and think tankers. In Q&A, the only question that threw me was from an old bloke who looked to me like he'd spent forty years in the Pentagon. 'You've talked about how to defend Australia from PRC intrusion. But successful defence requires attack. What can be done to attack?' As Australians, from a middle power, we don't think like that.

Later I met up with the admirable Sophie Richardson of Human Rights Watch. A long-time global activist, she knows better than anyone the positions taken by nations at the UN on China's worsening human rights situation. No nation, she said, is more indifferent to human rights abuses in China than Australia, then adding, 'except New Zealand'. She's a Kiwi.

On the previous Saturday, a free day, I had spent the morning hanging out at the landmark Kramerbooks at Dupont Circle. Over coffee, I read a long feature article in *The Wall Street Journal* by Cambridge don David Runciman, titled 'China's challenge to democracy'. Runciman asked whether citizens of Western democracies would be tempted to support the PRC's authoritarian model in their own countries because it delivers results. But this is the wrong question. The question is: will the political systems of the West be able to resist the influence and interference operations of the CCP, which aim to subdue them *without changing* the democratic model of governance?

At Kramerbooks, I picked up a copy of a new edition of the *I Ching*. It fell open at hexagram XXV, Wu Wang, Freedom from Guile: 'It profits to be steadfast. Absence of truth leads to disaster.'

26
Enemy of the state

Fℴℛ ˢᴵˣ ᴹᴼɴᵀᴴˢ since November 2017, I had been on high alert with elevated levels of cortisol in my body. Now back in Canberra, I had lost my mojo and had to drag myself through the day. People were already asking me what I would be doing now that *Silent Invasion* was out of the way. It was a question I'd been wondering about. To be honest, I wanted to take myself out of the firing line and return to the safer territory of the climate crisis. But whether I liked it or not, I had obligations now to all kinds of people, especially Chinese Australians, who were looking to me to speak up. And there were only a handful of us able to feed the media's mounting interest in CCP interference, which I wanted to sustain if I could. There could be no clean break from this episode in my life.

A week or two after I returned from the US, I met up with a cyber-warfare thinker from the defence department. Of all the conversations I'd had about what the PRC was doing, this was one of the most fascinating. Our defence establishment barely realises what it is up against, she said, a new kind of adversary engaged in coordinated cyber operations, psychological operations, human intelligence gathering and information warfare. Although several people had told me defence chiefs were reading my book, shifting a mindset entrenched in history takes years. Our problem, my contact suggested, is that China has a powerful national narrative built on a story of humiliation and rejuvenation, while our national narrative is … what? Some flabby, vague and contested story about a friendly island under the southern sun. She said that Australia was at risk of succumbing to 'learned help-lessness' in the face of a rising China, reflected in the view, widespread in DFAT and the Department of Prime Minister and Cabinet, that we can do nothing in the face of such a power.

A couple of months later, I was invited to give a talk at a forum on information warfare to people from the Five Eyes intelligence-sharing alliance. Held at the former RAAF Base Fairbairn, a handful of civilians talked to an audience of military officers about China's grey-zone warfare (coercive activities short of war). For me it was another 'what am I doing here?' moment. I never imagined my work intersecting with anything military. The truth is that China had changed the boundaries of what constitutes warfare – its practice of political warfare forces us to cross boundaries. Chatting with a senior US officer during a break, I said to her that I was assuming that if China invaded Taiwan then the US would use its cyber capability to shut down China's telecommunications and electricity networks. She replied, 'We would never do that.' I looked at her, surprised, and she added, 'We don't know what they have planted in our networks.' It was chilling. Cyber had replaced nuclear missiles in a game of mutually assured disruption.

Meanwhile, I had received an invitation from pro-democracy students at the Chinese University of Hong Kong to speak at a confer-ence. The student protests were escalating into mass demonstrations, with a mood of desperation in the face of Beijing's increasingly ruth-less assertion of power. Pro-democracy students were familiar with *Silent Invasion*, recognising in my analysis the CCP's aims and tactics in their city. After asking one or two others, I decided the risk of arrest was too high and declined the invitation, although I felt cowardly doing so. A few weeks later, a delegation of Hong Kong trade unionists arrived in Canberra. We gathered for lunch at Parliament

House, earnestly discussing the pro-democracy campaign that was taking to the streets. Eighteen months later, as the protests in Hong Kong reached a crescendo, I was asked by pro-democracy activists in Melbourne to speak at a fundraiser staged by the Australia–Hong Kong Link group. It was an extraordinary event. Anticipating Beijing-backed disruption, police were out in force and entry to the event was tightly controlled. Before a passionate audience of Hong Kongers, who broke out in ardent protest chants, the star of the show was the enormously popular Cantopop singer Denise Ho, with underground Chinese artist Badiucao and me as 'backup acts'. It was a hugely inspirational night, with the crowd's chants lifting the roof off. Still, I felt certain the protest movement would be crushed. Beijing would not tolerate it for much longer. When the end came, the only answer for those who wanted to remain free was to leave their home city. In May 2022, Denise Ho was taken into custody.

§

On 23 May 2018, Liberal MP Andrew Hastie gave a sensational speech in Parliament House. He identified Chau Chak Wing as the unnamed 'co-conspirator' in a US court indictment, the person who provided the funds to bribe the president of the UN General Assembly. Sheri Yan, who worked for Chau, paid the bribe and went to jail. Hastie said Chau had been 'in close contact with the United Front, the influence arm of the Chinese Communist Party ...'. Although he resides in a huge compound in Guangdong, Chau is an Australian citizen and has been a major donor to both main political parties.

At the time of Hastie's intervention, Chau was suing the ABC, Fairfax and Nick McKenzie for defamation, after a *Four Corners* program and associated news stories claimed Chau had united front connections and was linked to the UN bribery scandal. Chau hired Mark O'Brien, who had come after me on behalf of David Jones, and the case was having a chilling effect on news reporting on CCP influence. Eventually, the court ruled in Chau's favour, after Justice

Steven Rares, in his wisdom, ruled that evidence that came to light after the *Four Corners* program, to wit, the FBI report on the bribery case, could not be taken into consideration.

I was watching these events keenly because Chau's defamation suits (this one and the one against John Garnaut) had been the foremost reason for Allen & Unwin dropping my book. And I had learned that another publisher interested in publishing *Silent Invasion* had been warned by a well-connected person that 'Chau Chak Wing has deep pockets'. It's probably unnecessary to note that the sections in *Silent Invasion* dealing with Chau received special attention from our defamation lawyers.

Chau seemed to be cropping up everywhere. He donated $20 million for a new building, designed by celebrated architect Frank Gehry, at the University of Technology Sydney. He seemed to have become close to Michael Spence at the University of Sydney after donating $15 million for a new museum, so that now the first words one sees when entering the main gate of the university are 'Chau Chak Wing'.

The media was now publishing story after story about China's malign activities in Australia. They couldn't get enough of it. Fairfax, Murdoch, commercial TV and the ABC were all looking for good stories. The 'panda huggers' among Australia's political, business and academic elites found themselves for the first time receiving some serious pushback; the evidence kept mounting against their view that there is nothing to worry about, that China is no threat. Some of them worked harder to win back the initiative, but now they were seen in a different light. On social media, they were being denounced as CCP shills and traitors.

Over the next couple of years, I made submissions to parliamentary inquiries and gave evidence to committees. Working with my friend and research collaborator Amy Cheng, I looked closely into the links Gladys Liu, the federal Liberal candidate, maintained with united front figures, and I teamed up with China scholar Catherine Yeung in Perth to expose the united front network operating in Western Australia. The network has deep connections into both main political parties, but the state is so firmly under Beijing's sway that virtually no one in that part of the country seemed interested.

Early in June 2018, my CSU colleague Wayne Hudson dropped by my office to congratulate me 'for this morning's news'. I was perplexed but soon found he was referring to a story in *The Australian* reporting that the US Congress was introducing a law requiring closer monitoring of the CCP's subversive activities. The story attributed the impetus for the law to Australia's experience and mentioned the testimonies to Congress by John Garnaut and me. I wish I could have claimed the amount of credit I'd been given. John, on the other hand, was worthy of the influence attributed to him. After his report to Turnbull on CCP activities in Australia prompted our new law against foreign interference, Beijing had become obsessed with him. John and his wife were harassed and intimidated through conspicuous surveillance by Beijing's agents on the streets of Melbourne. When UTS academic Feng Chongyi was detained in China by the security services, they spent much of the time grilling him about John Garnaut. After his detention, DFAT urged everyone to shut up so it could pursue its 'quiet diplomacy', but Chongyi was released only after a public outcry. If I'm ever banged up in China, I hope people ignore DFAT's self-serving advice and make as much noise as possible.

§

Julie Pinkham at Hardie Grant was urging me to write a second book on China – a *Silent Invasion* for the rest of the world. The more I thought about it, the more worthwhile the idea seemed. And it would signal I was not going to be silenced by my critics. However, I didn't have the expertise to write such a book alone, so I parked the idea.

Meanwhile, people continued to approach me with information, snippets that at times deserved serious research. I began working more closely with Amy Cheng. Amy has a rare set of research skills – excellent Mandarin (of course), an ability to ferret out information from remote corners of the internet and, vitally, a thorough understanding of the modus operandi of the CCP and its united front system. The latter is essential because you need to know what you are looking for and how to interpret what you find. There are only a handful of people in Australia with these skills and who are committed to keeping the Chinese Communist Party out of Australia.

Together, Amy and I wrote background reports on united front networks in Australia, some of which led to stories in the media. We mapped a Melbourne network of united front operatives reaching up into Premier Dan Andrews' office. A couple of the central figures were criminals operating through Crown Casino, a company that struck me as a corrupt organisation knowingly working with crooks. One of the criminals had an ice habit and dressed like a gangster. He was bringing high-end customers from China to his property outside Melbourne with the promise of using high-powered weapons to kill native animals like kangaroos and wombats. The only person he deferred to in Melbourne was Ming Chai, Xi Jinping's cousin. Our work played a role in Nick McKenzie's devastating exposé on *60 Minutes* that led to the royal commission into Crown Casino.

Amy asked me if I were being followed. Some of my family members were receiving strange phone calls purporting to come from 'the Chinese embassy'. Perhaps they were trying to spook me, so I collected the details including the numbers of the callers. I even baffled the mechanics servicing my car by asking them to check underneath for tracking devices. Nothing was found, but I had no doubt I was being monitored by China's security apparatus in a campaign coordinated from the embassy in Canberra.

Late in May, I had lunch with a young Chinese Australian public servant in the cafe at the National Gallery of Australia. He had asked to meet because he was worried about CCP influence. As we talked, a man of Chinese appearance and dressed in motorcycle leathers sat down close to us and began playing with a phone. He then placed it on a spare seat and positioned it to point at us. My young friend noticed it too. Over the next months, this happened to me several times – someone would make a beeline for a seat next to me in a cafe and place a phone on the seat between us.

I described what had been happening to a surveillance expert, who said it was likely these people were trying to tap into my communications. I began switching off my phone and laptop when it happened. After the first few times, I became annoyed and began taking photos of them; they nonchalantly turned their faces away. I followed one man, whom I had recognised from a previous encounter, outside and watched him enter a secure public service building nearby. I sent a photo of him to one of my contacts and the image went 'into the system'. It helps to fight back.

§

With Labor's support, federal parliament enacted the new foreign interference law in June 2018. By criminalising foreign interference, the new law made Beijing's covert activities in Australia more difficult and risky. CCP bosses hated it, despite the fact that they insisted ad nauseam that China never interferes in the internal affairs of other countries. (CCP leaders sprinkle a spoonful of hypocrisy on their cornflakes every morning.) Opposition leader Bill Shorten had told Mark Dreyfus, who was still being obstreperous on the national security committee, to pull his head in. In 2021, in a public discussion on Zoom, Australia's high commissioner in London, George Brandis, said that the publication of *Silent Invasion* had made his life much easier when, as attorney-general, he was guiding the legislation through parliament. Powerful business groups and individuals wanted to shut down the debate to appease Beijing but my book and media attention made that impossible. As Beijing feared, other nations were soon sending delegations to find out about Australia's new law. In my talks overseas, the first question asked was usually about our foreign interference law.

I'd been invited to a private dinner at a Canberra restaurant for an intimate exchange of views between a handful of Australian analysts and journalists and Admiral Phil Davidson, commander of the US Indo-Pacific Command and several of his people. When I was introduced to the admiral, he immediately knew me as the author of *Silent Invasion*, offering hearty congratulations and indicating it was being read by the top brass. Of course, some of my critics will see this as consorting with the enemy. I think that betrays not only a blindness to Xi Jinping's militarisation and war preparation but also a poor understanding of grey-zone warfare.

Although it makes sense now, when I was writing *Silent Invasion* I didn't give any thought to the military implications. My political education had been in the cauldron of anti-Vietnam war activism in the early 1970s, so I felt out of place around people in uniforms. Yet I was also intrigued and, if I'm honest, flattered that the top brass were studying my ideas. Move over Sun Tzu.

The admiral shuffled through some business cards and gave me one with his mobile phone number and personal email. I couldn't imagine what I'd do with them, but it was an indication of the impact my work was having in challenging military thinking about grey-zone warfare. Still, I would keep that world at arm's length.

§

When I had returned from the US back in May, I decided I needed to regather my strength. A long, quiet break in an out-of-the-way place would be just the thing. So, through the good offices of Stephen Pickard, I was able to arrange a six-week sabbatical at a theology research centre at the University of Heidelberg, founded 1386. I'd not been to southern Germany and my image of Heidelberg was influenced by a memorable scene from the British sitcom *Blackadder*. Captured by the Germans, Captain Blackadder (played by Rowan Atkinson) is informed that, instead of a quick and noble death, he and his men will be taken to 'a convent school outside Heidelberg, where you will spend the rest of the war teaching the young girls home economics ... the humiliation will be *unbearable*'. Blackadder replies, 'Oh, I think you'll find we're tougher than you imagine.'

In mid-July 2018 I departed for Heidelberg, via Tokyo and Frankfurt. I'd left the arrangements too late and could find no accommodation. Through Airbnb, I came upon a quaint old house in an ancient walled village called Dilsberg, built atop a ruined fortress on a steep hill. It was hard to get to. Once I had worked it out, from my office in Heidelberg to the house took forty minutes by foot, train and bus.

I filled in the days in my creaky, third-floor office in an old building in Hauptstrasse, alone and ignored, which suited me. I looked across the ancient city and the Neckar River to the forested hillside and the famous Philosophers Walk, along which the romantic era poet Friedrich Hölderlin ambled. But what was I going to do here? My idea of looking further into the meaning of the Anthropocene now seemed like a dead end. Bruno Latour had sent me a couple of his latest papers, but they no longer did anything for me. The China experience had changed me. Although the last months had been energising and exciting, it was disturbing to live and breathe the CCP's malevolence every day. So I sat in my office with no enthusiasm for anything. Perhaps I just had to give myself time.

My host at the University of Heidelberg, Professor Michael Welker, had invited me and a dozen others to dinner at his very nice house in a village outside the city. There were half a dozen theologians and their wives. The theologians were brilliant and deep but their wives were much more interesting. They took a kind of anthropological view of their husbands. Chatting to one early in the evening, I explained that I had just arrived from Australia. Pointing out some of the men, she said: 'He's Old Testament, he's New Testament, and he's systematics. What are you?'

I often ask myself the same question, I thought, before mumbling something about not being a theologian.

Ten days later I took the six-hour train trip to Berlin to present a seminar at the Mercator Institute for China Studies (MERICS), the foremost China studies centre in Germany. There were a dozen present, all very well-informed. The story of *Silent Invasion* had preceded me. They were eager to hear of Australia's experience with CCP interference and the lessons for Germany, questioning me closely, sometimes sceptically. Pouring myself coffee before the event, I had chatted to an older gentleman who told me, quite openly, that he was from the BND, Germany's intelligence organisation. He said he and his colleagues had read *Silent Invasion* closely. Before attending the event, he'd been in touch with ASIO in Canberra and they had told him the book is very valuable and there are no errors in it. It was surprising, his ASIO contact had told him, how much there is in the book that they didn't know.

I went for lunch after the seminar with Jan Weideman, who had invited me to MERICS, and a younger China scholar, Mareike Ohlberg. Mareike impressed me. Her understanding of the CCP, its ambitions and its modus operandi was very similar to mine. And she was gutsy. With Hardie Grant asking about a second China book, the idea of teaming up with Mareike soon came to me. She knew a great deal more about the CCP than I did, having written a doctoral dissertation on the Party's external propaganda system. She'd spent years in China and Taiwan, spoke excellent Mandarin and worked in the centre of Europe. Mareike indicated there was vastly more CCP influence activity occurring in Europe than had been reported. I soon approached her and, after setting out how our collaboration would work, we agreed to write the book that would become *Hidden Hand*. For my sections of the book, Amy Cheng's research was indispensable. If she hadn't been working incognito, she could almost have been a third author.

On the way back to Canberra from Heidelberg I spent a couple of days in Taiwan at the invitation of a think tank called the Prospect Foundation. In Taiwan there was intense interest in *Silent Invasion* because I had described for Australia what they had been dealing with for years, so there was a kind of relief that the West was waking up to the CCP. I didn't understand this initially and was bewildered by my VIP treatment. An official car picked me up from the hotel to take me to a meeting at the Ministry of Justice. When we arrived, there was a greeting party of eight or ten people at the entrance with a large placard reading 'Welcome to Professor Clive Hamilton'. Perhaps they were working on me; if so, they were pushing against an open door. At a dinner that evening I was placed next to the foreign minister, Joseph Wu, an urbane and intelligent man and, by his manner, an introvert. We swapped notes about CCP interference and he was interested to hear that moves were afoot for a Chinese-language version of my book. Like others in Taiwan, when I told him that some in Australia were criticising *Silent Invasion* for being racist and anti-Chinese, he was mystified.

Before then, I'd never thought much about Taiwan, but my views changed sharply after the brief visit. I have noticed since then that those in Australia who are blasé about China occupying Taiwan have not been there and don't attach any value to the freedom of the island's 24 million people. As my colleague Wayne Hudson pointed out, Taiwan is more like Japan than China. Out on the streets of Taipei, one feels it; the people are more – what's the word? – well, free, that is, less fearful and more comfortable in themselves.

§

My parents were from Tasmania, so I feel an affinity for the place. While researching *Silent Invasion*, I had come across enough bits and pieces of information to know that CCP influence was a serious problem in Tasmania, where the political elite had been thoroughly groomed and captured. The Tasmanian infatuation with China followed the unlikely visit Xi Jinping paid to the island in 2014. He had his reasons and the whole place swooned. The Tasmanian government set up special units to attract investment from China, abandoning all due diligence, and giving rise to an unholy alliance between the state government, ex-politicians on the make and Chinese investors, some of whom were crooked, close to the PLA, or both. Soon, Tasmanians watched as asset sales and development proposals were waved through without any proper evaluation of what it all meant. The community didn't like it but were reluctant to criticise.

With the publication of *Silent Invasion*, Tasmanians felt permitted to express their concerns, and I was invited to present a lecture at the University of Tasmania, chaired by Taiwan scholar Mark Harrison, in October, 2018. Several hundred booked to attend, with many turned away. The university was a hotbed of CCP influence activity, so security was tight. With help from Amy Cheng and a couple of citizen investigators in Tasmania, I had been looking more closely at CCP influence on the island. I worked with community planning activist Sophie Underwood to expose an enormous and very dodgy resort development proposed for outside Swansea. It had all the markings of a scam to fleece elderly Chinese people, but local councils, not to mention the planning bureaucrats in Hobart, were ticking off developments without any idea of the backgrounds of those proposing them.

In contrast to some of their counterparts in Sydney, the Tasmanian Greens understood what was at stake – primarily, dark money flooding into Tasmania, corrupting state and local politics and facilitating developments or buy-ups that should never happen. In the face of fierce attacks on her, Cassy O'Connor, leader of the Greens in the Tasmanian parliament, has been clear-eyed and resolute in exposing the malign influence of the CCP and the capitulation of both the Liberal and Labor parties to Beijing's influence machine. Cassy was demanding proper due diligence and I was supporting her where I could. It was clear to me that the Chinese consulate in Melbourne, which oversaw Tasmania, was actively building up united front organisations. Our research showed that much of the activity centred on Wang Xinde, the leader of a Chinese Buddhist sect.

The CCP had been working systematically to control Chinese Buddhism abroad as well as at home, and Master Wang's Holy Tantra

Buddhist sect had persuaded a local council to allow it to build a vast 'Buddhist cultural park' featuring temples, accommodation and a university in sheep paddocks near Tea Tree, about an hour from Hobart. Having bought the property and held a gala opening with wide-eyed politicians acting out their multiculturalism, Holy Tantra began putting the squeeze on their neighbour, Craig Williams, who operated a quarry and did a bit of farming.

I went out to visit Craig, a salt-of-the-earth Australian who, though in debt and worried about his unwell wife, was dogged in his determination not to be forced off his land by various restrictions demanded by his unwelcome neighbours, including preventing him from the planned expansion of his quarry. He was up against powerful forces – a council in thrall to the sect, unfriendly planning bureaucrats in Hobart, and expensive lawyers hired by Holy Tantra with its bottomless bucket of money. I did what I could to help Craig – raise awareness among key groups and get his story into the media – but in the end it was too much. After years of fighting and mounting legal bills he could not pay, Craig had to put his property on the market.

§

Now deep into researching *Hidden Hand*, in October 2018 and again in April 2019 I travelled to North America to gather information and give talks. Trump's 'trade war' was in full swing. Only a handful then understood that the trade war was a smokescreen: the real war was over who would control the technologies of the twenty-first century. The American tech sector was not weighed down by any sense of patriotism and would just as soon work with the Chinese government as their own. In fact, Google had agreed to give China access to its data while refusing to work with the US government.

In Toronto and Vancouver I made contact with three Chinese Canadians who would be invaluable for explaining how the CCP operates in Canada, where Beijing's interference was even more deeply entrenched than in Australia. I spoke too with several journalists and experts invested in the issue. The Trudeau government was completely captured and in *Hidden Hand* I traced how the Trudeau family had over decades been groomed through its close links with the powerful Desmarais clan, itself in Beijing's orbit.

While in Canada I listened to a very disturbing story. I met up with a Canadian (of Anglo heritage) in an old wooden church hall. She had been documenting China's influence. One day while at home, she had suddenly felt an intense pressure on her head and a kind of fluttering sensation in her ears. It lasted a few minutes. Her husband and child experienced it too and, she learned, so had the neighbour in the apartment below. It left her with dizziness, disorientation, headaches and memory loss. It was debilitating. She could not drive or work and was out of action for six months, recovering only after rehab. The doctors could not isolate the probable cause but said her inner ears had been damaged. They told her it was like concussion.

I immediately thought of the Canadian diplomats who had reported the same symptoms, subsequently known as 'Havana syndrome', named after the location of the first attacks. US diplomats and intelligence agents had also reported similar 'brain injuries' acquired in China and Russia. A thorough investigation in 2020 by the US National Academy of Sciences would conclude that the most likely cause was some kind of sonic device emitting pulsed microwave energy, although mystery still surrounds the phenomenon. More recently, studies have suggested ultrasound.

My interlocutor appeared to be a sensible, credible person who gave no sign of paranoia. She had not been to the authorities because she didn't think they would believe her – the Canadian diplomats had met with official scepticism. In fact, she had told only a couple of people about her experience. I left the old church hall feeling deeply unsettled, worried for her and wondering about my own vulnerability. We subsequently had two or three phone calls where I acted as a sounding-board, and she later hired a lawyer and made contact with the relevant authorities.

§

In Washington I met up with Josh Rogin in the faded 'old world charm' of the guests' lounge at the Tabard Inn, where I was staying. A columnist at *The Washington Post*, Josh was one of only two or three journalists in the United States writing about China. He'd read *Silent Invasion* and was well-informed about Australia, lamenting the absence of a similar understanding of China in DC, despite the recent awakening to the massive tech theft and unfair trade practices. We agreed that Trump was a dangerous buffoon, but after decades of US weakness in responding to China, with Obama most culpable, Trump was the first president to push back. When I mentioned I had drafted an article setting out how China under Xi Jinping displays all the elements of a fascist state – a dictatorship built on ethnic nationalism, historical grievances, a leadership cult and state capitalism – Josh recounted the story of an intimate dinner he had been invited to at the Australian embassy. After a few drinks, while chatting to a senior Australian diplomat he responded to one of her questions with, 'I think China is a fascist state.' She was shocked to hear this, and after a moment replied, 'I think the United States is a fascist state.'

This moral equivalence thinking in DFAT was seemingly con-firmed by Trump's presidency. Trump dreamed of being an autocrat but, unlike Xi Jinping, he operated within a system with checks and balances, including a diverse and noisy media, a congressional opposition, a largely independent judicial system and elections, all of which, despite their flaws, came together to kick him out. Trump was a manifestation of the changing American psyche. In Freudian terms, he is America's id, its impulsive urges, which had for a long time been kept under control by its ego (the reality principle) and its super-ego (the ideals of liberalism). In Trump, the id broke free and went on a rampage.

I had received an invitation to present a seminar to staff at the Naval War College in Newport, Rhode Island. It sounded intriguing. It turns out the college is like a well-regulated university and I spoke with bright and earnest historians and political scientists. Still preoccupied with Russia and the Cold War, and with a recent history of friendly exchanges with China's Naval Analysis College, most were not too concerned about China's ability to rival the United States militarily, although they worried about America's fractured politics weakening the country's position in the world. They had amended their curriculum to include China as a major military-strategic challenger only a year or two earlier.

With a few exceptions, they were stuck in a traditional way of thinking, where 'political warfare' was someone else's responsibility, even though Beijing had been recruiting retiring senior American officers through exchanges and positions on boards, like Huawei's. In short, I could see that the United States was lumbering along in its conventional ways while Beijing was outmanoeuvring it in all domains.

27

Aftershocks

ALTHOUGH MY EXCURSION into the China question had won me many supporters – some eminent persons had even nominated me for an 'upgrade' from the AM I'd been awarded in 2009, but it was knocked back – politically I felt I was in a kind of no-man's-land. Maybe it didn't matter so much anymore. The left had become increasingly divided between a traditional left worldview that was stuck in the past and identity politics, fragmented into sometimes fanatical tribes. The outdated left politics lay behind a review of *Silent Invasion* by Jeff Sparrow, one of the more thoughtful intellectuals of the left. I'd known Jeff for a while, though not very well. In his review, he asked how it was that 'a principled, respected writer like Clive Hamilton' could write a book like *Silent Invasion*. The rest of the article argued by a series of inferences and innuendos: America is bad therefore China is not; US Admiral Harry Harris says China is a threat ergo China is not a threat; Australia has a history of anti-Chinese racism therefore (somehow) China will not attempt to dominate us; Australia has done bad things in Nauru so whatever the PRC does here should not worry us.

Jeff didn't answer his question about my motive. For any impartial reader, the answer is staring them in the face. It's the facts; the world changed. Anxiety over Australia's history of xenophobia and anger at the destruction wrought by US's imperial adventures should not blind us to the emergence of a new and frightening threat. It's a threat to the left's fundamental commitments – to democracy, human rights and national self-determination.

It was a fact, though, that many doubted my motives for writing the book, including directors of writers' festivals. Apart from Adelaide, the only invitation I received was from the Byron Bay festival. For its ambience and setting, it's the most agreeable on the festival circuit. When I arrived in August 2018, the festival director had arranged for me to have my own security guard. 'Woody' had done security at local pubs and, although a very likeable bloke, was not the kind you'd mess with. It felt weird wandering around the festival site two paces behind Woody and just to his right, as instructed. During my sessions in the big marquees, he stationed himself conspicuously at the side of the stage, watching out for any trouble. I felt like a git, but it signalled that this China stuff was serious.

My session on the CCP in Australia was not well attended, but the panel events I did with others on the Anthropocene and on 'Western values under siege' were full houses. The former human rights commissioner Gillian Triggs was on the latter panel along with Anna Clark, a young ANU historian, and the ABC's Paul Barclay in the chair.

Gillian was very popular after a bruising battle with *The Australian*. When she described the new foreign interference legislation as an unwarranted restriction on rights, I couldn't help intervening, saying she did not understand the new situation. Outlawing interference by foreign powers in the democratic process and in the exercise by citizens of their political rights, as the new law did, was in fact *protecting* rights. Like so many well-meaning but blinkered people, she didn't get it. I suggested she speak with pro-democracy Chinese Australians about their rights. She was not amused.

After Gillian had expatiated at length on threats to free speech in Australia, Paul asked me about my experience with *Silent Invasion*.

I set out the facts bearing on the suppression of my right to free speech when I could not find a publisher, noting that one of the publishers that was too afraid to take up my book for fear of an autocratic foreign power was Melbourne University Press, whose board had overruled the CEO. I then turned to Gillian and noted that she was a member of that board and asked how she reconciled that against her defence of free speech. Tension rippled through the audience as they looked to Gillian for a response. Smiling through gritted teeth, she gave a half-defensive, half-condescending reply, suggesting I had my facts wrong. The decision to turn down the book, she said, was made not by the board but by the CEO.

'That's not what Louise Adler told me,' I retorted, prompting laughter from the audience.

Paul Barclay intervened, asking Anna Clark what she thought of the exchange.

She replied, 'My parents are fighting.'

The audience loved the cut and thrust of the session. As we left the stage at the end of the session, I said to Gillian, 'Sorry to put you on the spot there, Gillian.'

Turning to me with an icy expression, she said, 'I think you are a very rude man.'

Oh well. MUP had misled me and Gillian was keeping up the pretence. I was justified in asking her to come clean.

Gillian Triggs was not the only person on the left alienated by my China stand. It pains me to say that my friend Rob Manne lost faith in me. I don't want to go into the details of the break but, after a couple of attempts to revive the friendship, I came to the view that the differences between us were irreconcilable.

As I see it, my warnings about the subversive intentions of the CCP have been more than vindicated by events since the publication of *Silent Invasion*. If I had seen the historical trend before most others, I had been in the game long enough to know that facts are puny in the face of deeply entrenched beliefs. I also knew from experience that, sooner or later, my arguments would be borrowed by others and reproduced without acknowledgement. But, hey, what matters is the influence.

Nevertheless, the punters could see what was happening. According to polling by the Lowy Institute, Australians' trust and warmth towards 'China' collapsed in the three years after 2018. In 2021, only 16 per cent of Australians said they trusted China to act responsibly in the world, down from 52 per cent in 2018. In 2018, eight in ten Australians saw China as more of an economic partner than a security threat, with one in ten taking the opposite view. In 2021, two thirds saw China as more of a security threat.

§

At the same time, our universities were proving just how useful they were to Beijing by refusing to take seriously CCP influence on campuses, stridently opposing the foreign interference laws and, later, resisting measures requiring them to report on their agreements with foreign governments. With a handful of honourable exceptions, China experts and executives across the universities were either uninterested in CCP interference or actively worked as apologists for the Party. Gareth Evans, while chancellor of the ANU, was one of the worst offenders. From 2017, he was out in public characterising warnings of China's malfeasance as 'Sinophobia'. Conflating the CCP with Chinese people, he pooh-poohed advice from the intelligence agencies, dismissed as wildly exaggerated claims of CCP influence in universities, blamed Australia for Beijing's bullying ('our actions are generating reactions') and urged the government to sign on to the One Belt, One Road Initiative. Of course, he was hailed by CCP media. As foreign minister in the Hawke–Keating era, Evans is remembered as an apologist for the brutal suppression of East Timorese by the Suharto regime, describing the murder of two hundred people by Indonesian troops as an 'aberration', and then clinking champagne glasses with his Indonesian counterpart while flying over the oil and gas fields that had been stolen from newly independent East Timor in a carve up with Jakarta.

The most dramatic instance of the capture of Australian universities took place on the campus of the University of Queensland after a large group of patriotic Chinese students, almost certainly led by trained Chinese security operatives, used force to break up a small and scrappy demonstration in support of pro-democracy students in Hong Kong. The demonstration was organised by twenty-year-old philosophy student Drew Pavlou, who was assaulted by the operatives. It set off a chain of events that saw the university administration go to extreme lengths to silence and expel Drew Pavlou because of his criticisms of the university's close links with Beijing. The vice-chancellor, Peter Høj, was especially embedded. When the Chinese consul-general in Brisbane praised the violent attack by patriotic students, Høj, who had received an award from Beijing, refused to nullify the consul-general's honorary professorship at the university (an appointment itself unheard of). The university's new chancellor, former diplomat Peter Varghese, backed the university's attempt to expel Drew. Drew secured the pro bono services of a top Brisbane QC, Tony Morris, and after a long struggle, the university suspended him for six months. Its reputation suffered severe damage, not least in the federal parliament.

I had great admiration for Drew. Yes, his pranks and social media commentary could be out there, but he was absolutely committed to defending democratic principles and the rights of those oppressed by the Chinese regime. And he was brave. The university put severe pressure on him, magnifying the stress caused by the frightening threats Drew and his family were receiving from Beijing's trolls. And as a committed left activist devoted to opposing the CCP regime, he was subjected to vicious attacks by 'tankies', far-left defenders of totalitarianism. I met Drew when, at the invitation of a student organisation, I gave a lecture on the UQ campus on CCP influence in universities. I thereafter tried to provide mentoring and support. I wish Australia had more people with Drew Pavlou's courage.

§

In June 2019 I travelled to Berlin to spend several weeks at MERICS working with Mareike on our book. I rented an apartment in the Prenzlauer Berg district, formerly in East Berlin and transformed into an artistic and alternative neighbourhood after the wall came down. The CEO of MERICS, Frank Pieke, a Dutch anthropologist and old China hand, had agreed to my visit to MERICS, but when I visited him in his office, he told me that he thought my work was, in effect, shit. A sharp exchange ensued, cut off only by the awkward intervention of the third person in the room. Let's just say that Frank was more sympathetic to the CCP than Mareike and I were.

Mareike was in a difficult position. Frank had decided that she was not to work on our book while being paid by MERICS. He had criticised her work in the Chinese media. And since we were writing a chapter on the cooptation of think tanks in the West, we felt obliged to make critical comments about MERICS itself, including Pieke. Fortunately, my co-author had a great deal of intellectual integrity and courage. After a time, Mareike's position become too difficult, and she found a job at the German Marshall Fund, a US-funded think tank with offices in Berlin.

Hardie Grant had sold northern hemisphere rights to *Hidden Hand* to Oneworld, a small London publisher with a strong reputation for literary fiction, including two Booker Prize winners. Oneworld would publish in the United Kingdom and the United States. I don't think they realised what they had bought – a book that would enrage a powerful regime with tentacles everywhere. As Covid took hold around the world, in April 2020 Oneworld decided to postpone publication from June until September.

No author likes a delay in publication, and I tried to persuade them that delay was a bad idea – if we waited too long, some of the book would begin to date. Besides, bookshops were still open, Hardie Grant would be publishing in Australia in June and the German publishers had said they were going ahead with planned publication in May. There was a risk some of the British revelations would leak into the British media before the book was available, and the first rule of book marketing is never to publicise a book before it is available to buy. But my entreaties were to no avail.

Then we had a stroke of luck. In June, Oneworld received a letter threatening defamation action from the London legal firm Druces representing Stephen Perry, chairman of the 48 Group Club, a pro-Beijing networking organisation for Britain's elites set up in the 1950s by secret members of the Communist Party of Great Britain, one of whom was Perry's father. In the book, we described Perry's slavish reproduction of CCP propaganda and the way he is fêted in Beijing, including meeting with Xi Jinping himself. It had been fascinating to piece together this story from old books and documents in the National Library of Australia and match it with more recent Chinese-language sources. The German edition of *Hidden Hand* had been reviewed strongly and was selling well, and a rough translation of certain passages had found its way to Perry, who phoned his lawyers.

Meanwhile, Oneworld had sublicensed publication of the book in Canada to a small company called Optimum Publishing, run by a bloke named Dean Baxendale. Dean, an enthusiast for the book, was already distributing copies to booksellers in preparation for the Canadian publication day in July, but Oneworld instructed him to desist. When Dean sent an email to bookshops telling them that a legal threat had been made and they were not to sell the book, the email found its way to *The Globe and Mail*, which on 19 June 2020 published a news story under the headline 'Legal challenge halts Canadian, US and UK release of book critical of Chinese Communist Party'.

Of course, as I had learned with *Silent Invasion*, nothing does more to stimulate demand for a book than attempts to stop people reading it. The Canadian news story was soon picked up by the media in Britain and interest erupted. Why did Stephen Perry in London want to block a book about the Chinese Communist Party? The news articles about the legal threat were publicity gifts and caused

Novin Doostdar, Oneworld's co-founder and publisher, to decide that *Hidden Hand* had to be rushed out. *The Times* in London began reporting on the British elite 'being groomed by China' based on *Hidden Hand* and soon had its teeth into the 48 Group Club, outing various members of the great and good for being members, including Tony Blair. But it was the *Daily Mail* that really locked onto the issue with a string of stories about CCP influence in Britain. Just before publication, it ran a series of long extracts from the book, presented in a sensational style. Okay, I thought, it's the *Daily Mail*, but what the hell: the system needs to be shaken up, and if it takes Britain's biggest tabloid to do it, so be it.

Although it did me a favour, I was irritated by Perry's threat; he was so thoroughly compromised that the only question was why he acted in a way that drew more scrutiny to himself and his club. Still, we needed to respond, and so, with help from my sources, I wrote a detailed forty-page, thoroughly referenced dossier laying out Perry's history of associations with top CCP figures and his commentary praising Xi Jinping and the Party. Oneworld's lawyers incorporated the dossier into their response to Druces and we heard nothing more from him. As a rule, publishers don't like being threatened and, as long as the authors have done the right thing, will push back hard. Like Hardie Grant, Oneworld were staunch in their backing of the book.

After publication of the *Daily Mail* extracts, another threatening letter arrived, this one from top defamation firm Carter-Ruck on behalf of Lord Bates and Lady Bates, formerly Li Xuelin. Lord Bates was a Tory peer, Sinophile and sometime junior minister. Li Xuelin was an immigrant from China who made large donations to the Conservative Party then married Bates. The letter claimed their clients were seriously harmed by material in the book and that unless all reference to them was withdrawn they would sue us. Mareike and I had documented Xuelin Bates's links with united front officials, her high-level contacts in the British elites from prime ministers down, and her trips to China to report on her activities in Britain.

I responded to the legal threat in the same way – facts. With help from my brilliant researchers, especially Amy Cheng, I compiled another forty pages of detailed information elaborating on Lady Bates's CCP links, along with those of her hapless husband, Lord Bates. The information was included in the reply from our lawyer, David Hooper at Howard Kennedy, to theirs, sending the message that *Hidden Hand* included only a small part of the information that could be much more damaging were it to be made public in court proceedings. In this kind of work, it all comes down to evidence and credible sources.

In the process of preparing our response, we noticed that, on the day the *Daily Mail* extract appeared, someone had deleted pages from the website of Xuelin Bates's united front organisation. In fact, everything that looked incriminating was gone. It was a serious mistake. When our lawyers replied to Carter-Ruck, they made it clear that, should the matter end up in court, we would be demanding an explanation of why vital evidence (which we had archived) had been tampered with in a way apparently designed to deceive the court. Any judge would take a very dim view of one party attempting to conceal evidence. After a half-hearted response, our opponents then beat a retreat and were not heard from again. To be transparent, we had in fact made a couple of minor errors in the book, which we corrected in future printings. Our 'concession' probably acted as a face-saver for the other side.

For years, Britain – basking in the glow of David Cameron's 'golden era' of UK–China relations – had been naïvely unaware of the true nature of the CCP and how it had been operating there. Information on united front activity was virtually non-existent, so we had to start from scratch. When writing the parts of *Hidden Hand* concerning Britain, I hoped to shock Britons out of their complacency. On publication, some in the media saw it immediately, although the BBC and *The Guardian* were slow to pick up on it. Aided by events in Hong Kong, the former British colony, in 2020 public opinion shifted sharply and the government, despite the influence of powerful Beijing apologists, was following suit.

Xuelin Bates was one of two British women highlighted in the book with close united front links and high-level political connections. The other was Christine Lee, whom we believed was more senior in the united front hierarchy. In January 2022, MI5 sent shockwaves through Britain's political establishment when it issued a public alert identifying Christine Lee as a covert influence agent of the CCP, warning MPs to avoid her. It was a sensational tactic, one ASIO might consider using to out CCP influence agents in Australia. All of the information in MI5's alert, with one exception, could be found in *Hidden Hand*, published eighteen months earlier. I fielded a surge of calls from British journalists wanting to understand what it was all about. The first question was usually why it had taken MI5 so long after the publication of *Hidden Hand*. I don't think there was anything untoward, just caution.

Beijing was of course receiving reports from its diplomatic mission in London. In particular, the coverage of *Hidden Hand* in the *Daily Mail*, the UK's biggest-selling newspaper, must have alarmed them. In August 2020, Mareike and I were denounced in official Chinese media as 'black hands', that is, secretive agents of foreign forces attempting to bring down the Chinese government. We were now in the worst category of CCP enemy. The article began by referencing the *Daily Mail* extracts, praising Xuelin Bates for fighting back against 'hate propaganda' and saying the 48 Group Club is no more than a trade association, before launching into a denunciation of me. While some scoffed and congratulated us on our new designation as black hands (Mareike noted she had been upgraded from 'misguided academic'), it would be foolish of us to forget how vicious the regime can be against its designated enemies.

In September, the *Global Times* published a story announcing that the Chinese government had banned two Australian academics from entering China – Alex Joske and me. It was unexpected but followed the Australian government's revocation of the visas of two Chinese academics frequently in Australia, including the notorious Chen Hong, a Party propagandist. We were described as 'anti-China scholars' who engage in 'connivance and denigration'. It quoted Chen Hong labelling us 'actors of the smear and slander campaign'. He complained his own exclusion was unjustified because all he had ever done was promote friendship between Australia and China. Our ban was heavily covered by Australian media, and many messages flowed in about 'badge of honour' and so on. We were apprehensive, though, wondering if there might be more to it.

§

When, in January 2020, news of a strange new virus outbreak in Wuhan began trickling out, I started a daily timeline of events based on Chinese and Western media, journals and government reports. By the end of March, with the Covid pandemic on the verge of rampaging across the world, I thought I might write a book about it. I sensed, though, that such a book would have value only if it included information from on the ground in Wuhan. My friend Amy Cheng suggested I speak with Murong Xuecun, a famous novelist and censorship critic in Beijing. He'd been silenced by the regime for several years. With Amy interpreting, I phoned Murong and put to him the idea of a co-authored book. He would need to go to Wuhan. He was captivated by the idea and three days later caught a train, virtually the only passenger, to a city under the harshest lockdown conditions.

It was an extremely hazardous mission. The media had been banned from Wuhan and several citizen-journalists reporting what they saw in the hospitals and on the streets were being arrested and disappearing. I think the mission inspired Murong because at last he would be writing again, and about something that truly mattered. He had many friends – fellow writers and human rights lawyers – who had been imprisoned, a fate he had evaded, and was perhaps feeling a bit of survivor guilt.

Murong found some Wuhan citizens willing to tell their stories, interviews held in secrecy. After some weeks, the calls to his phone from the secret police asking him what he was doing in Wuhan and telling him to be careful spooked him, and with enough stories collected anyway, he left for a remote place in Szechuan province to write them up. As he completed each story, drawing on his powers as a novelist, he sent them by encrypted email to Amy. After they had been translated into English, it was my task to edit them. I soon realised that, taken together, the stories he was telling were dazzling and it made no sense to combine them with my mundane material. It should be Murong's book.

I approached Julie Pinkham at Hardie Grant, who immediately saw the appeal of the book. And so in great secrecy, over the next year or so we prepared the book for publication. We knew the regime would punish Murong; he would probably vanish into prison for decades. He had to get out, although he sent a message telling us that if he disappeared then we must publish the book. In August 2021, we monitored events with hearts in mouths as he boarded a flight from Beijing to Hong Kong, then another to London, expecting at any moment to hear nothing more from him. Perhaps because the secret police system is not well coordinated with customs, they let him leave.

After publication he could not return to China, so we organised an application for a visa that would give him permanent residency in Australia. He arrived in January 2022 on a three-month visa, and on 5 March he and I launched his book, *Deadly Quiet City*, to a large and attentive audience at Adelaide Writers' Week, four years and one day after *Silent Invasion* had been launched at the very same place.

28
Beginning again

S OON AFTER *Hidden Hand* was published in the middle of 2020, I began to wonder what I would do next. This memoir was one idea. I also felt called back to my first passion, the natural world and the assault on it by humans. *Defiant Earth* had offered a vision of the Anthropocene and its meaning. Between the lines, it also hinted at theological themes because it seemed to me that the Anthropocene forces us to consider ideas absent from contemporary secular thought. My colleagues at George Browning House had taken notice and, in 2017, 2018 and 2020, arranged three colloquia on the theme of 'theology at four degrees'. It was gratifying to see *Defiant Earth* inspire so much creative thinking from some of Australia's leading theologians. The US scholar of religion Lisa Sideris, who shares with me a deep interest in reckoning with finality (eschatology), initiated the debates at two of the colloquia, which led to a book, *Theology on a Defiant Earth*, edited by Peter Walker and Jonathan Cole.

I valued these sessions because I believe we have largely lost the ability to go to the depths of things. In the 1950s, books about 'the human condition', 'the destiny of man' and 'the search for meaning' were common. No one writes books on these themes today and yet the climate crisis is thrusting these ideas at us and prompting a subterranean discussion among the more thoughtful observers of the state of the world. And so it was that in June 2022 I travelled to Copenhagen to present a lecture at the university on the question 'What is the human being in the Anthropocene?', a question that, disconcertingly, has no obvious answer.

§

One day in February 2020, as my Qantas flight was landing at Melbourne airport, the cabin services director thanked the bushfire and emergency personnel who had been fighting the catastrophic bushfires of Black Summer. The passengers applauded in a heartfelt way. The Black Summer fires were a shattering event for the nation, enshrouding the eastern states with dread. It was impossible to turn one's eyes from the horror unfolding on TV and in the papers. In Canberra, the nearest fires were a hundred kilometres away, unlike the 2003 fires that roared from the hills across the parched grassy plains to our west and devoured five hundred houses within a couple of hours. Through the weeks of the Black Summer, Canberra was engulfed by impenetrable, choking smoke. With the highest pollution index in the world, we too were sharing in the event that was traumatising so many communities.

For the most part, Australians don't have the concepts to grasp what is happening to the climate. When I saw one Saturday that the temperature in Penrith, on the outskirts of Sydney, had reached 49°C, it felt as if every dark warning I had made in my books and articles was coming to pass, except that they had arrived a decade or two too soon. It was too awful to feel vindicated, and it was impossible to suppress a seething rage against the political leaders, newspaper editors and coal lobbyists who had for years only pretended to take the scientific warnings seriously or had dismissed them altogether. I shared the relief of all those who worry about climate change when the Albanese government was elected in May 2022 and hoped the Greens and independents could push it to go further. Yet we know that if the Australian public has woken up, it's ten or twenty years too late.

In my early years of tracking the rise of climate science denialism, I argued that deniers would realise their error and accept climate science only when they were affected directly by extreme weather events due to a warming Earth. Later I realised that even facts as monstrous as the Black Summer fires would not burn through the carapace of ignorance. Repudiation of science is at the core of the deniers' identities; changing their minds about climate science would require them to change who they are. For all but a few, that would be too psychologically painful. So, in the face of the best science, and now the desperate appeals of the most credible fire and emergency chiefs for a change of course, deniers found reasons to pretend the fires were not linked to a warming climate. *The Australian*, whose primary task over two decades has been to supply the arguments and excuses for use by deniers, twisted and misinterpreted figures to make the case that the fires were all down to arson and made up stories about greenies being to blame for allegedly opposing fuel-reduction burns. With whole towns and hundreds of millions of animals burning, it was beyond despicable.

Having switched to China, by the time of Black Summer the Australian media had stopped coming to me for comment on climate change, although I had a few opinion articles about the fires published abroad, including in *Le Monde*. The fires seemed to incinerate hope, which made the resolve of youth climate activists around the nation all the more fascinating and inspirational. I decided my next book would be about those young activists – who are they, what drives them, what are their fears, how do they think about the future, and how does being an activist help? I wanted to know about their inner lives. I spoke with my well-connected friend Luke Taylor, for some years the director of the Sustainable Living Festival in Melbourne. From there I began to make contact with youth activists in Australia and, later, abroad. To form a full picture, I needed to conduct long interviews with fifty or sixty activists and went about the frustrating but unavoidable process of seeking ethics approval from my university.

After conducting twenty-two interviews, several in Europe and the United States, I was forced to call a halt to the project. The Covid pandemic had swept the world, bringing lockdowns and despair. Climate activism was suspended and young activists were no longer volunteering to be interviewed. Yet those twenty-two encounters made a deep impression on me, so a year later I returned to them and wrote an essay for *Meanjin*. The dominant emotion in those interviews was fear. As one thirteen-year-old girl put it, 'I'm just so worried that I don't really talk about it that much. But I think about it a lot.' Others spoke of eco-anxiety and a 'spiral of helplessness'. A nineteen-year-old activist said, 'It's a lot of shit to dump on you when you're just trying to find your way in the world and the world is falling apart around you.' What have we done?

§

According to the authorised narrative, we should expect our lives to be happy and fulfilling, and for most people the art of life is to enjoy the pleasures where they are available and cope with the obstacles as best they can. The odds are stacked against us, though. We do not experience our good health as a great pleasure but a sore toe can ruin our day. Yes, there are brief episodes in which we feel contented and satisfied, even joyful, but it is a fact that we feel life's slights, humiliations and failures more intensely than we feel their opposites. In relationships, psychologists tell us, we need five positive strokes to offset each negative one, and the same applies to life generally.

A few people have commented to me that I should feel pleased with what I have achieved, but I don't feel satisfaction or contentment. I just did what I did. Besides, as I sit here in my office wondering whether I should feel pleased looking back over three or four decades of life as a public intellectual, a man with a roaring leaf blower is walking around the building. He's wearing industrial earmuffs. The racket forces me to shut the windows. I try to ignore it, hoping it will end soon, but the irritation worms its way into me until I have to stop. I can't work with that noise, so I go outside and, with as much politeness as I can muster, ask his workmate to stop him. The racket soon ends but my repose has been fractured.

In truth, life is a struggle. The restless discontent that drives some people never dissipates, even if towards the end of a life they can say they attained their goals. Some are driven by a need to achieve, for whatever reason; some, including public intellectuals, are driven by a passion. There's no stopping it, despite the truth of Schopenhauer's words: 'When our real practical life is not moved by passions, it is tedious and humdrum; but when it is so moved, it becomes painful.'

I have described my life as a public intellectual as one of 'advocacy scholarship'. The life of the mind is endlessly entertaining; as long as the mind remains tuned, there are always available the small joys that come with new knowledge and new insights. For someone easily bored, the ability to immerse myself in the world of ideas has been a blessing, a lifesaver, one might say.

However, if pure learning is pleasurable, as soon as it gives rise to a desire to change the world it becomes painful, riddled with anxiety, outrage and conflict. In other words, in a life of advocacy scholarship, the pain of advocacy outweighs the pleasures of scholarship. Beyond that, the more one knows of the world, the more one is distressed by it, a truth many people understand. And yet, we cannot leave it; we feel obliged to remain engaged with the world. It's an old idea, to be found in Ecclesiastes: 'In much wisdom is much vexation.' And it has a corollary for people like me: 'Those who increase knowledge increase sorrow.'

Perhaps endorsing this thought says more about me than other increasers of knowledge because of the subjects I have decided to work on, which have illuminated and depressed others just as they have illuminated and depressed me.

I'm not done yet, with two books underway and new ideas taking shape. But perhaps I ought to devote more time to the great consolations of life. Apart from the love of those closest, one of life's greatest consolations is nature.

§

In March 2021, Janenne and I spent a few days at Lake Mungo in western New South Wales. We had hired a guide, an expert birder who knew every bird and how to find it. With much of Australia locked down, we had Lake Mungo virtually to ourselves. The wonders of the local avian world appeared before us, among them the blue-winged parrot, the yellow rosella, the black-faced cuckoo-shrike and the beautiful bluebonnet. Of course, we hoped to see the spectacular but elusive pink cockatoo, or Major Mitchell's cockatoo as it was known before we appreciated the role of Major Thomas Mitchell in the Mount Dispersion massacre of 1836 that left at least seven Aboriginal people dead.

One cool morning, we trekked across the lonely rilled sand dunes at the back of the dry lake's expanse, behind the lunettes of the Walls of China. Absorbed in the primordial silence of a landscape seemingly untouched for thousands of years, we heard an unfamiliar falsetto *creeek* call, turning to see a flock of some thirty pink cockatoos wheeling through the air then landing, not a hundred metres from us, on the splayed branches of a long-dead tree. Our guide immediately pointed his long-lens camera and the cockatoos rose and zigzagged over our heads, their plaintive calls fading to leave us alone in the silence, feeling blessed by such a rare visitation. I've known that silence since I was a boy, walking out beyond the last street into the grassy woodlands – the deep, uncanny quiet of the Australian bush.

Acknowledgements

MEMORY IS A slippery thing, as much inclined to deceive as inform. Where possible, I have held it to account with documents. At other times, various people have challenged my recollections with theirs, or prompted memories to return from the unconscious, and I thank them all for making the time to reminisce with me.

Ben Oquist at the Australia Institute was happy to give me access to old archives.

The team at Hardie Grant Books, led by Arwen Summers, provided invaluable support throughout the process. I'd like to specially thank the editors, Emma Driver and Simone Ford, whose close attention to the text did so much to improve the end product.

Finally, boundless gratitude to my partner in life, Janenne Hamilton, who watched it all happen from the inside.

Index

Note: P1, P2, etc. refer to the pictures so numbered in the picture section.